LATINO/A POPULAR CULTURE

EDITED BY MICHELLE HABELL-PALLÁN
AND MARY ROMERO

LATINO/A POPULAR CULTURE

New York University Press • *New York and London*

NEW YORK UNIVERSITY PRESS
New York and London

Library of Congress Cataloging-in-Publication Data
Latino/a popular culture / edited by Michelle Habell-Pallán and
Mary Romero.
p.   cm.
Includes bibliographical references and index.
ISBN 0-8147-3624-6 — ISBN 0-8147-3625-4 (pbk.)
1. Hispanic Americans—Ethnic identity. 2. Hispanic Americans and
mass media. 3. Popular culture—United States. 4. Hispanic Americans—
Social life and customs. 5. Hispanic American arts. 6. Hispanic American
athletes.   I. Habell-Pallán, Michelle.   II. Romero, Mary.
E184.S75 L3554 2002
305.868′073—dc21   2001007962

10   9   8   7   6   5   4   3

Contents

Theater and Art

Sports

Acknowledgments

We have many people to thank for their help in editing this volume and in shaping *Latino/a Popular Culture* into a multiethnic and multidisciplinary project. Our greatest appreciation goes to our contributors for their fine work and willingness to be part of this project. We are grateful for the encouragement Eric Zinner offered us as we developed our ideas into a proposal and eventually into this volume. We are indebted to the scholars who generously participated in roundtable discussions at the American Studies Association and Latin American Studies Association: Frances Aparicio, Susana Chávez-Silverman, Ricardo Ortiz, Jaime Cárdenas, Keta Miranda, Margarita Barceló, Adrian Burgos, Luz Calvo, and Deborah Vargas. Challenging questions and comments were helpful in shaping this collection, particularly those from Eric Avila, Ed Morales, Rick Bonus, and Catriona Esquibel. We acknowledge the insightful work of LatCrit scholars who have journeyed into popular culture in their quest to understand justice. We are particularly grateful to Kevin Johnson, Steve Bender, Ediberto Roman, and Pedro A. Malavet for sharing their recent publications and forthcoming articles. Kevin Johnson offered valuable suggestions and generously shared resources. Eric Margolis and Raul Villa graciously provided last-minute comments. We received institutional support from the Department of American Ethnic Studies, University of Washington, the School of Justice Studies, and the Publication Assistance Center in the College of Public Programs at Arizona State University. Finally, we would like to thank our partners, Jaime Cárdenas and Eric Margolis, without whose support, encouragement, and patience this project would not have been possible. A special thanks to Diane Gamboa for creating the art that appears on the cover of this book. No other artist could have expressed the spirit of our work as well as she.

Introduction

Mary Romero and Michelle Habell-Pallán

Headlines:

"2000 Census Shows Latino Boom"[1]

"Census Jolts Business World: Corporate America Suddenly Discovering the Latino Market"[2]

"Bush: Respect Mexican Immigrants; President and Responding Democrats Broadcast in Spanish"[3]

"Guard Stopped the Mexican Pediatrician Because of 'Profiling,' Her Attorney Charges"[4]

"Activists Say Border Patrol Targets All Latinos"[5]

"Martin Kicks Off Inaugural Festivities; Bush Shares Stage with Pop Sensation"[6]

WHILE LATINO AND Latina images in mainstream news and in commercial and oppositional popular culture in the United States suggest a Latin explosion at center stage, the representations and circulating symbols are contradictory—celebrated and contested. How are we to understand the image of Ricky Martin shaking his inaugural bonbon with George W. Bush at the foot of the Lincoln Memorial or Bush's Cinco de Mayo proclamation that "mi Casa Blanca, es su Casa Blanca"?[7] How do the symbolic embrace of and dance with Ricky Martin—Latino pop star par excellence—by the leader of the nation (and the so-called free world) contradict and mask the nation's current and historical record of treatment toward Latinos at home and abroad?[8] Such public symbolism compels us to mark a new period in the struggle to represent "Latinidad." Let us consider the provocative image of Ricky and George W.'s dance as a supreme example of the politics of image employed by the dominant culture to define the place of Latinas and Latinos at this historical juncture.[9] Within this image of the dancing men—one the son of a powerful, wealthy WASP family, the other a sexually ambiguous and powerful pop icon from the former U.S. colony and current commonwealth of Puerto Rico—lies what George Lipsitz described as "the sedimented historical currents within popular culture."[10] Concentrated within the image are layered histories of imperialism, racism, class domination, patriarchy, and heterosexism. At the same time, the image speaks to new geopolitical and economic realities that implicate Latinos and Latin America.

The volume's aim is to examine the ways American popular culture has been defining "Latina" and "Latino" during this millennial transition period. The various essays were selected, in part, because the authors interrogate the ways popular culture provides narratives about the roles Latinos have played as part of the national body in the past, as well as the roles they may or may not play in the future. As emergent signifiers, "Latina" and "Latino" have no fixed definition; historical and social locations create shifting fields of meaning. The power to define these terms is political and economic and plays out symbolically in the imaginative products of the popular culture machine. While recognizing the apparatus of cultural production as a central industry of capitalism, we also note that popular culture takes no fixed form or necessary ideological message. It is a contested terrain; historical circumstances shape production, reception, and appropriation, determining how plays, films, videos, and music operate in the spheres of popular culture. Popular cultural expressions range from blatant appropriation of cultural stereotypes for mass marketing like Chiquita Banana and the Frito Bandito to powerful oppositional forces like the Teatro Campesino and hip hop. The volume comfortably moves beyond the task of defining Latino popular culture once and for all, into the more fruitful juxtaposition and cross-examination of the mosaic of contradictory and congratulatory images thrown up by the mass media.

Images circulated through popular culture are an important part of the contested terrain in the struggle to define the place of Latinos in North America. On one hand, the collage of images contains everything: from Taco Bell's heavily accented Chihuahua "dinky"[11] to Jennifer Lopez's Versace dress at the 2000 Grammy Awards ceremony,[12] from Cinco de Mayo at the White House (including all the cultural condiments—food, *ballet folklórico*, and master of ceremonies Don Francisco, host of Univisión's *Sabado Gigante*)[13] to the taciturn Edward James Olmos of *Miami Vice* and *American Me*,[14] and from the Elián González custody battle[15] to evening news reports of roundups and deportations of illegal aliens.[16] On the other hand, the media pastiche reports protests against the navy bombing tests on the island of Vieques,[17] World War II Bracero workers filing legal action against the U.S. government for breaching contractual and fiduciary duties,[18] the dismantling of affirmative action,[19] and growing support for Ron Unz's well-financed attack on bilingual education.[20] Meanwhile, Santana wins record of the year,[21] Latin crossover succeeds in the music industry,[22] and livin' la vida loca is becoming an American pastime.[23] And though limited by their exclusion from commercial distribution networks, independent filmmakers and performance artists labor to redefine images and invent new narratives that contest the former.[24] We began this project from the premise that the issues of popular culture and the construction of Latina and Latino identity cannot be separated from issues of class, labor, and political economy—language, nationality, and citizenship. As such, each essay explores power relations embedded in different forms of popular culture. Each essay examines the "power to define," whether in Broadway plays or grassroots theater. In addition, each contributor explores how popular culture is shaped by the economic and/or social matrix from which it emerges.

This anthology purposefully links two highly contentious and problematic terms—"Latino" and "popular culture"—in order to embrace the contradictions within each and argue against (1) the conception of Latinos as a monolithic cultural group sharing the same language, geographical space, and political struggles; (2) the conception that "popular culture" refers to "authentic culture of the people" existing independently from the capitalist production of consumerism; and (3) the conception that popular culture is only produced as mass media. The essays demonstrate the manifold ways audiences "make their own meanings with the texts of popular culture and resources."[25]

CONSTRUCTING LATINAS AND LATINOS:
¿QUÉ SOMOS Y CÓMO SOMOS?

The term "Latino" is politically charged and has been defined by various communities in diverse geographical locations and at different moments in U.S. history in order to achieve a variety of objectives. Our goal is not to establish consensus, but to understand the concept's usefulness and dangers. We examine the conversations the term "Latino" enables and the discussions it prohibits. As editors, we find that our stake in the term emerges from a desire to speak across differences of class, structural placement, racialization, national identity, and gender. At the same time, we assume that particular Latino communities—Chicano, Puerto Rican, Cuban American, Central American, and so on—are themselves heterogeneous. This makes discussion of the term especially vexing and provocative. The essays presented in this collection bring to the fore some of the political investments in the term "Latino" that find expression through different forms of popular culture. Recognizing the fluidity of race and ethnic identification, our contributors analyze representations of Latinidad and Hispanization in relation to Chicanas, Chicanos, mestizos, Puerto Ricans, *boricuas*, Cubans, Dominicans, Caribbeans, Colombians—not essentializing, but rather interrogating the ways popular cultures rethink, refigure, and (re)produce narratives of nation, citizenship, class, racialization, gender, and sexuality.

The 2000 U.S. Census proclaimed that the 35.5 million Latinos have become the largest ethnic minority group in the United States—surpassing 30 million African Americans.[26] The political meanings being imposed on these demographic shifts are particularly acute, forcing re-examinations of the binary Black/White characterization of race relations that has marked (or marred) American history to date.[27] For Latinos at this millennial moment, as well as for members of the dominant Anglo and African American cultures, popular culture takes center stage in struggles over defining meaning. Within the magic, ritualistic, and symbolic realm of popular culture, narratives are constructed about the role Latinos will or will not play as part of the national body. Intergroup relations are played out in tabloid romances between Jennifer Lopez and Puffy Combs or Peruvian American Benjamin Bratt and Julia Roberts. Multiracial and other hybrid racial and ethnic identities of individuals and groups are highly debated and the political consequences of new categorizations remain unclear.[28]

Even though the history of colonialism serves as a point of unity among groups, within the poly-cultural construction "Latino" there is an endless circulation from similarity to difference: Mexicans, Puerto Ricans, Cubans, Salvadorans, Nicaraguans, Dominicans, Guatemalans, Costa Ricans, and others bob and weave between solidarity and distinction. Among U.S. residents classified as Latino, different political meanings attach to the Mexican American War, the Spanish American War, the Bay of Pigs, and the U.S. military occupations in Nicaragua, Dominican Republic, and Panama. Sharp distinctions still exist between immigrants and their descendants, and those who became involuntary Americans through conquest and (land and culture) appropriation. Particular immigrant and conquest experiences also mark sharp political boundaries—those who faced the Texas Rangers and the Border Patrol as "Mexicans" (legal or illegal)[29] have different interests and political perspectives from those who were embraced as political refugees, were granted permanent residence in the U.S., and received extensive benefits and social services.[30] In general, historical ties between Cubans and Republicans and Chicanos/Mexicanos and the Democratic Party are just the surface manifestation of deep cultural and ideological fault lines. Furthermore, the topic of color and the ability to pass as white have played an important role in the segregation or assimilation of certain Latino groups. In these ways and others, the U.S. history of colonialism and imperialism serves to unite as well as separate Latinas and Latinos, subdividing groups along waves of immigration, class, color, and generation.[31] Moreover, the American experience in the twenty-first century has produced new identities, coalitions, and adaptations to the specific racialization that popular culture recognizes as Latino.

Does the fact that Ecuadoran American Christina Aguilera, Chicano Carlos Santana, Tejana Selena, and Nuyorican Jennifer Lopez have become mainstream artists make any difference in larger struggles for social justice?[32] While there is no doubt that Latinos have achieved unprecedented visibility in popular culture (for example, Geraldo Rivera, Cristina Saralegui, Jimmy Smits, and even Bob Villa), this remains to be seen. It is highly likely that heightened media visibility, coupled with the growth of Latino populations throughout the nation, is contributing to anxieties about who or what Latinas and Latinos are and how they fit into the nation (if they do at all). The catchall term "Hispanic" adds to the confusion, lumping all "Spanish-speakers" into one indistinguishable category even if many of them do not actually speak Spanish. At the same time, people and artists marked as Latino or Hispanic work against these invented labels—redefining themselves, articulating histories, locating their specific place in the nation, and in the process redefining U.S. culture itself.

MAPPING LATINA/O POPULAR CULTURE AND
CULTURAL STUDIES

We cast our lot with scholars who argue that popular culture constitutes a terrain where not only ethnic and racial identity is contested, reproduced, and transformed, but also where the struggle for and against social equality is engaged. As Stuart Hall asserted, "Popular culture is one of the sites where this struggle for and against a culture of the powerful is engaged: it is also the stake to be won or lost in that struggle. It is the arena of consent and resistance."[33] Cultural politics played out in Latino popular culture provides an entree for understanding the double stake in popular culture, the dialectical movement of appropriation and resistance. Discourses produced in popular cultural production created and distributed by the dominant culture industry (from the beginning to the end of the twentieth century) have fabricated conceptual blueprints about Latinos that continue to be reproduced and contested into the twenty-first century.

The essays in this volume reiterate that cultural politics is important because it is an increasingly important element of the struggle to acquire, maintain, or resist power. As Angie Chabram and Rosa Linda Fregoso argued over ten years ago, narratives about cultural images and icons are key in struggles to define superior or inferior cultures, to establish what is central and what is marginal, to dictate official and forgotten histories, and to reinforce and police external and internal representations of social relations.[34] Cultural politics engages this struggle over meaning within the context of the real political economy of scarcity and inequality. This anthology investigates Latino and Latina popular culture as social and artistic phenomena through which major cultural and political debates, conflicts, and social expressions of identity, gender, sexuality, community, and nation are staged and performed.[35]

The increasing centralization of and hegemonic control over media outlets, visible in the commercial popular music industry's crushing of Napster, reveal that this historical moment is one of shrinking public and noncommercial outlets for the circulation and discussion of alternative and oppositional perspectives. Even as new technologies make possible independently produced forms of popular culture and facilitate both the critique of the status quo and dialogue concerning progressive social transformation, mass media limit this type of exposure. As artist and cultural critic Coco Fusco reminds us, "[c]ultural identity and values are politically and historically charged issues for peoples in this country whose access to exercising political power and controlling their symbolic representations has been limited within mainstream culture."[36]

Representations of life constructed in comics, live music, improvisation, and spoken word do not merely reflect everyday life, but help us imagine and construct what it could be in the future. Those who have limited access to the production and distribution of the dominant modes of representation—television, commercial film, popular music, and so forth—can find more accessible formats, such as live performance and independently produced compact discs and videos, to gain voice in discussions about everyday life in the United States and to represent themselves and their concerns, fears, and hopes for the future. Formats such as art performance, music, and local sports organizations are crucial because they open spaces, counter-sites, and conditions of possibility where Latinas and Latinos can publicly imagine new ways of constructing racial, ethnic, gendered, and economic identities. In the construction of new subjects for political identification, new movements for social equality can be articulated.[37] While such productions of popular culture may not have been considered traditional modes of political action, they constitute social territories where it is possible to engage in cultural politics. All cultural production "plays a constitutive, not merely a reflective role" in the production of everyday life.[38]

Finally, given the rapidly changing migration patterns of Latinos, motivated in part by new political and economic shifts, we agree with other scholars that there is the need to amplify the investigation of the production of Latino popular culture within a larger context of the Americas. Building on such work as Frances R. Aparicio and Susana Chávez's edited collection on how U.S. culture has been transformed by Latinos (a process they call tropicalization),[39] many of our contributors emphasize transcultural representations that link Latin America and Latinas/os in the United States. In our volume, we have included essays crossing both southern and northern borders. Thus the collection pays attention to the ways popular culture is "negotiated and becomes an object of transaction in a variety of contexts." As an object of transaction, we are interested in the ways popular culture, even as it is produced within a national context, resonates in transnational settings and produces a transnational imaginary.[40]

We solicited essays that exhibit a broad range of popular forms, various geographical and temporal spaces, as well as diverse Latina and Latino groups in North America. We organized the book along the lines of genre—media, music, film, theater, art, and sports—not so much out of lack of imagination, but rather with the intent of offering a user-friendly format conducive to interdisciplinary studies such as Latina/o studies and cultural studies. In addition, we hope the format meets the needs of scholars and students from a wide range of multidisciplinary backgrounds. While we know that some readers will be attracted to specific essays on particular types of genre, we encourage a broader reading to grasp significant issues central to Latinos and popular culture. The cross-fertilization of themes among contributors as they address the diverse forms of popular culture—music, dance, film, visual art, sports, and performance art—is enriched by the variety of sites of production, representations, and multiple social contradictions presented in each essay. The range of themes includes the complications of cultural citizenship in a border context; reconstructing a notion of the Americas; tensions around English, Spanish, and linguistic varieties in between; interrogations of the contours of the current "Latin boom"; and U.S. conceptions of race, transnational culture, gender and sexuality, and language and identity and the particularities of Cubanness, Caribbean-Latinoness, Mexicanness, and Puerto Ricanness. The essays are similarly linked by the critical analysis of cultural creations: Who creates? What images and symbols are employed? How are they interpreted? By whom? For whom?

ISSUES OF REPRESENTATION, AUDIENCE, AND PRODUCTION

Central to the investigation of Latina and Latino popular culture are questions of representation, audience, and production: How do self-representations differ from images produced in mainstream culture?[41] Are self-representations sources of empowerment or do these images subordinate others?[42] To what degree have crossover performers arrived without having to portray cultural archetypes: Latin spitfire or suffering Madonna, exotic erotic or hot-blooded super-macho, stoop laborer or drug warlord, illegal immigrant or exiled freedom fighter?[43] Do Latino/a artists and filmmakers deconstruct images and offer alternatives to mainstream productions?[44] Do Latino audiences construct alternative meaning and value through actual usage of popular culture?[45] Do Chicanas, Puerto Ricans, and Dominicans share similar views of racialized, gendered Latina and Latino images produced by Telemundo or Univisión?[46] How do Latinos intervene, contest, or reproduce "already" circulating representations?

In her critique of media culture, Angharad Valdivia emphasizes the significance of representation as "an important theoretical and political component of any strategy that seeks to redress issues of cultural and material inequality."[47] Consequently, concern for the legal and political consequences of Latino and Latina ethnic and racial representations in film and other media in the so-called Latin explosion has been addressed by social science and legal scholars writing on current immigration,[48] welfare,[49] and racial profiling issues.[50]

A major issue of representation examined by the contributors in this volume is racialization and the intersectionalities of gender, sexuality, nationality, and citizenship, in particular racial formations. Essays by Adrian Burgos and Frances Negrón-Muntaner elaborate the ways U.S.-born Latinos disrupt racial categories, thereby revealing the socially constructed natures of such categories where the Black/White racial binary still reigns. Tanya Hernández's essay similarly investigates the stakes in maintaining the binary by asking who benefits from such discursive divisions. Juan Velasco's analysis of Guillermo Gómez-Peña's performance illustrates the complexities of mestizo in constructing a racial, cultural, and national identity. In her analysis of Latino focus groups in New York City, Arlene Dávila finds distinct differences in issues of color that are revealed in audiences' reactions to "the whiteness of the world of Spanish TV." Each of these essays implicates the history of U.S. colonization of Latin America and its effects on U.S. racial formation.

Adrian Burgos's "Learning America's Other Game: Baseball, Race, and the Study of Latinos" highlights baseball as a quintessentially "American" institution and analyzes the turn-of-the-century classification of Latinos in the racial scheme of baseball leagues. Yet Burgos deftly demonstrates baseball as another instance of popular culture playing out U.S. struggles to determine the place of U.S.-born Latinos within the Black/White racial binary. Burgos then traces how early-twentieth-century debates over the racial categorization of Latinos continue to haunt present-day representations of U.S.-born Latinos in baseball. Moreover, Burgos's analysis points to long-standing ways the U.S. national imagination has confused and been confused about the racial designation of U.S.-born Latinos. Equally important, he draws attention to how white team owners benefited from this racial ambiguity. What is striking is how this racial confusion militates against including U.S. Latinos in baseball history; U.S.-born Latino players are not seen in the context of Latin American baseball, and since they were never considered a separate category, as black players were, their history of participation was lost in American baseball annals.

Tanya Katerí Hernández's essay, "*The Buena Vista Social Club*: The Racial Politics of Nostalgia," moves to a contemporary moment that is no less historically shaped. Hernández argues that U.S. popular press circulated narratives about the recent film *Buena Vista Social Club* that reproduced racialized colonial myths that Cuba was unable to exploit its "national resources"; such discourse helps justify reentry of U.S. corporate interests into the affairs of Cuba. Hernández notes the conflation of "primitive other" and "noble savage" discourses that news narratives superimposed on the figures of the Afro-Cuban musicians. The narrative further serves to reproduce a colonial myth by presenting Ry Cooder as "'discoverer/conqueror' of native resources that have gone unappreciated and are more effectively channeled by a North American figure" (a role he played earlier in "discovering" Flaco Jiménez). This "nostalgia for a prerevolutionary Cuba that was presumably more appreciative of its Black talent than socialist Cuba" omits the prolific, if not easily marketed, contemporary Afro-Cuban musical production. It defines Afro-Cuban musical production as belonging to the past.

Frances Negrón-Muntaner's essay, "Barbie's Hair: Selling Out Puerto Rican Identity in the Global Market," discusses the impact of class location on notions of ethnic and racial identity in the context of the Puerto Rican Barbie. Negrón-Muntaner argues that the Mattel Corporation's figure of the Puerto Rican Barbie colluded with the ideology of Puerto Rico's ruling class, representing the "consummate nationalist elite product bred by the contradictions of the commonwealth: a modern packaging (plastic) of a premodern essence (rural Puerto Rico), for postmodern nationalists (colonial survivors)." The struggle to define the Puerto Rican Barbie as an Anglicized image of what Puerto Ricans are supposed to be, as a "wavy-haired mulatta," points to the "real and perceived power of different Puerto Rican communities to invent, control, and deploy their cultural specificity."

In "Performing Multiple Identities: Guillermo Gómez-Peña and His 'Dangerous Border Crossings,'" Juan Velasco critiques the cultural construction of mestizo and indigenista in the video documentaries *The Couple in the Cage* and *Border Brujo*. Both performances address the complexities of linking the notion of "Indian" to the "new world order" and the reconstruction of the border trope so commonly used by Chicana/o writers and artists. Velasco argues that the value of these performances is "to destabilize the very specific idea of creating a new identity" and demonstrates the distinction between the U.S. appropriation of the multiracial (or mestizo) identity and the new Xicanistas, such as Ana Castillo.

Debates surrounding language usage within Latino communities are long-standing and contentious. The retention or loss of Spanish is sometimes employed as a cultural barometer to register the supposed "authenticity" of a given Latino group or individual within a group. While we believe that retention of Spanish is not a requirement for "authentic" Latino identities in the United States, public debate about the issue takes many points of view. Tensions in constructing a Latina/o racial and cultural identity are central to Arlene Dávila's chapter, "Talking Back: Spanish Media and U.S. Latinidad." Here, both skin color and language, as well as national and transnational symbols of class, are revealed in the opinions expressed by different Latino subnationalities. Dávila takes the heated language debate to heart. By exploring Latino responses to corporate Spanish-language media in the United States, she argues that Latinos' self-conceptualization of their identity is not reducible to the issue of language. However, her essay calls attention to, and problematizes, the strict association that corporate media promote between Spanish language and Latinidad.

Amplifying the discussion of language, Raquel Rivera's "Hip Hop and New York Puerto Ricans" examines how English-speaking U.S. Latino rappers challenge the strict association of language and culture, but at a cost. Rivera's argument, that Latino rap artists who write in English are overlooked by the music industry, sheds new light on the multiethnic core of the New York hip hop scene. Latino rappers' challenging of racial and linguistic binaries compels them to share a similar fate of invisibility with Burgos's U.S.-born Latino baseball players. In addition, Rivera's focus on language launches debating points concerning assimilation, diaspora, and intra-ethnic relationships. Rivera's piece demonstrates the ways representations of oppositional masculinity in forms such as rap (and by implication punk) and rock lose their transformative force as they reproduce misogynist and homophobic discourses.

Alberto Sandoval-Sánchez's essay, "Paul Simon's *The Capeman:* The Staging of Puerto Rican National Identity as Spectacle and Commodity on Broadway," compels readers to look beyond Spanish as a barometer for the authenticity of Latino cultural production. Sandoval-Sánchez claims that the marketing of *The Capeman* as an "authentically Puerto Rican" production was misleading and that *The Capeman's* consumption by audiences as "authentically Puerto Rican" was problematic as well. His critique turns on three issues: (1) the production of *Capeman* itself, (2) the racist assumptions of Anglo reviewers, and (3) Puerto Rican audiences' ecstatic reception of the piece. He discusses the power of the genre of the Broadway play to reproduce stereotypes and the willingness of Latinos to accept them. However, he carefully points out that Latinos do this within a social structure that offers very limited representations of Latinos.

In, "Bidi Bidi Bom Bom: Selena and Tejano Music in the Making of Tejas," Deborah Vargas critiques the notion of "crossover" artist that has been used by the U.S. media to describe the posthumous success of Tejana pop star Selena. Vargas asserts that Selena's major crossover was not her move from Tejano markets to major U.S. pop markets, but from Tejano markets to Latin American markets. Vargas also claims that Selena crossed gender borders in the Tejano music industry. Vargas explores the cultural implication of debates around U.S.-born Selena's fluency in English, her first language, and her acquisition of Spanish in her adult life.

As these essays demonstrate, the complex relation to language that is negotiated through Latino popular culture was shaped by the history of Spanish colonization, diasporic displacement, and interaction with hegemonic U.S. middle-class white culture. Essays by Ana Patricia Rodríguez, Josh Kun, Christopher Shinn, Michelle Habell-Pallán, and William Nericcio continue "the shift away from a sense of popular culture as products and traditions to a complex idea of signifying 'practice,' performance, and institutional process."[51] These essays document the practices and processes of transculturation of popular culture. They demonstrate that just as Latino popular culture is transformed by the dominant culture, so is U.S. mainstream culture being transformed by Latino cultural production. Transnational practices of cultural production often call, from a North American perspective, for solidarity coalesced around the desire to reinvent a critical culture of the Americas. Ana Patricia Rodríguez's profound essay, "Encrucijadas: Rubén Blades at the Transnational Crossroads," addresses the cultural effects of the Central American diaspora in the United States and Panama. Rodríguez argues that Rubén Blades's musical production is a site where the struggle to make visible Central Americans as U.S. Latinos takes places and also highlights the "particular legacy of colonialism and imperialism in Panamá." Moreover, Rodríguez charges, Blades's musical production marks a moment when "military warfare has given way to the violence of global capital and neoliberal rule in the region" and locates Blades within the "extensive corpus of Central American social protest discourses and genres, which include anti-occupation novels, anti-imperialist literature, and testimonial narratives."

In "'The Sun Never Sets on MTV': Tijuana NO! and the Border of Music Video," Josh Kun exposes the contradictions and possibilities of anti-imperialist discourse circulating in border music videos against the context of MTV's discursive celebration of global domination and conquest. Kun demonstrates that the videos are scenes where the fates and futures of Latinos in the United States are rehearsed and struggled over.

Christopher Shinn's "Fútbol Nation: U.S. Latinos and the Goal of a Homeland" links Latino identity with soccer and investigates the transformation of local communities in the Pacific Northwest by transnational migrants from Latin America. Shinn suggests that international, national, and local struggles to define "homeland" have led to the development of national and local leagues made possible by the service/farmer/worker migrant circuit that supports local communities throughout the United States.

Michelle Habell-Pallán's "'Don't Call Us Hispanic': Popular Latino Theater in Vancouver" continues Shinn's exploration of the U.S. northern borderlands area by focusing attention on the situation of Latino youth in Canada. Young Latino Canadians are competing to define themselves in a North American context in which stereotypical images of Latinos produced by U.S. media endlessly infiltrate their everyday lives. Grassroots theater in Canada offers Canadian-born Latina/o youth a place to imagine how solidarity across the continent of the Americas might eradicate second-class citizenship in North America.

William Nericcio's "A Decidedly 'Mexican' and 'American' Semi-[er]otic Transference: Frida Kahlo in the Eyes of Gilbert Hernandez" points to ways artistic sensibilities cross the U.S.-Mexico border. His essay is also an innovative model for students of the *Love and Rockets* graphic novella series by Los Bros. Hernandez. Nericcio provides an excellent model for interpreting "mestizo art" as a form whose history is richly layered and textured.

Although almost all the essays implicitly deal with questions of gender and representation, the following chapters highlight the ways categories of ethnicity/race, class, gender, and sexuality always intersect. Advances made by Latina[52] and women of color[53] feminist intellectuals compel scholars to recognize these intersections and have, in part, created the possibility for analysis such as the following by Luz Calvo, Gregory Rodriguez, and Melissa Fitch.

"'Lemme Stay, I Want to Watch': Ambivalence in Borderlands Cinema," Calvo's exploration of three key "border" films that visually collapse racial hybridity, sexuality, and violence, is a powerful analysis of unconscious colonial fears and desires. Calvo charts new theoretical territory by juxtaposing Chicana feminism and psychoanalysis in exploring the unconscious reproduction of "the colonial scene of sexual and racial violence" that continually surfaces in forms of popular culture. Equally important, Calvo's discussion suggests that recent border narratives offer an escape from that colonial imaginary: the figure of the mestiza can narrate a story outside the logic of patriarchy, the logic that frames colonial relations, by embodying sexualities not sanctioned by the patriarchal order.

If Calvo's analysis turns on the figure of prohibited mestiza sexuality, Gregory Rodriguez's "Boxing and Masculinity: The History and (Her)story of Oscar de la Hoya" focuses on boxing as a cultural site that attempts to fix a rigid and limited version of ethnic and gender identity, specifically heterosexual masculinity. Rodriguez analyzes audience responses to de la Hoya's presentation of masculinity from the perspective of spectators, including state officials, businessmen, journalists, but especially Latino fans, specifically women. As a contemporary incarnation of a "Mexican" boxing idol, de la Hoya represents both change and continuity in the century-long tradition. Debates about his public display of masculinity have been framed and fueled by his female fans. Though Latino spectators tend to question his manhood because de la Hoya refuses to perform a working-class inflected style of masculinity, Latina fans judge de la Hoya's manhood and "manliness" based on perceived intimate relations with important women in his life.

Melissa A. Fitch's essay, "Gender Bending in Latino Theater: *Johnny Diego*, *The His-panic Zone*, and *Deporting the Divas* by Guillermo Reyes," takes assumed ethnic and gender identities to task as it examines the Chilean playwright's compelling development of gay and bisexual characters who open the spectrum of Latino representation in contemporary theater. Fitch's essay elucidates Reyes's cautionary tales about the dehumanizing effects of both the dominant cultural and the politically correct notions of ethnicity, gender, and sexuality. Fitch suggests that the strength in Reyes's work is to make ordinary the diversity of human sexuality.

CONCLUSION

This collection's innovative discussions of popular culture are intended as a launching point to challenge our imaginations about the way issues articulated in Latino popular culture resonate in both the northern (United States and Canada), southern, and Caribbean reaches of the hemisphere. Since the passage of the North American Free Trade Agreement (NAFTA), mass media discourse has focused almost exclusively on the economic implications of trade policy, that is, on how easing restrictions of capital and goods flow across national borders affects business in the United States. The cultural implications (in both everyday and artistic realms) of the economic ties engendered by NAFTA are rarely given public airing. Even as xenophobic discourse advocates the increased militarization of borders dividing the United States from Mexico and Canada, the demilitarization of the border for the sake of human rights, suggested by Vicente Fox, president of Mexico, is being discussed in mainstream American media. Public debate is just beginning to recognize the unparalleled *need* for undocumented migrant labor that supports local economies in the United States, ranging from the orchards of the Yakima Valley to Nebraska meatpacking facilities, Pennsylvania mushroom caves, and the construction industry in the booming Southwest.[54] The collection investigates cutting-edge public, if not mainstream, debates about these issues in the most unexpected forms of popular culture. Moreover, the cultural impacts of NAFTA are furthering a social dynamic strengthening preexisting ties of immigrants from the Americas to the United States and Canada, while simultaneously compelling U.S.-based Latinos to imagine and invent new cultural ties to Latin America.

We hope this anthology contributes to the ongoing discussion concerning U.S. Latinas and Latinos and their use of popular culture as a site of invention, critique, and pleasure. There is still much more work to be done in this area of inquiry. For the most part, in the United States, popular culture is aimed at, and is influenced by, young people. Our hope is to inspire graduate students and undergraduates to analyze Latino popular culture in a manner that captures the interests, hopes, and fears of their generation. Thanks in part to the unprecedented demographic increase in the Latino population, the sheer impact of Latino culture, whether first or twenty-first generation, will continue to transculturate and transform the definition of "American." While it is our fervent hope that collections such as this one will challenge social inequality, marginalization, and cultural denigration that continue to exist in the economic, political, and cultural spheres, we look forward to the day when such themes will no longer have a place in the study of Latina and Latino popular culture.

NOTES

1. Robin Fields, "2000 Census Shows Latino Boom," *Los Angeles Times*, 22 March 2001, 27A.

2. Bob Golfen and Hernan Rozemberg, "Census Jolts Business World: Corporate America Suddenly Discovering the Latino Market," *Arizona Republic*, 31 March 2001, B1.

3. Mike Allen, "Bush: Respect Mexican Immigrants; President and Responding Democrats Broadcast in Spanish," *Washington Post*, 6 May 2001, A07.

4. Johnathon E. Briggs, "Woman Was Brutalized at Store, Suit Alleges; Courts: Guard Stopped the Mexican Pediatrician Because of 'Profiling,' Her Attorney Charges," *Los Angeles Times*, 17 March 2000, B3.

5. Lee Romney, "Over the Line? Citing Questioning of Mayor, Activists Say Border Patrol Targets All Latinos," *Los Angeles Times*, 2 September 1993, J1.

6. Jessie Halladay and Blake Morrison, "Martin Kicks Off Inaugural Festivities; Bush Shares Stage with Pop Sensation," *USA Today*, 19 January 2001, 4A.

7. Jeff Jacoby, "Mr. Bush, Encourage Hispanics to Learn English," *Boston Globe*, 10 May 2001, A21.

8. Dance is described in the following newspaper articles: David E. Sanger,

"Transition in Washington: The President-Elect; G.O.P. Begins a Party 8 Years in the Making," *New York Times*, 19 January 2001, 1A; Alan Sipress and Manny Fernandez, "First Dance at the Party; For President-Elect and Ricky Martin: Cold Rain, Warm Welcome," *Washington Post*, 19 January 2001, A1.

9. Stuart Hall's rumination on the contested definitions and historical emergence of Black popular culture prompts this collection to consider the current historical moment as both a productive and vexed moment to analyze the "Latina/o" in popular culture. See "Where Is the Black in Black Popular Culture?" in *Black Popular Culture*, ed. Gina Dent (Seattle: Bay Press, 1992), 21–33.

10. George Lipsitz, *Time Passages: Collective Memory and American Popular Culture* (Minneapolis: University of Minnesota Press, 1990), 4.

11. Reports of protests and commentaries on stereotypes are reported in newspaper articles. See George Hunter, "Ads Often Miss for Minorities: In Touchy Industry, White- and Black-Owned Agencies Struggle to Overcome Stereotypes," *Detroit News*, 18 October 1998, B1; Richard Estrada, "Taco Bell TV Ads Aren't as Harmless as Viewers Think," *Rocky Mountain News*, 27 April 1998, 36A.

12. Isis Artze, "2000 in Review," *Hispanic: Business, Career, Politics and Culture*, December 2000, 36.

13. Jacoby, "Mr. Bush, Encourage Hispanics to Learn English."

14. In the television series *Miami Vice* (NBC TV from 1984 to 1989), Olmos played the role of Lt. Martin Castillo. Olmos directed and played the lead character (the street gang leader Santana) in the film drama *American Me* (Universal, 1992).

15. Neil A. Lewis, "Miami Relatives Seek Review of Decision That Would Let Boy Return to Cuba," *New York Times*, 16 June 2000, A22.

16. A recent and highly publicized case involved the five-day 1997 "sweep" in Chandler, Arizona. Using racial and economic profiling to target people, thirty-five Chandler police officers joined U.S. Border Patrol personnel and entered residential areas to bust illegals, arresting 432 undocumented immigrants and several U.S. citizens. See Melissa L. Jones, "Officials Overstepped Authority in Chandler Roundup: Policies Violated, INS Report Says," *Arizona Republic*, 6 August 1999, B2.

17. Adam Nagourney, "Ferrer to Go to Puerto Rico to Join Protest of Navy Bombings," *New York Times*, 1 May 2001, B2.

18. Ana Mendieta, "Mexican Workers Seek WWII Wages," *Chicago Sun-Times*, 2 March 2001, 28.

19. Steve Bousquet, "Affirmative Action Up for Debate in Florida; Proposal Akin to California's Proposition 209," *Houston Chronicle*, 5 December 1999, 2A.

20. B. Drummond Ayres, Jr., "Political Briefing: Sizing Up Colorado for a Bilingual Battle," *New York Times*, 1 April 2001, sec. 1, 24.

21. Neil Strauss, "Santana Dominates Grammy Awards," *New York Times,* 24 February 2000, A20.

22. Alisa Valdes-Rodriguez and Geoff Boucher, "Martin's Music Catapults Latin Crossover Success," *Times Union,* 21 May 1999, D5.

23. Leila Cobo, "Here to Stay?" *Miami Herald,* 20 February 2000, 1M.

24. Coco Fusco, ed., *Corpus Delecti: Performance Art of the Americas* (New York: Routledge, 2000); Chon A. Noriega and Ana M. López, eds., *The Ethnic Eye: Latino Media Arts* (Minneapolis: University of Minnesota Press, 1996); Alicia Arrizón and Lillian Manzor, eds., *Latinas on Stage* (Berkeley: Third Woman Press, 2000).

25. Chris Barker, *Cultural Studies, Theory and Practice* (Thousand Oaks, CA: Sage, 2000), 47.

26. Jonathan Tilove, "Census More Than Black and White; African-Americans Vying with Hispanics for No. 1 Status," *Times Picayune,* 8 March 2001, 1.

27. Silvia Pedraza, "Beyond Black and White: Latinos and Social Science Research on Immigration, Race, and Ethnicity in America," *Social Science History* 24, no. 4 (winter 2000): 697–726; Angela Y. Davis, "Gender, Class, and Multiculturalism, Rethinking 'Race' Politics," in *Mapping Multi-Culturalism,* ed. Avery F. Gordon and Christopher Newfield (Minneapolis: University of Minnesota Press, 1996), 40–48.

28. For instance, the debates and controversy surrounding the recent census counts indicating that Latinos now outnumber African Americans in the United States. See Zev Chafets, "Changing Races: Eventually America Treats All Its Ethnics as Whites—Except Blacks," *New York Daily News,* 25 March 2001, 39; Tilove, "Census More Than Black and White."

29. In the case of Mexicans, see Rodolfo Acuña, *Occupied America* (San Francisco: Canfield, 1972); and Timothy J. Dunn, *The Militarization of the U.S.-Mexico Border, 1978–1992* (Austin: University of Texas Press, 1996). In the case of Salvadoran immigrants, see Sarah J. Mahler, *Salvadorans in Suburbia: Symbiosis and Conflict* (Boston: Allyn and Bacon, 1995); Sarah J. Mahler, *American Dreaming: Immigrant Life on the Margins* (Princeton: Princeton University Press, 1995); and Cecilia Menjívar, *Fragmented Ties: Salvadoran Immigrant Networks in America* (Berkeley: University of California Press, 2000).

30. In the case of Cubans and Nicaraguans, see Alejandro Portes and Alex Stepick, *City on the Edge: The Transformation of Miami* (Berkeley: University of California Press, 1993).

31. Waves of immigration from Mexico have been an important topic of research in cultural studies. See María Herrera-Sobek, *The Bracero Experience: Elitelore versus Folklore* (Los Angeles: UCLA Latin American Center Publications, University of California, Los Angeles, 1979); and David R. Maciel and María Herrera-Sobek, eds., *Culture across Borders: Mexican Immigration and Popular Culture* (Tucson: University of Arizona Press, 1998).

32. Ediberto Roman, "Who Exactly Is Living la Vida Loca? The Legal and Political Consequences of Latino-Latina Ethnic and Racial Stereotypes in Film and Other Media," *Journal of Gender, Race and Justice* 4 (fall 2000): 38–39; Steven W. Bender, "Will the Wolf Survive? Latino/a Pop Music in the Cultural Mainstream," *University of Denver Law Review* (forthcoming); Kevin R. Johnson, "Comparative Racialization: Culture and National Origin in the Latino/a Communities," *University of Denver Law Review* (forthcoming).

33. Stuart Hall, "Notes on Deconstructing 'The Popular,'" in *People's History and Socialist Theory,* ed. Raphael Samuel (Boston: Routledge and K. Paul, 1981), 239.

34. In their groundbreaking introduction to a special issue in *Cultural Studies on Chicana/o Cultural Representations,* Angie Chabram-Dernersesian and Rosa Linda Fregoso compelled scholars interested in the politics of representation to consider the intersections of race, class, gender, and national identity. Their work helped shaped the field of Chicana and Latina cultural studies and intersectional studies in general. Angie Chabram-Dernersesian and Rosa Linda Fregoso, "Chicana/o Cultural Representations: Reframing Alternative Critical Discourses," *Cultural Studies* 4, no. 3 (1990): 203–12.

35. This collection's discussion of the uses of Latina and Latino popular culture is in conversation with Herman Gray's compelling discussion of how debates about "Blackness" are staged, contested, or reproduced through and with commercial forms of popular culture. Herman Gray, *Watching Race: Television and the Struggle for "Blackness"* (Minneapolis: University of Minnesota Press, 1995).

36. Coco Fusco, *English Is Broken Here: Notes on Cultural Fusion in the Americas* (New York: New Press, 1995), 27.

37. Michelle Habell-Pallán, "No Cultural Icon: Marisela Norte," in *Women Transforming Politics: An Alternative Reader,* ed. Kathy Jones, Cathy Cohen, and Joan Tronto (New York: New York University Press, 1997), 256–68.

38. Hall, "Notes on Deconstructing 'The Popular,'" 239. See also Michel de Certeau, *The Practice of Everyday Life* (Berkeley: University of California Press, 1984).

39. Frances R. Aparicio and Susana Chávez-Silverman, eds., *Tropicalizations: Transcultural Representations of Latinidad* (Hanover, NH: University Press of New England, 1997).

40. Philip Schlesinger, introduction to *Communication, Culture, and Hegemony: From the Media to Mediations,* by Jesús Martín Barbero, trans. by Elizabeth Fox and Robert A. White (Newbury Park, CA: Sage, 1993), xiii.

41. Lillian Jiménez, "From the Margin to the Center: Puerto Rican Cinema in New York," and Liz Kotz, "Unofficial Stories: Documentaries by Latinas and Latin American Women," in *Latin Looks: Images of Latinas and Latinos in the U.S. Media,* ed. Clara Rodríguez (Boulder: Westview, 1997), 188–213; Melissa A.

Johnson, "Pre-Television Stereotypes: Mexicans in U.S. Newsreels, 1919–1932," *Critical Studies in Mass Communications* 16, no. 4 (1999): 417–35; Adriana Olivarez, "Studying Representations of U.S. Latino Culture," *Journal of Communication Inquiry* 22, no. 4 (October 1998): 426–37.

42. In calling for a "reframing of Chicano cultural identity," Fregoso and Chabram identify the limitations of the Chicano student movement representations. "Chicana/o Cultural Representations: Reframing Alternative Critical Discourses."

43. For instance, in film, see Chon Noriega, "Citizen Chicano: The Trials and Titillations of Ethnicity in the American Cinema, 1935–1962," *Social Research* 58, no. 2 (summer 1991): 413–28. In the area of sports, see Don Sabo, Sue Carry Jansen, Danny Tate, Margaret Carlisle Duncan, and Susan Leggett, "Televising International Sport: Race, Ethnicity, and Nationalistic Bias," *Journal of Sport and Social Issues* 20, no. 1 (1996): 7–21.

44. Coco Fusco, "Latin American Performance and the Reconquista of Civil Space," in Fusco, ed., *Corpus Delecti: Performance Art of the Americas*, 1–20.

45. Building on Paul Willis's argument that meaning and value are constructed through actual usage and on John Fiske's writings on creative meaning-producing activities of consumers. Paul Willis, *Common Culture: Symbolic Work at Play in the Everyday Cultures of the Young* (Milton Keynes: Open University Press, 1990); John Fiske, *Reading the Popular* (Boston: Unwin Hyman, 1989).

46. Arlene M. Dávila, *Latinos, Inc.: The Marketing and Making of a People* (Berkeley: University California Press, 2001); Diana I. Ríos and Stanley O. Gaines, Jr., "Impact of Gender and Ethnic Subgroup Membership on Mexican Americans' Use of Mass Media for Cultural Maintenance," *Howard Journal of Communications* 8, no. 2 (1997): 197–216.

47. Angharad N. Valdivia, *A Latina in the Land of Hollywood and Other Essays on Media Culture* (Tucson: University of Arizona Press, 2000), 90.

48. Kevin R. Johnson, "The Case against Race Profiling in Immigration Enforcement," *Washington University Law Quarterly* 78, no. 3 (2000): 675–736; Kevin R. Johnson, "Race, the Immigration Laws, and Domestic Race Relations: 'A Major Mirror' into the Heart of Darkness," *Indiana Law Journal* 73, no. 4 (1998): 1110–59.

49. In his discussion of stereotypes that shaped his students' interaction with a Latina client, Ms. Esperon, Peter Magulies writes,

> Our blind spots were numerous. Most seriously, we did not acknowledge that Ms. Esperon's situation as a single Latina receiving AFDC emerged from the intersectionality of ethnicity, class, and gender. The combination of these three factors marginalized Ms. Esperon not only within the larger society, but also within groups who share one or two marginalizing factors with Ms. Esperon. For example, Anglo society has never viewed Latinas as participants in the polity, but instead has

typically relegated them to the caricatured role of the "hot-blooded" female.

Peter Magulies, "The Mother with Poor Judgment and Other Tales of the Unexpected: A Civic Republican View of Difference and Clinical Legal Education," *Northwestern University Law Review* 88 (1994): 695–732.

50. Mary Romero, "State Violence and the Social and Legal Construction of Latino Criminality: From El Bandido to Gang Member," *Denver University Law Review* 78, no. 2 (forthcoming).

51. Juan Flores, *From Bomba to Hip-Hop: Puerto Rican Culture and Latino Identity* (New York: Columbia University Press, 2000).

52. See Cherríe Moraga and Gloria Anzaldúa, eds., *This Bridge Called My Back: Writings by Radical Women of Color* (Watertown, MA: Persephone Press, 1981); Yvonne Yarbro-Bejarano, "The Female Subject in Chicano Theater: Sexuality, 'Race,' and Class," *Theater Journal* 38, no. 4 (1986): 389–407; Mary Romero, *Maid in the U.S.A.* (New York: Routledge, 1992); Angie Chabram-Dernersesian, "I Throw Punches for My Race, but I Don't Want to Be a Man: Writing Us—Chica-nos (Girl, Us)/Chicanas—into the Movement Script," in *Cultural Studies,* ed. Lawrence Grossberg, Cary Nelson, and Paula Treichler (New York: Routledge, 1992), 81–95.

53. Trinh T. Minh-ha, *When the Moon Waxes Red: Representation, Gender, and Cultural Politics* (New York: Routledge, 1991); Rayna Green, "The Pocahontas Perplex: The Image of Indian Women in American Culture," *Massachusetts Review* 16 (autumn 1975): 698–714; Lisa Lowe, "Heterogeneity, Hybridity, Multiplicity: Marking Asian American Difference," *Diaspora* 1, no. 1 (spring 1991): 24–44; bell hooks, "Dialectically Down with the Critical Program," in Dent, ed., *Black Popular Culture,* 48–55.

54. Eric Schmitt, "Ambivalence Prevails in Immigration Policy," *New York Times,* 27 May 2001, A12.

MEDIA/CULTURE

I

Talking Back

Spanish Media and U.S. Latinidad

Arlene Dávila

FELIPE: The problem is those *novelas* in Spanish television. They are all white. It's like, I'm a dark-skinned Puerto Rican. And in these stations they are all white. They all look South American. They are racist. (*All interrupt*)

ARLENE (moderator): Let's hear one at a time.

FELIPE: If you watched TV you would think that Latinos are all white or looking like fucking, I don't know . . .

TRINY: That we all looked Mexican.

FELIPE: But Mexicans are Indian looking. It's all ridiculous.

TRINY: Yeah, we all have different elements in us, we have whites, Africans, you know, we are a mix of all those people, but even in commercials, all you see is white people eating Goya beans. It's crazy.

JENNY: Yes, we are a mix, you know.

TRINY: You don't see a lot of dark-skinned Latinos on *novelas*, just the housemaid.

—Exchange among Latino youth during a focus group

WITH LATINOS BEING targeted by more and more Spanish-language and Latino-oriented media, it is evident that these initiatives have been central to the development and conceptualization of U.S. Latinidad. In addressing Latinos as a single encompassing group, these initiatives have certainly helped shape and refurbish the existence of a common Latino/a identity, but seldom have we looked at the ways people respond to these culturally specific media and to the "Latinness" so promoted by their programming and representations.[1] This chapter explores this void by providing a brief examination of the views and opinions voiced by a group of New York Latinos about some of the media directed at them and what their comments revealed about how Latinos position themselves within the all-encompassing category of identity in which these representations are predicated. My aim is to expose some of the range of issues that color people's consumption of these texts and, in particular, to analyze what the opinions of different Latino subnationalities with regard to the existence of a common "Latino media market" suggest about these media's impact on the public consolidation of U.S. Latinidad.

My discussion is based on a year-long ethnographic research project on the making of Hispanic advertisements for Spanish TV, which included some focus group discussions exploring their reception by the people toward whom they were geared.[2] They consisted of six groups of self-identified Latinos from different nationalities and displaying different levels of proficiency in Spanish, from nonspeakers to bilinguals to active users of "Spanglish," that is, code switching between Spanish and English (Zentella 1997). All participants had lived in New York from three to fifteen years and many had been born in the city and were quite knowledgeable about the U.S. Hispanic media environment. The discussions were intended to focus primarily on Hispanic advertisements, but they soon turned to the Spanish TV networks, Univisión and Telemundo, as well as to the city's Latin-formatted radio stations, such as La Mega (97.9 FM) and Amor (93.1 FM), providing revealing insights about people's views on different Latino-oriented media.

What follows are excerpts of these discussions and my analysis, which I offer not as conclusive statements of how all U.S. Latinos think about these media and their representation of "things Latino," but rather as "positioned stories" (Ang 1996), that is, as contextualized observations gained primarily from New York Latinos that are suggestive of how U.S. Latinos react to representations of Latinidad, an issue rarely studied. I stress "contextualized," because as will be evident below, participants' engagements with the media were always mediated by regionally specific considerations. In particular New York City's race/ethnic hierarchies, where the city's largest Latino subgroups, Puerto Ricans and Dominicans, are placed at the bottom of the hierarchy, were a dominant reference in these discussions. Specifically, during their discussions of the media, participants would consistently draw on their perception of their place and that of others within these existing hierarchies while simultaneously expressing and communicating particularized identities along the lines of race, class, or ethnicity using the same conventions of Latinidad disseminated by the Spanish and Latino-oriented media. I will therefore suggest that while Spanish and Latino-oriented media have undoubtedly contributed to Latinization—the consolidation of a common Latino identity among different Latino subgroups—they have also helped forge and trigger existing hierarchies of evaluation among members of ostensibly the same group.

One of the most generalized beliefs advanced in different forms by focus group participants was that the Hispanic/Latino-oriented media are representative of U.S. Latinos and that their growth is indicative of Latinos' achievement and enfranchisement.[3] Again and again, participants would mirror the discourse of representation that the U.S. Spanish networks are so dependent on, attesting to the extent to which this discourse permeated almost all of my informants' diverse interpretations or evaluations of these media. These media were alternately praised or criticized, but always in relation to their position as an ethnic-specific (or culture-specific) product whose growth attests to Latinos' growing power and visibility. This view was succinctly voiced by a Puerto Rican participant who, when recalling with pride the rapid growth of the Hispanic media in New York City, insisted that this demonstrated that "They've had to adapt themselves to us, and could not survive if we stop consuming." Viewers' association of Hispanic media with Hispanics' "coming of age" in the public eye, however, does not mean they were oblivious to the exclusions generated by these representations, and it is this much less known fact that concerns me here.

Participants were particularly critical of the "foreignness" of the Spanish TV networks' programming, which they felt made the networks irrelevant to their everyday reality. One participant bemoaned the fact that there was too much Mexican programming, leaving little room for shows targeted to other nationalities. Most felt that the stations were geared only to audiences in the West, not to them, inasmuch as they featured ranchero music, Mexican artists, and soccer rather than programs from other Latin American countries where they could learn what was happening "back home," or even watch baseball, which is favored over soccer by the city's Dominican and Puerto Rican Latino audience. To contextualize these comments we must note that, though the U.S. Hispanic TV networks project and sell themselves as the representative media of U.S. Latinos, they have historically functioned as a "transnational," not "ethnic," media, importing cheaper Latin American programming or else producing shows for export to Latin America, and hence with primarily the transcontinental Latin American, not the U.S., audience in mind.[4] In particular, the U.S. Spanish networks have tended to draw most of their programming and talent from the largest media exporting countries in Latin America, such as Mexico and to a lesser degree Venezuela, leading to a preponderance of Mexican actors and talent in the U.S. Spanish airwaves. The networks have tended to justify this trend on the grounds that Mexicans constitute 65 percent of the Latino population, but in New York City, where within a highly heterogeneous Latino population it is Hispanic Caribbeans who are predominant, the exclusion of other Latino subgroups ensuing from the network's reliance on exported programming was easily noticeable by most participants. Also highly represented in the U.S. networks are Cubans, as a result of the early entry of Cuban actors and media entrepreneurs who had been previously involved in Cuba's media and publicity industry, in the development of the U.S. Hispanic media and marketing industry since the 1960s. Again, such dominance of some Latino subgroups and the ensuing exclusions of others did not go unnoticed by focus group participants, who were quick to draw a connection between the whiteness of the world of Spanish TV and the dominance in it of some Latino groups over others. Thus, revealingly, when participants bemoaned the dominance of whiter and Mediterranean Hispanic models, it was Cubans and Mexicans who some participants blamed for this trend. As one stated, these groups had "shaped these images after themselves," a view I believe speaks less to participants' belief that Mexican and Cubans are indeed closer to these images, than to their awareness of the dominance of some Latino subgroups over others in the making of these representations.

Interestingly, the whiteness of the world of Spanish TV was of greater concern among the U.S.-born Latinos than among recent immigrants, reminding us that immigration and length of stay in the United States are central variables affecting an individual's experience and awareness of U.S. racism, and hence the likelihood that they would express dissatisfaction with the lack of racial representativeness in the

Spanish TV networks. Additionally, among U.S.-born Latinos, it was Hispanic Caribbeans, primarily Puerto Ricans and Dominicans, who were most concerned with issues of color. This, in turn, is not surprising, given the greater African racial influence in the Caribbean—a product of the islands' history of slavery. What I would like to suggest here, however, is that Hispanic Caribbeans' greater concern with this issue was suggestive of viewers' awareness that when black Latinos are shown on Hispanic TV, it is Hispanic Caribbeans (mostly Puerto Ricans and Dominicans, and to a much lesser degree Cubans) who have been made to stand for "color." For example, when dark-skinned maids are shown in Mexican soap operas, they tend to be from the Caribbean (such as in *La Usurpadora*). Another example is the casting of the black Puerto Rican actor Rafael José for the multinational team of *Despierta América*, Univisión's version of *Good Morning America*. Yet another example is provided by the short-lived Spanish version of *Charlie's Angels* by Telemundo, featuring a multiracial/multinational team of angels—a blonde, a brunette, and a black Latina, played by an Argentinean, a Mexican, and a Colombian actress respectively. Echoing what is a common trend in representations of Latinidad, the angels' skin color is increasingly darker among the actresses originating from the countries closest to the Equator as Spanish TV consistently leaves us with the impression that there are no blacks in Mexico, blondes in the Dominican Republic, or brunettes in Argentina.

Indeed, representations of Latinidad in the Spanish TV networks, when not revolving around generic representations that prioritize white Mediterranean Hispanic actors and talent, have generally reduced each Latino subgroup to a particular cultural index, be it music, race, or an artist. Accordingly, appealing to Puerto Ricans becomes tantamount to showing a Puerto Rican salsa group, and to Colombians to featuring Colombian model/actress Sonia Vergara, and so forth. This strategy of representation, however, as simple as it may make the networks' mission of appealing to different Latino nationalities, is no more inclusive than their regular programming fare of white models or Mexican shows. Thus, we are left with the following predicament: on the one hand, the dominance of Mediterranean Hispanic types in Spanish TV negates and leaves no room for acknowledging Latinos' racial and ethnic diversity, while diversity is accordingly reduced to iconic and essentialist representations that are presented as "belonging" neatly to some groups but not others.

Viewers were not oblivious to the networks' strict assignment of cultural traits, in this case color, to particular Latino nationalities. A particularly revealing example here surfaced during a discussion of a JCPenney ad for the Hispanic market that presents a multiracial collage of Latino youth of different nationalities, which we are led to deduce by the distinct words each uses for "cool" (*macanudo* used in Argentina, *chévere* in Puerto Rico and Central America, *padrísimo* in Mexico, and so forth). A Puerto Rican participant demanded to know why it was that when black Latinos were shown, if at all, they were always Puerto Rican, when in fact there are Puerto Ricans of all races and, like Argentineans, Puerto Ricans can also be blonde. Interestingly, nothing except the word *chévere* marks the black kid as Puerto Rican in the ad. In fact, the same character also says *órale*, more characteristic of Mexicans, while the creative staff who had done the ad confirmed to me that the model had been cast to be a generic Caribbean Hispanic, not Puerto Rican. This participant's comment was one more example of how participants' own backgrounds were always summoned as part of their interpretation of the ads, in this case, the informant's awareness of his own racialization and that of Puerto Ricans both in the greater U.S. society and in the "Latino" community. To put it another way, he had seen through the fact that the ad, though claiming racial and ethnic integration (its punch line reads, "It does not matter who you are or where you come from. We can all be cool by dressing JCPenney"), is predicated on assignments of color and race and even language idioms to particular nationalities that hinder the acceptance of racial diversity as intrinsic to all Latinos, not solely some groups, be they Puerto Ricans or other Hispanic Caribbeans.

Moreover, by associating different nationalities with particular ethnic indexes, the Spanish and Latino-oriented media end up negating the actual cross-fertilization that does occur among and across Latino subgroups. After all, Latinos do not live and operate from neatly defined ethnic enclaves isolated from other subgroups, and nowhere is this more evident than in New York City, which features one of the most heterogeneous U.S. Latino populations. In the past years, New York has seen a growing diversification of the city's Latino population: Puerto Ricans, who made up 80 percent of the city's Latino population in the 1960s, are now only 43 percent of all Latinos; a rapid growth of Dominican, Mexican, and Central American populations has rendered the city an important "homogenizing pot" of Latinidad. In this context, and at the level of practice, popular culture emerges as a cross-fertilizing medium among and across Latino subgroups that cannot be neatly associated to any particular subgroup in the manner intended by the networks' strategies of customization.

Most significant, the media's strategies of customization become vehicles that expose and in so doing, help shape and naturalize essentialist conventions concerning cultural traits that are supposedly characteristic of particular Latino subnationalities. A good example of this trend is provided by a discussion of the city's Latino-formatted radio stations, regional media that easily lend themselves to customization, evidencing the media's "naturalization" of difference among Latino nationalities. The discussion revolved around La Mega (97.9 FM), targeted to Puerto Ricans and Dominicans through a fare of salsa, merengue, and bachata, and Amor (93.1 FM), geared to a pan-Latino audience through baladas, pop tunes, and Latin soft rock. It was triggered by recent programming changes adopted by the city's most popular radio station, the salsa- and merengue-formatted La Mega, to target more directly the city's growing Dominican community by playing more bachata and merengue and by featuring Dominican language mannerisms in spoken segments. The overall tone of the stations is irreverent—imagine a Latin Howard Stern full of sexual imagery and innuendos—and consequently, the goal of appealing to the Dominicans became tantamount to the D.J.s' use of Dominican slang and accent when speaking to *mamis* (girlfriends) over the airwaves. Thus, during a discussion among a group of Spanish-dominant Latinos, mostly South American (Colombian and Ecuadorian) and one Cuban as well as one Dominican participant, not surprisingly La Mega and the Dominican participant were soon turned into the embodiment of Dominican culture and hence of the stereotypes about Dominicans and Hispanic Caribbeans. Briefly, one of the Colombian women denounced the sexual innuendo that pervades the dialogue between the D.J.s' and their call-in public, to which an Ecuadorian man responded by evoking the stereotype of the hot Dominican male and the more open and eroticized Caribbean culture: "that's Caribbean culture for you. Change the station to Amor and you'll see that they speak different because they are not from the Caribbean." In this group, the Dominican female participant had previously explained, in relation to a similar insinuation of Dominicans' unrepressed sexuality, that Dominican culture is not the way it is represented in the Latin media and that such profanities would not be heard in the Dominican Republic, where, she claimed, a Commission of Public Entertainments would prohibit them from being aired. Such objections notwithstanding, the issue continued to surface, with the salsa-merengue radio station serving as the indisputable proof of Caribbeans' lustfulness versus South Americans' more "restrained" sexuality, which one would encounter on another station. Again, I stress that participants made these distinctions concerning the so-called morals and sexual dispositions of different Latino subgroups by contrasting the merengue/salsa-formatted La Mega with the pop-formatted Amor, and through associations that were predicated on the strict and essentialist equations between different types of music and particular Latin countries and nationalities.

In reality, however, such strict associations of countries and particular types of music are quite superfluous. In fact, the same participants who shunned La Mega would later reveal that they did in fact listen to salsa and merengue, and appeared to be quite familiar with the station's programming—as did most participants irrespective of their nationality. Obviously, then, people's negative comments on La Mega did not necessarily reflect their listening habits, but rather their generalized association of salsa/merengue stations with Dominicans and Puerto Ricans, who in these discussions were treated as the embodiments of low culture against which other New York Latinos would distinguish themselves as more moral, respectable, and authentic. Moreover, such comments were also intertwined with issues of class, which were similarly indexed and negotiated in relation to various media and in reference to particular nationalities. Specifically, while all groups admitted liking and listening to La Mega, it was common for people to make claims about their status and class for themselves and others by shunning or taking issue with the station's vulgar and offensive content, or else by being more or less open about their listening to this station. Again, the former stance was embraced by many irrespective of nationality, although relative to Puerto Rican and Dominican informants, who constitute the station's main target groups, Central and South Americans were more likely to shun the station, as evident in the above discussion.

To grapple with these responses we need to acknowledge the existence of particular ethnic and racial hierarchies at play among Latinos, informed and affected by their different histories, the specific conditions leading to their immigrations, such as the prior relationships between the United States and the immigrant countries of origins, as well as each group's position within the city, variables that are also regionally specific (Flores 1996, Grosfoguel, and Georas 2001). In New York City, for instance, Hispanic Caribbeans, particularly Puerto Ricans, the oldest large-scale Latino immigration to the city, are positioned at the bottom of the city's ethnic and racial hierarchy, necessarily constituting the group against which other Latinos distance themselves in the process of claiming a space in the city. These dynamics have been documented by Robert Smith (1996) and Philippe Bourgois (1995), who have analyzed interethnic relations between Mexicans and Puerto Ricans in New York City. As they note, the negative perceptions of Puerto Ricans by Mexicans and presumably other recent arrivals to the city suggest, among other factors, Puerto Ricans' historical subordination in the city, which has vested them with the stigma of being the ultimate marginal minority, and their long-time association with African Americans, with whom they share similar positions in the city's racial and ethnic hierarchies.

At the same time, I am not suggesting that New York Puerto Ricans were mere victims of these hierarchies of representation. They too asserted their standing and identity in ways that simultaneously demeaned other Latino subgroups, and these dynamics were also communicated through their discussion of particular media. A general trend among U.S.-born English-dominant youth was to embrace hip hop and rap and their media as legitimate sites of Latinidad, where Latinos could prove their contribution to mainstream culture. Hip hop and rap served as reflections of their everyday realities, which they conceived in terms of alterity and marginality vis-à-vis mainstream culture. During these discussions, participants would identify Latin hip hop artists whom they had discovered were Latin, such as Fat Joe or Big Punisher, or African Americans they had thought were Latin, but in fact were not, pointing out in this way the mutability and cross-fertilization between black and Latino youth culture, and so highlighting the contributions of Latin artists to rap and hip hop. In particular, discussions of the media by young U.S.-born Latinos provided clues to alternative definitions of Latinidad beyond the dominant definition of "Latino/ Hispanic" projected by the Spanish TV networks, which emphasizes knowledge and mastery of the Spanish language, whiteness, and direct connections to a specific Latin American country. Some even overtly criticized the dominant Hispanophilic representations in the Spanish TV networks (recall our earlier discussion), asserting instead an anti-

Hispanic version of Latinidad rooted in a mixed black and mestizo culture. As one young Puerto Rican participant explained, "I don't have Spanish blood so I am no Hispanic." Their views and lack of self-recognition in the Spanish media are evidenced in the discussion quoted in the chapter opening, this discussion continued by touching on the representation of women as symbols of hypersexuality.

> FELIPE: I feel that they misrepresent us. And I don't like to watch it.
> ARLENE (moderator): How about you, Manuel, what do you think?
> MANUEL: No, I don't like it. It's boring, all they give is soap operas.
> HERB: Just for older people.
> MANUEL: I was catching myself the other day. I am twenty-five, you know, and I was thinking that every time I pass my sister [i.e., any Latina] on the subway I catch myself looking at their ass, I just do it. (*All laugh*) 'Cause all you see is women in bathing suits every time.
> SANDY: Like in *No te duermas*, caliente and with the big butt.
> HERB: No se ve más [You don't see anything else].
> MANUEL: Always is like hoochy mama, you know, something like that.

Yet, as critical of these representations as the youth were, some of them also gave evidence that they have internalized dominant definitions of Latinos promoted by the networks (that Latinos speak Spanish and have some connection and rooting with Latin America), by assuming that they lacked or may be perceived by others to lack the "appropriate" cultural capital of Latinidad. While I was recruiting participants for the focus groups, more than one English-dominant youth declined to participate on the grounds that he or she spoke no Spanish, until I explained that my study included all Latinos, be they code switchers or Spanish- or English-dominant. Another recruit (who failed to appear in the focus group) had identified herself as a second-generation Puerto Rican and a Latina, but was ready to add that she may not be the right person for this study because she neither spoke Spanish nor watched the Spanish-language channels, as if qualifying her own authenticity as a Latina on the grounds that she lacked the right language and media skills. It is therefore important to problematize the strict association promoted between Spanish and Latinidad by the Spanish media. Indeed, not surprisingly, putting down the Spanish TV networks surfaced as a common strategy among U.S.-born and English-dominant Latinos with which to reverse their peripheral position within this strict association. As was evident in the exchange above, they saw Spanish-language media as predictable, boring, and alien to their everyday realities. This stance, however, was not without problems. It was at the cost of the Spanish TV media, which along with its viewers were put down as unsophisticated and tacky, that the youth communicated their greater sophistication and street smarts.

In conclusion, it is evident that discussions of the media would lead not only to critical assessments but also to the expression of particularized forms of identification, be it along the lines of race, class, or nationality, destabilizing in this manner the neatness of "Latinness" as an all-encompassing category of identification. It is important to recognize, however, that this category was always a central reference in all the discussions, functioning as a recourse that participants mobilized as needed. After all, all comments were made in terms of a generalizable Latino culture, bringing to the forefront the fact that despite all their critical assessments of the U.S. Hispanic media and their representations of Latinidad, participants ultimately identified themselves with the same category that merged them into that "Other" Latino that everyone had been trying so hard not to be.

Separately and collectively, the responses suggested that, despite their criticisms of the category of Latinidad and its representation in the media, participants have in fact internalized, or made theirs, particular dynamics and conventions of Latinidad disseminated in the media. As we saw, commercial representations were actively used by participants to assert their own and others' place and level of "belonging" to this category or to distinguish particularized forms of identification along the lines of class, race, morality, and nationality. The irony is that all of these insidious distinctions deployed by participants to differentiate among themselves fall short of challenging—and in fact re-inscribe—the preeminence of whiteness and of the "nonethnic" as the abiding reference against which one of them is rendered suspect. After all, an overarching assumption in these discussions was that the Spanish and Latino-oriented media were beholden to and needed to be representative of all Latinos. This concern, as unfeasible as it may be for any type of media, is one fueled by the all too real omission of Latinos in the general "mainstream" media. My guess is that participants were all too aware of this predicament; hence their abiding concern with the representativeness or lack thereof of these productions.

NOTES

1. Noted exceptions include Aparicio (1998) and a recent study by the Tomas Rivera Policy Institute on Television (1998).

2. The groups included three Spanish-dominant groups ranging from the late twenties to mid-sixties, with an average age of thirty-eight, one of South Americans, mostly Colombians and Ecuadorians, another of Puerto Ricans and Dominicans, and a third made up exclusively of Mexicans. There was also an English-dominant group of youth (ages eighteen to twenty-five), most of whom were Dominican, Puerto Rican, but which also included Central Americans, and a fifth group of bilingual/English-dominant adults (Dominicans and Puerto Ricans). All the groups were moderated by me, except the focus group with the Mexican informants. For a longer discussion of my use of focus groups, see Dávila 2001.

3. For the purposes of this essay I use "Hispanic and Latino-oriented media" to denote media that are geared to the U.S. Latino population. These media encompass a range of formats and genres, but my analysis will focus primarily on the most popular media sources among New York City Latinos: the nationwide Spanish TV networks, Telemundo and Univisión, and the FM radio stations La Mega and Amor.

4. The distinction between transnational and ethnic media is discussed by Naficy (1993) and the Latin American foundations of U.S. Hispanic media by Rodríguez (1999) and Wilkinson (1995).

BIBLIOGRAPHY

Ang, Ien. *Living Room Wars: Rethinking Media Audiences for a Postmodern World.* London: Routledge, 1996.

Aparicio, Frances R. *Listening to Salsa: Gender, Latin Popular Music, and Puerto Rican Cultures.* Hanover, NH: University Press of New England, 1998.

Bourgois, Philippe. *In Search of Respect. Selling Crack in El Barrio.* New York: Cambridge University Press, 1995.

Dávila, Arlene. *Latinos Inc.: The Marketing and Making of a People.* Berkeley: University of California Press, 2001.

Duany, Jorge. *Los Dominicanos en Puerto Rico: Migración en la semiperiferia.* Río Piedras: Ediciones Huracán, 1990.

Flores, Juan. "Pan-Latino/Trans-Latino: Puerto Ricans in the 'New Nueva York.'" *Centro* 8, nos. 1–2 (1996): 171–86.

Grosfoguel, Ramon, and Chloe S. Georas. "Latino Caribbean Diasporas in New York." In *Mambo Montage: The Latinization of New York,* Agustin Lao and Arlene Dávila. New York: Columbia University Press, 2001.

Naficy, Hamid. *The Making of Exile Culture: Iranian Television in Los Angeles.* Minneapolis: University of Minnesota Press, 1993.

Rivera, Raquel. "Hip Hop, Puerto Ricans and Ethno-Racial Identities in New York." In *Mambo Montage: The Latinization of New York,* Agustin Lao and Arlene Dávila. New York: Columbia University Press, 2001.

Rodríguez, América. *Making Latino News: Race, Language, Class.* Thousand Oaks, CA: Sage, 1999.

Smith, Robert. "Mexicans in New York: Memberships and Incorporation in a New Immigrant Community." In *Latinos in New York, Communities in Transition,* ed. Gabriel Haslip-Viera and Sherrie L. Baver, 57–103. Notre Dame: University of Notre Dame Press, 1996.

Tomas Rivera Policy Institute on Television. *Talking Back to Television: Latinos Discuss How Television Portrays Them and the Quality of Programming Options.* Research Report. Claremont, CA.: Tomas Rivera Policy Institute on Television, 1998.

Wilkinson, Kenton. "Where Culture, Language and Communication Converge: The Latin American Cultural-Linguistic Television Market." Ph.D. diss., University of Texas, Austin, 1995.

Zentella, Ana Celia. *Growing Up Bilingual: Puerto Rican Children in New York.* Malden, MA: Blackwell, 1997.

2

Barbie's Hair

Selling Out Puerto Rican Identity in the Global Market

Frances Negrón-Muntaner

[Toys] cannot bear witness to any autonomous separate existence, but rather are a silent signifying dialogue between them and their nation.
—Walter Benjamin, "The Cultural History of Toys"

Era una chica plástica
de esas que veo por ahí.
—Rubén Blades, "Plástico"

Vikki Carr, Katerina Valente . . . They're not women. Plastic Puerto Ricans!
—Rita Moreno as Googie Gómez in *The Ritz*

A YEAR BEFORE the life-size Puerto Rican "Ken" doll—Ricky Martin—jolted a jaded Grammy Awards audience to their feet with Latin pop,[1] Puerto Ricans from both the Island and the United States had been tearing their hair out over the impact of another "plastic" globalized commodity bearing the sign of *boricuaness*: the Puerto Rican Barbie. Mattel seemed genuinely surprised at the unforeseen entanglement. After all, the company had already manufactured dozens of dolls representing countries from the world over without any complaints, including such close cousins in the ethnic and colonial divide as Hispanic Barbie, American Indian Barbie, and Hawaiian Barbie.[2] As with many other objects of *boricua* wrath or affection, however, this Puerto Rican doll is unique if only because it comes with anticipated political baggage. No assembly required.

The notorious "PR" Barbie was introduced to eager Island consumers with some fanfare at a ceremony held in the capital city of San Juan in February 1997. The first doll, in what many saw as a biased political performance, was presented to Irma Margarita Rosselló, the wife of Pedro Rosselló, pro-statehood governor who at the time was investing considerable energy to obtain binding congressional legislation on the Island's political status.[3] The convergence of capital's ingratiating gaze at Island consumers and a congressional wink toward a process of decolonization, which some feared favored statehood as the "final solution," prompted an anxious response, particularly on the mainland: "This toy can be seen as something of a pro-statehood move, and certainly a tricky issue when it comes to the question of identity," stated Concordia University professor Víctor Rodríguez, with apparent seriousness.[4]

Rodríguez's take was, however, far from universal, and instead became part of one of the most furious debates on Puerto Ricans and pop culture since *West Side Story*.[5] While most U.S.-based *boricuas*—who already live in a state of the Union but still consider themselves Puerto Ricans—feared Barbie as a Trojan horse of identity destruction, Island intellectuals and consumers—who often denounce the eroding effects of Americanization on Puerto Rican culture—gleefully embraced the doll and their right to enjoy it. Evidently both communities wrapped a different narrative around the plastic and made the Barbie a desirable playmate—silent, but endowed—to engage in the increasingly high-stakes game of interests and intrigue called "Puerto Rican identity."

Barbie is one of the most globalized toys in history—"every second, somewhere in the world, two Barbies are sold"[6]—as well as the most transnational of American icons. Barbie play constitutes a privileged site to convey discontent and to negotiate conflicts in (and with) the United States, particularly around race, ethnicity, and gender. Indeed, one of the aspects that made this contest exceptional is that it took place on the pages of mainstream American and Puerto Rican newspapers, rather than in the usually more rarefied halls of academia and organizational newsletters. Furthermore, the Barbie skirmish reiterated for all to see that key sites of cultural rearticulations of Puerto Rican identification are increasingly sponsored by American-made and/or -distributed commodities—even when they feature "plastic" Puerto Ricans.

The few weeks that intellectuals debated the dangers and charms of the Puerto Rican Barbie can also be revisited as a virtual play-therapy session through which each community used Barbie to tease out its location regarding its disenfranchised colonial status, both avowed (most U.S. Puerto Ricans) and disavowed (most Islanders), on the same playing field of (national) cultures, albeit with different resources and from varying capital(s). Significantly, although both groups used the tools of globalization to tell their story, Islanders engaged in a game of make-believe—we are Barbie—as U.S. Puerto Ricans focused on the violence and pain of intercultural exchange. They positioned themselves as "masters" of another game—the political domain—and pointed out that Barbie was an inappropriate plaything for Puerto Ricans. Angelo Falcón, director of the Puerto Rican Policy Institute based in New York, defended this oppositional stance in urgent terms: "Over here, there's a real question of how we're presented because the negative stereotypes hit us hard."[7]

That one of the most public disputes between Puerto Ricans in recent years took place around a toy rather than more worldly matters stresses that "play" allowed specific subjects and groups to "model and experiment with personhood, [and] different contexts in which we may be selves" without the risk associated with binding political action.[8] This is precisely what Rosselló was after in seeking a congressionally sanctioned plebiscite to determine Puerto Rico's ultimate status. Play became politics as a way to negotiate inclusion—and exclusion—within several national imaginaries, not coincidentally through a feminized object that all aimed to control, but ultimately no one could quite pin down.

The striking divergence among pro- and anti-Barbie camps quickly became evident in the field of vision itself as highly educated and hence arguably good observers could not agree on what the doll actually looked like. Writer Aurora Levins Morales—who is of Puerto Rican and Jewish descent, was raised in Puerto Rico's countryside and New York City, and currently resides in California—claimed that the Puerto Rican Barbie was "an Anglicized image of what we're supposed to be."[9] On the other side of the Dream House, however, light-skinned, Island-based, and pro–associated republic advocate Juan Manuel García Passalacqua saw quite the opposite, a doll that resembles who "we are" as Puerto Ricans: "mulatto complexion . . . almond eyes . . . thick nose . . . plump lips . . . raven hair."[10] As in most lengthy conversations about

Barbie, through which "one usually learns more about the speaker than about the doll,"[11] a distinct pattern emerged from the fray. Those who identified as Island Puerto Ricans saw the doll as a *wavy-haired mulatta*, while most U.S. Puerto Ricans disagreed: the doll was *straight-haired* and *white*.

The most documented exception to the U.S. trend—Puerto Ricans in Florida—poignantly establishes, however, that less than a dichotomy between Puerto Rico and the United States, at issue was the real and perceived power of different Puerto Rican communities to invent, control, and deploy their cultural specificity within hostile or relatively auspicious contexts. Puerto Ricans in Florida, who in the last decade have migrated directly from the Island and/or come from upwardly mobile backgrounds, tended to view themselves as either part of a Hispanic cultural majority in Miami or as a dominant (largely middle-class) Hispanic group in Orlando and, thus, less likely to mobilize around racial disenfranchisement. Although inter-Latino conflicts exist —particularly with the more influential Cuban Americans—Florida Ricans can live in environments where bilingualism is an appreciable commodity and can also enjoy a significant presence in politics and the media. In fact, Florida is currently the home of many prominent Puerto Ricans, including singers Ricky Martin and Chayanne; television personalities María Celeste Arrarás and Rafael José, former Miami mayor Maurice Ferré, and even astrologer Walter Mercado.

Curtly excluded from the imaginary created by the Puerto Rican Barbie, U.S. Puerto Ricans outside Florida (and to some extent Washington, D.C.) refused to play with it in the way that it was intended and proceeded to "remove the sting," to quote Walter Benjamin,[12] by validating their own brand of (neo)Puerto Rican experience, using the weapons stored up by decades of civil rights struggles in the United States. That so many men felt compelled to play with the Barbie as a way publicly to express themselves politically also recalls what José Quiroga has argued in relation to the increasing popularity of gay dolls. As for some gay men who long to caress queer plastic, for some Puerto Ricans who faced Barbie glaring from its box at Toys R' Us, "childhood is not necessarily something that is looked back on with affection, but hostility. They remind the subject of all those dolls that were never given and never received, all those prohibitions."[13] The irony of this strategy, however, is not only that they were aiming all their guns at the wrong enemy (as I will explore later), but also that the U.S.-based intelligentsia hurled at Puerto Rican Barbie the one charge that Islanders had traditionally—and painfully—thrown at them: inauthenticity. As a *Miami Herald* journalist put it, "Le imputan [a Barbie] que su 'puertorriqueñidad' no es genuina."[14] And this had hairy consequences.

RAISING HAIR! BARBIE'S LOCKS AND PUERTO RICAN–AMERICAN IDENTITY

The cultural knowledge that Barbies are "essentially" white, despite their outward appearance, constitutes the first clue to the seemingly untenable color blindness. As Erica Rand has observed, "Although some 'ethnic' dolls now get the name Barbie, a 'nonethnic' Barbie still occupies the center stage."[15] Most consumers seem to be able to accept an ethnic Barbie doll simultaneously as both culturally specific and "white" at heart, since the essential Barbie is unarguably light-skinned, blonde, and blue-eyed. The lingering impression that the Puerto Rican Barbie was essentially white and that its "mulattoness" was a cultural masquerade was reinforced by the box's ethnic "origin" story for Puerto Ricans: "My country was discovered in 1493 by Christopher Columbus who claimed it for Spain." In only mentioning that the island was discovered by Columbus, Mattel and its allies connote that all Puerto Ricans are fundamentally Europeans and banish the influence of Natives and Africans to the back of the bus. Due to the category of race's preeminence in the regulation and management of minorities, Puerto Rican struggles over representation tend to demand "realistic" depictions (epidermal and demographic) as a measure of democratic inclusion. If Puerto Ricans in the United States have traditionally visualized themselves as "of color" in the struggle for enfranchisement, the Barbie could be authentic only if it were "brown."

Remarkably, Puerto Rican Barbie's perceived skin color was not the doll's most controversial physical aspect for *boricuas* in the United States, particularly women. Although in Puerto Rico and Florida the doll's racial makeup was deemed acceptable, representative, and even beautiful, much of the U.S. discussion focused on a specific Barbie feature: its hair, or more specifically, the *texture* of the doll's hair, not color (black) or length (long). Lourdes Pérez, a Puerto Rican Chicago-based, San Juan–raised interior decorator, was horrified at what she saw: "I don't care that she's white. Puerto Ricans come in all colors. But when I saw that hair, I thought 'Dios mío' ('my God'), we just passed a terrible legacy to the next generation."[16] Despite exasperated responses from some Puerto Rico–based (white) men—"[t]his woman is saying that the prevalent lack of respect, the lawlessness, drugs, driving conditions, domestic and child abuse aren't as terrible a legacy as a straight-haired Barbie"—the charges stuck.[17] Journalist Louis Aguilar, who wrote several stories on the topic, pointed out that Lourdes' response was not isolated: "For some Puerto Rican women who have spent countless hours ironing the curl out of their hair before going to the office or school, it's Barbie's hair that makes them cringe."[18]

Playing with the doll's hair is reportedly the most popular activity that children engage in with Barbie, and the grown-up argument over the doll's locks raged on for weeks in print and on the Internet. Hair became, as anthropologist Patrick Olivelle has theorized, a "condensed symbol": "so powerful that it encapsulates all the diverse aspects of the symbolized, which under normal circumstances would require separate symbolic expressions."[19] That the dead weight of Puerto Rican identity fell on Barbie's weave should not be surprising on at least three counts. The ways hair is coiffured are universally used to signify cultural identity, social status, age, and gender. "Hair worn in a polarized manner has served to indicate the masculine and the feminine, the slave and the ruler, the young, the old, the virgin, the married, the widowed, the mourners."[20] Across many cultures and historical periods, hair is also linked to the power of women to destroy, kill, and seduce their own and others, hence its care and representation are not trivial matters. Most important in this case, the Barbie's Puerto Rican roots could only really show up in its intractable hair.

In Puerto Rico, unlike the United States, a person's race is not solely dictated by a single African ancestor. "El color y las facciones," writes the appropriately surnamed Tomás Blanco, "valen más que la sangre."[21] Whereas one drop of "black blood" makes you African American in the United States, one of "white" can have the opposite effect on the Island, where a person does not need to claim exclusively European lineage to access the benefits of whiteness. The greater value attributed to white blood in the Puerto Rican scheme allows for a larger number of mixed-race people to qualify as *blancos*, yet this does not diminish the fact that Puerto Ricans of African descent are socially encouraged to seek upward mobility by flushing out the inauspicious "black" blood in each subsequent generation, as the infamous "mejorar la raza" mantra implies. Given the possibility of *becoming* white—which is denied in the United States—"racial" identification (and attribution) in Puerto Rico is partly determined by a combination of phenotypical factors, including thickness of lips, skin tone, broadness of nose, eye color, cheekbones, and—most important—hair texture, which is physically coterminous with the skin and hence often symbolizes the entire body's "race."

The lavish attention given to "black hair" in Puerto Rican racial discourse—it has considerably more (mostly demeaning) names than any other racialized corporal matter—prompted anthropologist Sidney Mintz to claim that "Puerto Rican cultural standards for racial identity appear to place the most weight on hair type, less on skin color."[22] However, it is not so much that hair is more important than color, but that once hair is called upon to stand up for (the) race, it is not necessary to also mention the skin's hue. Mulatta poet Julia de Burgos, for example, identifies hair first in defining blackness in "Ay ay ay de la grifa negra" (not the *negra grifa*),[23] while Francisco Arrivís's mulatta character Cambucha describes herself as "Pasúa, hocicúa y bembúa"—not darkskinned—in his "liberal" play on racial relations, *Sirena*.[24] Consequently, Luis Palés Matos's foundational opera magna celebrating Caribbean syncretism and black (mythic) sensuality could only be aptly titled *Tuntún de pasa y grifería*—tuntún of kinky and mulatto hair.[25]

Despite the deceiving laxness (from a U.S. standpoint) in determining race among Puerto Ricans, the emphasis on hair remits to biologically based understandings of difference that are shared with Americans. Anthropologist Franz Boas, who once testified in a 1914 case in which a white man sued for divorce on the grounds that his wife was not really white, argues for both sides when he claims that "You can tell by a microscopic examination of a cross section of hair to what race that person belongs."[26] In fact, because it can be altered or hidden, hair is the object of much scrutiny in liminal social situations, particularly if background information is not self-evident or forthcoming. As Renzo Sereno bluntly phrased it, "la contextura del pelo—bueno o malo—puede decidir el matrimonio mixto."[27] Advocate Isabelo Zenón confirms the crucial role of hair when he recalls a "test" through which "whites" can detect whether someone is a "grifo" (racially mixed) or simply an "oliveskinned" white, by placing him in front of a fan to see if the hair follows the wind: "Si no se despeina, queda fuera del grupo de privilegiados."[28] Hair is, undoubtedly, the thin wavy line that separates the "authentic" whites from the deceiving upwardly mobile mulattos.

At the same time, although U.S. Puerto Ricans repudiated Barbie's straight hair, these discriminating—and discriminated—consumers were not demanding that the doll have "bad" hair, as if a Black Puerto Rican Barbie could not be representative of all Puerto Ricans. Ironically, a Black Puerto Rican Barbie, particularly one who wears contemporary clothes, could not have looked much different from Black (African American) Barbie, thus undermining the notion of essential differences between both groups, and any modest racial capital that light-skinned Puerto Ricans may wish to claim in the colonial metropolis.

Due to the many cultural convergences between Puerto Ricans and African Americans in cities such as New York, a black Puerto Rican Barbie could have ended up legitimizing poet Willie Perdomo's motto that an Afro–Puerto Rican is just a black man—or woman—with an accent.[29] As Rodríguez affirmed, "to introduce a doll . . . that looks like it has no *trace* of African ancestry, to a group of young Puerto Rican females who are at a crucial age in the formation of their identity, this becomes a very serious issue" (my emphasis).[30] What U.S. critics were after, then, was the "correct" ethnic representational formula that could prevent Puerto Ricans from being confused with *either* African Americans or Anglos. In this, they converged—perhaps inadvertently—with the Island elites, who would likely agree that it's tough to play at being *boricua* with the "wrong" kind of hair, because as Elsie Crumb McCaeb and Anne H. Stark agree, "[Y]ou don't feel good until your hair looks good."[31]

Considering that Puerto Rican ethnic identity in the United States has often been produced within racial discourses, and upward mobility in Puerto Rico implies a willed loss of racialized identity, the mainland's response to Puerto Rican Barbie's hair evokes a social distress over losing control of an important identity sign. The fears of cultural consumption and political dissolution triggered by Puerto Rico becoming the fifty-first state of the Union—and Puerto Ricans morphing into "Americans"—were hence curled around tropes of de-ethnification such as "straight hair." The organizing assumption was that the Barbie's hair could only have been straight because it had been "straightened," an act of self-hatred or conformity that would also be judged by American whites derisively. Critics focused on the wavy hair to protect the specificity of the group against changes already taking place in the United States, such as language dominance (to English), territorial residence, intermarriage, and hyphenated children. Ultimately, pulling Barbie's hair was a way to manage anxieties about the transculturation of future Puerto Rican generations, for as Walter Benjamin has written, "toys are a site of conflict, less of the child with the adult than of the adult with the child."[32]

The fears of giving up your hair (to Mattel) also recall the importance that many cultures assign to the custody of hair. In Africa, for instance, only trusted friends and relatives may touch or have access to your hair since "in the hands of the enemy, it could become an ingredient in the production of a dangerous charm or 'medicine' that would injure the owner."[33] The relationship between hair and potential harm is not confined to actual people's hair, but also to hair found in sculptures—which the Barbie arguably is. Puerto Rican popular sayings also stress the importance of keeping hair in its proper place—*cuídate los pelos*—but also of getting rid of it if you need to defend yourself: *sin pelos en la lengua*. To allow the Puerto Rican Barbie to have the wrong hair and to put it into the wrong hands can then be quite dangerous to a group: it signifies social submission, can bring about shame, and even lead to (cultural) death—the "terrible legacy" alluded to by the Chicago decorator. But as some observers noticed (though they preferred to stay at least a hair away) one community's bristly nightmare was another's synthetic fantasy.

PLAYING WITH YOUR SELF: WHY ISLANDERS LOVED BARBIE

Barbie was a reliable—if frustrating—toy used by U.S. *boricuas* to imagine Puerto Ricanness as a distinct ethnic identity, and to make demands on American public culture as a politically disenfranchised minority. The doll's wild success with Islanders—by December 31, 1997, one Carolina store alone had sold over five thousand dolls[34]—asserts, however, that for many Islanders, the Puerto Rican Barbie was the *perfect* doll for playing with the "self." In playing with Barbie, these consumers not only "enjoyed" themselves, but also enacted the material and symbolic conditions that make their (limited) identity play intelligible.

Significantly, although Island intellectuals and cultural institutions often make use of cultural differences as part of a struggle to expand or protect local political control within camouflaged colonial parameters, the Puerto Rican Barbie was not perceived as threatening to the main pillars of national identity as defined by the state apparatus and the elites: Spanish language (Barbie does not speak), symbols such as *el jíbaro* (which it is), and sports sovereignty (which does not apply).[35] While a rampantly "commercial" product made by an American multinational (as opposed to the "purely" folkloric art dear to the intelligentsia), the Puerto Rican Barbie is more consistent with dominant discourses of *puertorriqueñidad* on the Island than many "real" Puerto Rican–produced art forms that have undergone different degrees of commodification, such as salsa or hip hop. In this sense, the Puerto Rican Barbie is the consummate nationalist elite product bred by the contradictions of the commonwealth: a modern packaging (plastic) of a premodern essence (rural Puerto Rico), for postmodern nationalists (colonial survivors).

The emphasis on Barbie's hair and the attack on Mattel as a symbol of corporate whiteness facilitated a dialogue on race, but overlooked Puerto Rican agency in the doll's production as a symbolic good (or evil). As Néstor García Canclini writes, "David did not really know where Goliath was."[36] Most notably, these critics did not engage with the significant fact that the doll was fashioned as a *jíbara*—the mythical nineteenth-century, mountain-dwelling, white Spanish creolized peasant—with all that this implies within hegemonic elite discourses. U.S. critics did not address how *jibarismo* excludes them as much as—and perhaps more than—Mattel with its dreadlocked Hispanic Barbie and the broad-nosed Quinceañera Teresa. This critical slip can be partly attributed to the acceptance and reworkings of the *jíbaro* myth in the United States, and the popularity of this icon to the virtual tribe in multiple contexts, including Internet sites such as jíbaro.com, ("el lugar Boricua más jíbaro del Interné"). In hindsight, Mattel's contribution was relatively minimal, albeit practically indestructible: it commercialized the already officialized *jíbaro* myth by casting it in plastic and giving it worldwide commodity status.

As has been noted with a mixture of scorn and disbelief, the Institute of Puerto Rican Culture—the official voice of government-sanctioned Puerto Ricanness created by the commonwealth—was the corporation's chief advisor in designing the doll's accessories and writing the box's copy (which, nevertheless, contains several mistakes and typos). Interestingly, the pro-statehood administration seemed to have supported the doll, underlining the success of *jibarista* discourse among all ideological sectors. The hold of *jibarismo* is, in fact, so strong that statehooders refer to their brand of federalism as *estadidad jíbara*, a specifically Puerto Rican "way" of becoming a state of the Union; and the supporters of commonwealth still use a silhouetted *jíbaro* as a beacon, even when their party's economic policies were largely responsible for the obliteration of the peasants' way of life. The obviousness of why Barbie had to be a *jíbara*—and not a "Return Nuyorican Barbie" or a "Sugar Cane Babe Barbie"—begins to untangle the question of who belongs (and who calls the shots) in *jíbaro* country.

From the nineteenth century, the mostly male, white, affluent intellectual elites have been elaborating the myth of the *jíbaro* as the repository of the Puerto Rican people's true (white) soul. "El 'denso contenido espiritual,'" writes Luis Zayas, "es legado del alma hispana."[37] As Francisco Scarano argues, early identification with the *jíbaros* by the elites can reasonably be interpreted as a progressive gesture to include the peasants into a proto-national imaginary in the face of a retrograde colonial regime.[38] After the Spanish-American War, however, this investment became increasingly problematic as a sign of national democratic inclusion. Despite the fact that the term *jíbaro* was generally used to refer to a (mixed) racial category in several regions of the Americas (a usage not unknown in Puerto Rico), this knowledge was conveniently disregarded as living peasants became paper icons in the hands of nationalist writers.

The *jíbaro* was the symbol of choice for a wide range of reasons, including the peasants' alleged "whiteness" as the presumed (pure) descendants of the Spanish. The insistence on the *jíbaro*'s uncorrupted Europeanness suggests that the *jíbaro* became the "great white hope" for the elites in defending a separate and unique national identity from the United States. "En él vinculamos nuestros júbilos," wrote one of Puerto Rico's (still) most influential intellectuals, Antonio S. Pedreira, "nuestros favores y nuestras aspiraciones."[39] Investing in the *jíbaro*'s whiteness served (and continues to serve) at least two contradictory political impulses. On the one hand, it affirmed that Puerto Ricans shared an equally civilized (European) culture as that of the new colonial ruler, who branded them racially inferior. On the other, it allowed elites to ward off uncomfortable associations with the emerging working class, whose members, despite increased capitalist exploitation, were savoring previously unavailable political rights and challenging their subordinate class status.

Drastically different from the passive *jíbaro* of the elite's imagination, the working class was combative in its demand for a decent wage and material comfort, had little trouble openly collaborating with Americans to achieve political objectives, and possessed its own intellectual traditions and modes of expression. Some of its leadership even rejected "nationalism" as an ideology. In other words, these flesh-and-blood proletarians resembled the elites in threatening ways. As Pedreira would say, the *jíbaro*—as the elite—had to protect himself "del atropello de la zona urbana y de la negra competencia de la costa."[40]

The more Puerto Ricans resembled Americans—in this *boricuas* share some terrain with Canadians—the more imperative it was for cultural discourse to create and police distance. As Lillian Guerra suggests, "[T]he elite needed the *jíbaro* in order to remind them of who they truly were—Spanish and Puerto Rican—rather than who their own actions told them they were trying to become—North Americans."[41] Despite appearances to the contrary—such as the growing statehood movement, the critical dependence on federal transfers, demographic shifts, and transculturation—the *jíbaro*, and with him the nation, remains intact, authentic, and unchanging. This is why Pedreira contributed to creating the equivalent of a national holy ghost that protects Puerto Ricans from themselves and their "suicidal" tendencies: "en cada puertorriqueño hay *escondido* un jíbaro" (my emphasis).[42] We may often "look" American, but Puerto Ricanness comes from the soul, not the body; it can only be heartfelt. Or collected.

Conveniently, twentieth-century elites called upon the *jíbaro*'s specter to serve their spiritual and political needs at a time when peasants were undergoing a rapid process of proletarianization. The vanishing *jíbaro* became the emblem of another time, in which the currently displaced elites faced less competition for control over bodies and resources. The *jíbaro*'s intimate relationship to the land is also crucial to this formulation, as not only did the soil change hands during this period (from Spanish and creole *hacendados* to American corporations), but also Puerto Rico was reduced to being a property of the United States: it legally belongs to, but is not part of, the metropolis. By exalting the *jíbaro*, the elites aimed symbolically to repossess the land and regain its control. The main irony of this identification, particularly for future generations, is that the elites fashioned identity as a simulacra—technically dead but symbolically alive—like a doll.

Although never a static discourse, *jibarismo*, however, has been primarily concerned with the *jíbaro*, not the *jíbara*. As Arlene Dávila observes, "An African contribution to the *jíbaro* is never acknowledged or emphasized, as neither is a female gender identity."[43] The (male) en-gendering of the national myth is, of course, not surprising, particularly when control over the *jíbaras* was taken for granted by men of all classes and the female proletarian represented doubly transgressive possibili-ties. As was not lost on most observers, women took advantage of American-sponsored modernity in ways that challenged social and re-productive structures, including labor, politics, and the patriarchal fam-ily. After 1898 *jíbaras* joined the workforce and then the unions in sub-stantial numbers, sought divorces, used birth control, publicly chal-lenged male authority, and gladly incorporated technology into their lives. If the *jíbaro* constituted a space/time of longing for the old labor regime, the *jíbara's* proper place could only be safely evoked as pas-sively below the belt.

As might be expected, dominant discourse about *jíbaras* tends to highlight their seductiveness, even amid the squalor. According to poet Virgilio Dávila, the *jíbara* is anemic and sad, "como una flor escuálida de malogrado abril," and her dress is "un harapo / que cubre a duras penas un cuerpo virginal."[44] Sociologist Salvador Brau describes the peasant woman who inspired him to write one of the first sociological texts on the *jíbara* as "pobre mujer indolente y sensual."[45] Writer Abelardo Díaz Alfaro also contributes his pity when he says that *jíbaras* are "Mujeres gastadas por la maternidad y el trabajo excesivo."[46] Yet, in welding the Barbie and the mythical *jíbara*, the contemporary elites modernized and let go of the crudest discourses of female subordina-tion in the interest of a globally recognized hegemony. As Mattel has made it clear, Barbie lives in a sanitized world of glamour and auton-omy, in which men are just one more accessory.

Given the meager, but fairly consistent, discourse on *jíbaras* and the hegemony of the male *jíbaro* myth, the Puerto Rican Barbie has rewrit-ten parts of the *jibarista* script for generations to come, giving it even more currency. If early *jibarista* discourse was concerned with the *jíbaro's* grave sociological, political, and economic problems, the Puerto Rican Barbie is fantastically free from want and openly transnational. Furthermore, it is American-financed and Malaysian-made, and it's definitely not going back to picking coffee. The doll's main concern is for you to "like the special white dress I am wearing. It is very typical of a dress I might wear to a festival or party." The use of the *jíbara* as a spectacle, however, is not new. As Guerra has argued, the *jíbara's* imagined "natural inclination toward promiscuity made her fair game for these intellectuals to put her body on display for their own amusement and to invade her gynecology for the sake of the public interest."[47] In fact, the back of the box is clear about the intent of urging the Barbie to put out a *jíbara* show: "Tourism is a very significant part of our economy. . . . Today, people from all over the world come to enjoy our beautiful country, delicious food and friendly people. I hope you can come and visit us soon."

The Puerto Rican Barbie's divorce from the realm of agricultural want is specifically signified by its accessories—a disproportionately large hairbrush, a pair of high heels, earrings, and a ring—and, above all, its "magnificently simple but gorgeous local folkloric dress."[48] The dress worn by the Barbie was criticized by some Puerto Ricans as forcing women to be "stuck in the feminine stereotype of the nineteenth century,"[49] but no one questioned its contribution to whitening Barbie or its status as an invented tradition from above. A Mattel spokeswoman defended it by affirming that "Barbie's dress is a traditional costume not meant to offend, and not meant to depict the clothes of today's women."[50] Still, the doll's elaborate costume does not conform to any dress worn by a peasant in the visual record. In an essay criticizing a 1953 competition to reward the best entry depicting a Puerto Rican "regional dress," writer Nilita Vientós Gastón categorically denied its existence and chastised those who seek this form of national validation by labeling it "un alarde de la fantasía, una invención. . . . Imagino que su destino será convertirse en disfraz."[51] Indeed, the dress definitely makes the Barbie a plastic *jíbara*, in the slang implication of the term: superficial, fake, and materialistic.

Barbie's dress is also an important part of the elaboration of a postmortem *jíbaro* myth as it incorporates a wide array of influences and patriarchal nationalist desires. For instance, the dress is low-cut (quite rare before the 1940s but emphasizing the *jíbara*'s femininity), and has five pieces of *encaje*, a very expensive material that only wealthy women could purchase during the first part of the century. By using *encaje*, the dress is fit to signify the Barbie as a "country" girl, but imagines it with the same affluence of the *hacendada*, the landowner or his wife. The extensive use of the *encaje* also brings the Barbie closer to Spain, as folkloric Spanish costumes usually exhibit large quantities of this fabric, including in the Mattel versions of Spanish Barbie. Furthermore, the dress's finery and elaborateness connote access to the city, not the mythic isolation of the countryside. The general acceptance of the doll's dress as historically accurate spells yet another victory for the elites by avoiding questions about the "authenticity" of the *jíbaro* myth, and affirming that "culture" is not a struggle over representation or participation, but a collection of essential accessories. Once more, corporate America and Puerto Rican colonial institutions see eye to eye: It's the dress that makes the *jíbara*.

The fact that Puerto Rican Barbie is a "collectible" doll further reinforces its colonial cast as well as certain *jíbara* imagined characteristics. In Mattel's universe, to be a "collectible" is to live as a folkloric object with limited agency (i.e., accessories). The doll's transformation into an aesthetic commodity also takes *jibarista* discourse further than even Pedreira intended when he wrote, "Por encima de su angustia económica pondremos su valor humano, su bella calidad representativa."[52] Puerto Rican Barbie confirms the *jíbara* as the symbol of a Puerto Rican essence, not a historically specific product of colonial relations and economic exploitation. Different from other black and white Barbies, but similar to most other Latin American ones, the Puerto Rican Barbie does not achieve anything but being itself, eternally and tirelessly "national." In culminating the *jíbaro* myth as an aesthetic commodity, Mattel rejects the economy of lack associated with the *jíbaro*, and actualizes an orgy of plenty in which the consumer in need of national affirmation is "free" to buy his- or herself some pleasure—and own it (if not own up to it).

This pleasure is further enhanced by the fact that the doll is perceived as a light-skinned mulatta, a departure from most historical accounts of the *jíbara,* who is often represented as sickly pale. Puerto Rican Barbie is, however, the kind of mulatta "that won't tap her feet" when it hears the drum, but instead, dances the *seis chorreao* wearing a very virginal white dress. The passion for the whitewashed mulatta among the middle-class elites, however, should not be confused with the questioning of racism as an ideology of exclusion. As Tomás Blanco remarks without a trace of irony, the mulatta "parece tener valor estético o de selección erótica" for creole men.[53] Not coincidentally, the embracing of a mulatto aesthetics comes at a time when the elites—more American and "modern" than ever—wish to distinguish themselves from (other) Americans by establishing that they are not racists. In fact, the educated elites, as Eduardo Seda Bonilla has written, tend to produce the most inclusive democratic public discourse, while exhibiting equally segregationist behavior in their familial lives, with the possible exception of (out-of-wedlock) sexuality.[54]

Simultaneously, the Puerto Rican Barbie established several lines of continuity with certain *jíbaro* texts, as the doll is sexually desirable, eager to do the work of the nation, and willing to serve as a (non)maternal reproductive machine.[55] The fact that the Barbie is gendered feminine also wards off associations with threatening mulatto sexuality (urban, male, and possibly homosexual). While never vulnerable within Mattel's gripping narrative, the Puerto Rican Barbie can be imagined as the seductive body—*sabrosamente femenina*—dreamed most forcefully by twentieth-century poet Luis Lloréns Torres. The Barbie fuses the passive (yet sensual) *jíbara* with the social climbing hot mulatta, transforming it into the ultimate user-friendly object of national excitement and interracial desires, queerly recalling the doll's historical predecessor, the post–World War II German novelty toy for men, Lilli.[56] In the elite's collaboration with Mattel, you could say that they had their way with the Barbie thrice: as a *gringa*, a *jíbara*, and a mulatta. Not surprisingly, many indignities projected onto the *jíbara* have been forced upon Barbie dolls by their (ab)users with a vengeance. Both bodies have been known to suffer the erotic urges (hard-ons, breast fondling), paranoia, racist rage, misogyny, amputated limbs, and decapitations of their owners—with a pasted-on smile. Ultimately, if as Lillian Guerra suggests, the elites have historically perceived the *jíbaro's* alleged passivity as a "deep reservoir of nationalism,"[57] the Puerto Rican Barbie is the most anticolonial object ever invented for the cause.

Furthermore, whereas Barbie's corporate "parents" do not encourage consumers to imagine it as a mother, the elites were able to transfigure the doll into a reproductive vessel—of *jibarismo*. Political analyst García Passalacqua, in fact, specifically praised the doll because it would help Puerto Ricans "explain ourselves, as we are, to all Americans."[58] In becoming a *jíbara* commodity, the Puerto Rican Barbie is unable physically to give birth to the *jibarito* of tomorrow, but does reproduce its myth to new generations, rephrasing the popular nationalist aphorism: *la patria es valor (en el mercado) y sacrificio (para el intelectual)*. Characteristically for the Island's elite, although the Puerto Rican Barbie is doing their symbolic work, it is mostly benefiting American capital and the colonial status quo.

TRAÍDO POR LOS PELOS: SELLING OUT
PUERTO RICANNESS

A Puerto Rican Barbie dressed as a *jíbara*, however, would not have been enough to draw thousands of *adults* to Island stores. To sell Puerto Ricanness out, the *jíbara* had to stand in the "right" political pose; it needed to affirm hegemonic ideas about Puerto Rico's (central) place in the world, not only local racial hierarchies. Luckily, Mattel was again able to capitalize on the winning formula. By including the Puerto Rican Barbie as part of the "Dolls-of-the-World" series, Mattel recognized Islanders' specificity as a distinct Spanish(only)-speaking, white, Latin American nation, with merely bureaucratic ties to the United States, and without a sizable diaspora, politically subaltern status, or financial dependency. Ironically, the series' main objective is to introduce "children in the United States to other cultures,"[59] as if there were not already three million Puerto Ricans in the United States, and the Puerto Rican doll was not based on the "Hispanic" one. In this, the elite's culturalist strategy of difference—manipulated for over one hundred years to obtain political concessions—coalesced with Mattel's marketing department to deny U.S. Puerto Ricans their market worth. But as we know, the Barbie aims to please—for a profit.

Mattel has always been aware of its Latin market, not only because one of its plants is located in Mexico, but also because it was born in a state that is home to millions of Hispanics: California. As early as 1968, the company came out with "Spanish Talker," a Hispanic Barbie with a Mexican accent. The first "Hispanic Barbie," launched in 1980, was dressed in a pseudo-Spanish costume called "fiesta-style."[60] Ironically, the Barbies' colorful wardrobes and risqué poses have been partially attributed to the dress codes of working-class Hispanics: "Whatever the fashion, the California version will be more extreme . . . much more colorful. . . . Clothes tend to fit more tightly than is considered elsewhere, and to expose more flesh."[61] No wonder Ken Handler, the son of two of Barbie's "inventors" and the reason the doll's male companion's name is Ken, calls Barbie a "bimba," not a bimbo.[62]

In 1996—a year before the introduction of the Puerto Rican Barbie—Latin America had been experiencing a higher rate of growth (47 percent) than the United States (32 percent),[63] consolidating itself as the doll's third largest market.[64] Puerto Rico's four million consumers do not constitute in themselves a substantial market—there are almost as many *boricuas* in the United States. Islanders, however, have the highest per capita number of Barbies in Latin America, the context in which Mattel and most of the Island's elites locate Puerto Rico. A whopping 72 percent of Puerto Rican children own at least one Barbie, as compared to the second highest, Chile, with 49 percent. Eight-year-old Amanda from Bayamón alone owns forty-three Barbies, but the Puerto Rican Barbie reigns "supreme in her collection."[65] The difference in Barbie penetration can be linked to closer economic and cultural ties to the United States, a higher per capita income than most Latin American nations (at twenty dollars, Barbie is considered an expensive children's toy), and higher consumption rates.

Since the changes Mattel makes to each doll are minimal—pure genius from a Warholian ethos—the company is able to change hair color, pigmentation, and costume and appeal to dozens of markets in their best (white) light, which tends to be appealing to the country's most affluent sectors. Puerto Rican Barbie may be a globalized product, but it is ably designed to cash in on the needs of many to affirm their national pride and prominence in the family of nations. "Globalization," in fact, tends to encourage a hunger for what is unique, local, regional, and national among certain social sectors. In many parts of the world, and notoriously in Puerto Rico,[66] advertising a product as if it was native or with native characteristics can spell impressive profits, even if changes to the product are nil. A disgruntled Nuyorican consumer, Andrés Quiñones, criticized the doll precisely on those grounds: "lo que hizo Mattel fue hacerle la nariz más grande y oscurecerle los ojos. Ahora nos quieren vender como boricua la misma muñeca de siempre."[67]

Although Andrés was not impressed, Mattel managed to do what Bacardí, Budweiser, and Winston had already achieved on the Island: sell Puerto Ricans an "American" product while affirming Puerto Rico's unassimilable difference and specificity (nationality) in sameness (capital). True to form, Mattel's boxed history makes it clear that the Island is separate and different from the United States, in every exoticizing way, including culinary traditions (*plátanos, arroz con gandules*) and wildlife (*coquí*). The doll was a triumph for Island elites: corporate America gave them what reality denies them—a purely plastic Puerto Rican identity—and they enjoyed it without financial or political responsibility. Unlike other, more impoverished markets, the Puerto Rican consumer is proud to verify his worth as a commodity, even if he doesn't financially benefit. Purchasing also highlights how hegemonic identity constructs—even if culled from elite culture—are today manufactured for mass consumption, and largely understood as an accessory: T-shirt, coquí souvenir, and CD car flag.

The tendency to construct identity as an accessory, however, points to the increasing complexity of the current cultural terrain for Puerto Ricans. The same year that the Puerto Rican Barbie was introduced to the world, a second *boricua* doll made an entrance fit for royalty. As *Latina* magazine tells it, "Now there's more to complain about with the debut of a Puerto Rican doll named Carlos: If Barbie wants to date this plastic *papi*, she can forget about it. He's gay. Carlos is the boyfriend of Billy."[68] Although *Latina*'s complaint suggests a lack of imagination, it also fails to take into account to what extent playing with Barbie, Ken, and G.I. Joe is always, already, a queer experience for most. Although this debate lasted less than the Barbie's and was not aired out in the *New York Times*, Carlos's existence makes seeing the Puerto Rican Barbie straight a difficult endeavor. As *Latina*'s campy prose put it, "[T]he *fashionistas* outraged over Barbie's clichéd *vestido criollo* should find solace. At least he's not wearing a straw hat."[69]

Queerly, the same year that the Puerto Rican Barbie came out, it occurred to Island-based drag performer Vanessa Fox to refashion the Puerto Rican Barbie's wardrobe to her own as a strategy to raise money for charity. After the introduction of Fox's personalized Puerto Rican Barbie, she was able to raise hundreds of dollars to purchase dolls for disadvantaged girls and boys: "O sea, que con una Barbie hemos podido hacer felices a muchos niños."[70] With Fox, the Puerto Rican Barbie brought about a miraculous state of affairs, akin to the biblical miracles of the loaves and fishes. Fox not only managed to make more children happy, she also created value for a doll that has not experienced any appreciation among Barbie collectors. Mattel may have made the doll for corporate profit, but it has ultimately been Puerto Ricans who have infused it with alternative values and made it theirs.

At the same time, Barbie's Aryan origins and "white" corporate parents certainly limit its capacity to stake new ground in decolonizing politics. But when Mattel put Puerto Rican Barbie within our mature reach, it forced us to relive our childhood as colonial survivors, racialized migrants, and/or queer kids, and to enact our frustrations toward whoever made us feel subordinate, ugly, and vulnerable. Symbolically teasing Barbie's hair let some blow off steam; lovingly combing it held fantastic pleasures for others. As a fairly well-adjusted child, I do not remember ever giving much thought to my Barbie, Ken, and G.I. Joe. I do vividly recall, however, the day when I stopped in the Barbie aisle in a Miami toy store and could not believe my wondering eyes, hurt in so many colonial battles for dignity. The big, corny, white and pink letters spelling PUERTO RICAN BARBIE drew me in, for they seemed to confirm what as a child I always knew, but as a migrant adult, had been denied: Barbie has always been Puerto Rican. Even as I delighted in the recognition of this archaic and secret code, I was mostly savoring the bittersweet constraints of my own political agency.

NOTES

This essay is dedicated to my mother, who inspired me to write it.

1. Frances Negrón-Muntaner, "Ricky's Hips," in *Passing Memories* (New York: New York University Press, forthcoming).

2. Mireya Navarro, "A New Barbie in Puerto Rico Divides Island and Mainland," *New York Times,* 27 December 1997, A1.

3. Louis Aguilar, "Barbie Stirs Debate in Puerto Rico," *Miami Herald,* 14 November 1997, 25A.

4. Ibid., 25A.

5. Frances Negrón-Muntaner, "Feeling Pretty: *West Side Story* and Puerto Rican–American Identity," *Social Text* 63 (summer 2000): 83–106.

6. M. G. Lord, *Forever Barbie: The Unauthorized Biography of a Real Doll* (New York: Morrow, 1994), 7.

7. Navarro, A9.

8. Margaret Carlisle Duncan, Garry Chick, and Alan Aycock, eds., *Play and Culture Studies,* vol. 1 (Greenwich, CT.: Ablex, 1998), 4.

9. Froma Harrop, "Ask Real Barbie Experts," *Miami Herald,* 6 January 1998, 7A.

10. Navarro, A9, A10.

11. Lord, 298.

12. Walter Benjamin, "The Cultural History of Toys," in *Selected Writings,* vol. 2 (Cambridge: Harvard University Press, 1999), 100.

13. José Quiroga, *Tropics of Desire: Interventions from Queer Latino America* (New York: New York University Press, 2000).

14. Jeannette Rivera-Lyles, "Boricuas divididos con la Barbie puertorriqueña," *El Nuevo Herald,* 31 December 1997, sec. 1, 16A.

15. Erica Rand, *Barbie's Queer Accessories* (Durham: Duke University Press, 1995).

16. Louis Aguilar, "Barbie Has Serious Implications for Puerto Ricans," *Miami Herald*, 9 November 1997, 127.

17. Adrian Febles, "Coming Soon: Political Activist Barbie," *San Juan Star*, 14 November 1997, 76.

18. Aguilar, "Barbie Stirs Debate," 25A.

19. Patrick Olivelle, "Hair and Society: Social Significance of Hair in South Asian Traditions," in *Hair: Its Power and Meaning in Asian Cultures*, ed. Alf Hiltebeitel and Barbara D. Miller, 40–41 (Albany: State University of New York Press, 1998).

20. Susan Brownmiller, *Femininity* (New York: Linden Press, Simon and Schuster, 1984), 57.

21. Tomás Blanco, *El prejuicio racial en Puerto Rico* (Río Piedras: Ediciones Huracán, 1985), 138.

22. Sidney Mintz, "Cañamelas: The Subculture of a Rural Sugar Plantation Proletariat," in *The People of Puerto Rico: A Study in Social Anthropology*, ed. Julián H. Steward et al. (Urbana: University of Illinois, 1956), 410.

23. Julia de Burgos, "Ay ay ay de la grifa negra," in *Poema en veinte surcos* (Río Piedras: Editorial Huracán, 1997), 52.

24. Francisco Arriví, *Sirena* (Río Piedras: Editorial Cultural, 1971), 45.

25. Luis Palés Matos, *Tuntún de pasa y grifería* (San Juan: Biblioteca de Autores Puertorriqueños, 1974).

26. Quoted in Noliwe M. Rooks, *Hair Raising: Beauty, Culture, and African-American Women* (New Brunswick: Rutgers University Press, 1996), 14

27. Quoted in Isabelo Zenon, *Narciso descubre su trasero: El negro en la cultura puertorriqueña*, vol. 2 (Humacao, Puerto Rico: Editorial Furidi, 1975), 79.

28. Zenón, vol. 1, 84.

29. Willie Perdomo, "Nigger Reecan Blues," in *Aloud: Voices from the Nuyorican Poets Café*, ed. Miguel Algarín and Bob Holzan (New York: Henry Holt, 1994), 111–13.

30. Aguilar, "Barbie Stirs Debate," 25A.

31. Elsie Crumb McCaeb and Anne H. Stark, preface to *Hair in African Art and Culture*, ed. Roy Sieber, and Frank Herreman (New York: Museum for African Art, 2000), 8.

32. Walter Benjamin, "Toys and Play," in *Selected Writings*, vol. 2 (Cambridge: Harvard University Press, 1999), 117-21, 118.

33. McCaeb and Stark, 11.

34. Rivera-Lyles, 16A.

35. Francisco A. Scarano, "The Jíbaro Masquerade and the Subaltern Politics of Creole Identity Formation in Puerto Rico, 1745-1823," *American Historical Review* 101, no. 5 (December 1996): 1398–431.

36. Néstor García Canclini, *La globalización* (Buenos Aires: Paidós, 2000), 11.

37. Luis O. Zayas Micheli, "La trascendencia como Coyuntura del jíbaro," In *El jíbaro*, ed. Manuel Alonso (Río Piedras; Edil, 1992), 16.

38. Scarano, 1398–431.

39. Antonio S. Pedreira, "La actualidad del jíbaro," in *El jíbaro de Puerto Rico: Símbolo y figura*, ed. Enrique Laguerre and Esther Melón (Sharon, CT: Troutman Press, 1968), 14.

40. Pedreira, 23.

41. Lillian Guerra, *Popular Expression and National Identity in Puerto Rico: The Struggle for Self, Community, and Nation* (Gainesville: University Press of Florida, 1998).

42. Pedreira, 20.

43. Dávila, 72.

44. Virgilio Dávila, "La jibarita," in *El jíbaro de Puerto Rico: Símbolo y figura*, ed. Laguerre and Melón, 100–101.

45. Salvador Brau, "La campesina," in *El jíbaro de Puerto Rico: Símbolo y figura*, ed. Enrique Laguerre and Esther Melón, 27.

46. Abelardo Díaz Alfaro, "El boliche," in *El jíbaro de Puerto Rico: Símbolo y figura*, ed. Laguerre and Melón, 206.

47. Guerra, 117.

48. Navarro, A1.

49. Rivera-Lyles, 16A.

50. Shelley Emling, "Barbie Creates Brouhaha, This Time among Puerto Ricans," *Charlotte Observer*, 30 December 1997, available www.charlotte.com/barbie1.htm.

51. Nilita Vientós Gastón, "El 'traje típico' puertorriqueño," in *Indice cultural*, vol. 1 (Río Piedras: Ediciones de la Universidad de Puerto Rico, 1962), 204.

52. Pedreira, 8.

53. Blanco, 130.

54. Eduardo Seda Bonilla, *Los derechos civiles en la cultura puertorriqueña* (Río Piedras: Ediciones de Bayoán, 1973), 189.

55. Guerra, 111.

56. Lord, 8.

57. Guerra, 102.

58. Navarro, A9.

59. Emling, www.charlotte.com/barbie1.htm.

60. Lord, 108.

61. Ibid., 190.

62. Ibid., 190.

63. "Mattel popularizó a Barbie mediante productos con licencias," *El Universal*, 13 Dec 2000, available http://noticias.eluniversal.com/1998/06/28/28502AA.shtml.

64. Ibid.

65. Navarro, A9.

66. Arlene Dávila, *Sponsored Identities: Cultural Politics in Puerto Rico* (Philadelphia: Temple University Press, 1997).

67. Rivera-Lyles, 16A.

68. "Boy Toy," *Latina,* July 1998, 20.

69. Ibid., 20.

70. Patricia Vargas, "Por la felicidad de un niño," *El Nuevo Día,* 23 December 1997, 77.

3

The *Buena Vista Social Club*

The Racial Politics of Nostalgia

Tanya Katerí Hernández

THIS ESSAY WILL examine the popularity and success of the *Buena Vista Social Club* documentary and music collection in the United States in order to evaluate the role of popular culture in shaping political discourse. It is my premise that the *Buena Vista Social Club* is a narrative of an ahistorical nostalgia for a prerevolutionary Cuba that was presumably more appreciative of its Black talent than socialist Cuba, and thereby ends up serving as a justification for the unilateral reentry of U.S. corporate interests into the affairs of Cuba.[1]

Cultural studies theorists have long observed that popular culture can "legitimate exploitative social hierarchies."[2] Specifically, popular culture can perpetuate societal power relations through the vehicle of narrative. Some scholars conceive of culture as a "contested narrative field" containing symbolically charged elements with ideological significance.[3] Culture is thus a valuable area of analysis even for legal academics such as myself who traditionally confine ourselves to the textual analysis of court opinions and statutes.[4] What is particularly rewarding about the inquiry into Cuban popular music is the manner in which it helps to elucidate issues of discrimination and racial conflict given the overrepresentation of Afro-Cubans within Cuban music.[5]

THE *BUENA VISTA SOCIAL CLUB* NARRATIVE

The *Buena Vista Social Club* is a 1997 album of newly recorded Afro-Cuban *son* pieces produced by the U.S. conglomerate Warner Music

Company. The album won a Grammy Award in 1998 and has become one of the best-selling world music albums of all time.[6] The *Buena Vista Social Club* is also the title of the documentary that was produced in 1999, which interviewed the musicians in Cuba and filmed them as they performed in the United States and Europe.

The popularly depicted narrative of how the *Buena Vista Social Club* came to be is as follows:

> North American guitarist Ry Cooder decided to seek out talented mu-
> sicians in Cuba to revitalize the forgotten music of *son* that made Cuba
> great before the socialist revolution.[7] If not for the intervention of Ry
> Cooder, the talented members of the ensemble he put together would
> have perished without national recognition. In fact, lead singer
> Ibrahim Ferrer would still be shining shoes for a living had it not been
> for the heroic efforts of Ry Cooder.[8] Ry Cooder discovered Cuban mu-
> sical treasures that the nation itself had overlooked.[9]

What is missing from this finely spun tale ("the *BVSC* narrative") is any demonstration of agency on the part of the Afro-Cuban musi-cians themselves and the respect they garnered within Cuban society of their own accord. For instance, the narrative completely omits the role of Afro-Cuban bandleader Juan de Marcos González, the individ-ual who masterminded and facilitated the collaboration. (de Marcos González briefly appears as a nonspeaking background figure in the documentary, leaving the viewer to conclude that he might be a friend of the musicians who wanted to listen in at the recording session). Yet, long before the arrival of Cooder, de Marcos González had contacted many of the veteran musicians who appear on the BVSC album for a project of the Afro-Cuban All Stars entitled *A todo Cuba le gusta* (All of Cuba likes it).[10] In fact, Cooder's original intention had been to record an album in Cuba with African and Cuban guitarists. But when the African guitarists were unable to arrive in Cuba, Cooder's record label approached de Marcos González for assistance. It was de Marcos Gon-zalez who then reconceived the project to focus on the Afro-Cuban musical tradition of *son* with the musicians who he already had a working relationship with.[11] In short, Cooder did not discover nor did he "pluck" the musicians off the streets of Havana as depicted in the U.S. popular press.[12]

Furthermore, the characterization of lead singer Ibrahim Ferrer as so unappreciated and destitute that he was forced to shine shoes over-looks the fact that his principal source of income was his government pension. Unlike musicians in the United States, Cuban musicians are state employees with the security of a pension and other government benefits when they choose to retire.[13] Ferrer himself explains, "I was re-tired. I didn't need to shine shoes for money. I've always been a restless guy. You can ask my wife. I have to stay busy."[14] Similarly, contrary to the *BVSC* narrative of atrophied musicians, pianist Rubén González had never stopped performing. His reduction in the number of per-formances was due to arthritis.[15] In addition to portraying the elderly musicians as discarded by Cuban society, the *BVSC* narrative refers to *son* as the forgotten music of the 1940s. Yet the one female vocalist on the album, Omara Portuondo, has explicitly affirmed that "there have always been people performing it, like Rubén, and Cachao, the bass player—all these people who have kept playing."[16] Furthermore, the Cuban government has facilitated the continued performance of *son* music as part of its overarching national commitment to the develop-ment of the arts.[17]

THE RACIAL POLITICS OF NOSTALGIA

So why is Ry Cooder glorified in the U.S. popular press and the *BVSC* documentary when the facts themselves contradict Cooder's self-ag-grandized role? The narrative's focus on Cooder serves to create a colo-nial myth of Cooder as "discoverer/conqueror" of native resources that have gone unappreciated and are more effectively channeled by a North American figure. Cooder's own descriptions of his attraction to working with musicians in the Afro-Cuban *son* tradition position Cooder as foreign explorer in opposition to an "unspoiled" indigenous Other. For instance, when interviewed on the television broadcast of *The Newshour with Jim Lehrer*, Cooder stated,

> I love the music because it is purely emotional, and then it has a cer-tain mysterious other side. . . . But when you are around him [Ibrahim Ferrer] or around these folks, what you begin to see is they have re-tained some humanity that is very out in front. It is very well-worn, you know. This guy comes in this aura of humanity. . . . His music comes from inside, it's from direct experience. . . . He didn't buy it in a

mall, so his culture has not been replaced, as people outside in the rest of the world have often forfeited and given up their culture, and they don't even know it.[18]

Cooder in effect equates the isolation of the U.S. trade embargo with being sheltered from the political and commodifying aspects of the international music industry.[19] Yet Cuban artists are quite cognizant of the commercial influences on their artistry. *BVSC* creator Juan de Marcos González himself has conceded that he implicitly acquiesced to Cooder's propagation of the colonial myth for the purpose of ensuring the commercial success of the collaboration.[20] Other Cuban artists have also expressed concern about the commercial pressure to "self-exoticize" in order to ensure financial success.[21]

The documentary furthers the image of the Afro-Cuban musicians as spiritual and emblematic of a more authentic humanity when singer Ibrahim Ferrer is interviewed in his home and the camera focuses great attention on artifacts and tokens symbolic of the Afro-Cuban religion Santería (which many Cubans maintain in their homes whether or not they are firm adherents of Santería).[22] Yet when Ferrer himself was questioned about spiritual issues, he stated, "I don't understand anything about Santería."[23] Nevertheless, the CD's liner notes go on to describe him as a "shy and unassuming man with a strong faith."[24] The reference to his presumed faith in Santería acts as a metonym for his authenticity that in turn facilitates the commodification of African-based spirituality for the sale of Afro-Cuban music.[25] Cooder is thus positioned as the foreign outside observer who can truly appreciate the authenticity of the Afro-Cuban indigenous "Other" constructed in the documentary. The *BVSC* narrative constructs the Afro-Cuban *son* musicians as "Other" precisely because their presumed authenticity stands in marked contrast to the ennui of the observer from an industrialized nation.[26]

It is in this way that the *BVSC* can be viewed as suffering from the same ills as ethnographic cinema so vividly depicted by cultural studies commentator Fatimah Tobing Rony.[27] In analyzing the films that have accompanied the development of anthropology as a discipline, Rony concludes that the ethnographic depictions of people of color as embodying and conferring authenticity and spirituality, best illustrated by the myth of the Noble Savage, serve as an antidote to the alienation engendered by industrialized modernity.[28] Central to the ethnographic spectacle that Rony describes is the nostalgic reconstruction of a more authentic humanity centered in the unspoiled primitive.

Indeed, the very musical form Cooder seeks to excavate like a colonial explorer in his self-described musical "treasure hunt"[29] is a genre of dance music created at the end of the nineteenth century by Afro-Cubans who were for the most part illiterate and not formally trained as musicians.[30] Their lack of formal education facilitates a characterization of *son* musicians as "feeling" artists who are "unspoiled" and thus subject to discovery. In contrast, contemporary Afro-Cuban music is being developed by musicians who have been formally trained with conservatory educations provided by the socialist government.[31] As a consequence, younger Cuban musicians have been disturbed by the level of international attention focused on older *son* musicians while contemporary Afro-Cuban music is ignored.[32] Cuban musicians note that the foreign interest in Afro-Cuban music "has been propelled by the Cuban music of a bygone era."[33] Furthermore, the *BVSC* focus on prerevolutionary musical styles completely overlooks the upbeat and nationalistic character of most popular songs in contemporary Cuban dance music that chronicle the life on the island today and its changes.[34] But of course the more politicized content of contemporary Afro-Cuban music does not lend itself as easily to the colonial fantasy of discovering unspoiled native talents.[35]

The *BVSC* colonial fantasy of discovery and conquest reverberates within the larger Cuban music industry context in which the United States and European countries compete to stake a claim in much the same way European powers once competed to establish territorial claims in the "new world." One music industry executive describes the race to claim a share of the Cuban music market as a "feeding frenzy" because "[i]t's like discovering a treasure that's been buried all these years."[36] Despite the U.S. trade embargo, U.S. record companies have been sending emissaries to Cuba on a regular basis and were a strong presence at the 1998 Cubadisco annual music industry trade show in Cuba.[37] (Although U.S. law prohibits U.S. companies from hiring Cuban musicians directly, U.S. companies can contract to be the U.S. distributors of musicians signed to foreign labels. In addition, Cuban musicians can be signed directly to the foreign subsidiaries of U.S. companies.)[38] And just as the colonial expansion of European powers was accompanied by legitimate concerns with economic exploitation, the competition for the Cuban music market has raised similar concerns with economic exploitation. In fact, there have been instances already of foreign record companies refusing to compensate Cuban musicians, of fraudulent concert promoters leaving musicians stranded in Europe, and of payment fees being set as low as twenty-five dollars for a recording session.[39] Furthermore, the ability of Cuban music companies to negotiate their own distribution deals has been periodically hampered by the denial of U.S. State Department travel visas to attend important music industry conferences.[40]

The construction of the colonial myth is furthered by the *BVSC*'s idealization of prerevolutionary Cuba as a magic time for music in which these musicians and the music *son* were appreciated. The choice of the album title itself is a fond look at Cuba from before the revolution, as the Buena Vista Social Club was a music hall from the 1940s, which has long been closed. Similarly, Cooder's constant reference to lead singer Ibrahim Ferrer as "the Cuban Nat King Cole" evokes apolitical visions of a lost musical elegance.[41] The nostalgic picture continues with the documentary's soulful shots of the now faded mansions and glamorous hotels of yesteryear as the camera searches for the architectural remnants of what was the Buena Vista Social Club, while omitting any depictions of the more developed and upscale areas of the island that do exist.

What is particularly disturbing about the *Buena Vista Social Club* longing for old-world Cuba is its oversight of the social ills that plagued prerevolutionary Cuba and motivated large numbers of Afro-Cubans to support Fidel Castro.[42] Even the use of the name "Buena Vista Social Club" fails to appreciate how the original Buena Vista Social Club was one of the few prerevolutionary Havana nightspots that allowed entrance to people of African descent.[43] De facto racial segregation was widely practiced before the revolution in public accommodations like restaurants, nightclubs, and beaches.[44] The racial segregation was also accompanied by extreme racial stratification:

> In the main Afro-Cubans occupied the lower end of the socio-economic order. Almost 30 percent of the population of color over twenty years of age was illiterate. Blacks tended to constitute a majority in the crowded tenement dwellings of Havana. They suffered greater job insecurity, more unemployment/underemployment, poorer health care, and constituted a proportionally larger part of the prison population. They generally earned lower wages than whites, even in the same in-

dustries. Afro-Cubans were subjected to systematic discrimination, barred from hotels, resorts, clubs, and restaurants.[45]

Only after the socialist revolution did the Cuban government publicly denounce these manifestations of racial hierarchy.[46] Yet the *BVSC* narrative is completely divorced from the realities of the time frame it so longingly wants to be transported back to. Moreover, the documentary's own evidence of prerevolutionary economic disparity is glossed over as romantic. For instance, Ibrahim Ferrer's birth in a social dance club in 1927 is characterized as a testament to his inherent ability as a singer, rather than as an indicator of his family's destitute economic status and lack of the nationalized health care system that presently exists for all Cubans.[47] Similarly, guitarist Eliades Ochoa's youth spent performing music in brothels and bars is presented as charming rather than demonstrative of the impoverished educational system that existed before the socialist revolution.[48] The complexities of racial hierarchy and desperate poverty do not lend themselves as well to the commercial ends of packaging "authentic" and "quaint" Cuba for sale.[49]

Instead, the *Buena Vista Social Club* idealizes the past and reinvents it to support the notion that socialist Cuba does not appreciate the talent of its populace in the way a White North American like Ry Cooder can.[50] Missing from the picture are the documented instances of contract exploitation of Cuban songwriters by U.S. music companies before the revolution, when musicians were paid one dollar for the legal rights to their songs and Afro-Cuban *son* musicians were targeted for copyright exploitation.[51] Also missing from the story is the racial discrimination that *son* musicians were subject to before the revolution, in which Afro-Cubans were denied admission to musician unions because they played the Afro-Cuban music of *son* or because they had no formal training or could not read music.[52] The erroneous depiction of Afro-Cuban music as frozen in time, isolated from outside influences, and populated by unappreciated dark natives re-envisions Cuba as a new frontier to be discovered and conquered as colonial imperialists did in the past.

History demonstrates that the construction of narratives is instrumental to the subjugation of people and thus should be carefully monitored. For example, when Native Americans began to use the courts to challenge their dispossession from their own lands, the U.S. Supreme Court justified the maintenance of their continued exclusion from legal title to property with the narrative that the poor character of the Native Americans as a people warranted their conquest and forceful expulsion.[53] Contemporary analysis of judicial opinions also demonstrates the continued use of ethnocentric and racially biased narratives in the application of the law.[54] Thus, even the racially harmless myth of how a North American "rediscovered" Afro-Cuban popular culture for the world can have an adverse effect on the sovereignty of Cuba and its economic power by providing ideological justification for contemporary colonial and economic conquest.[55] As cultural studies scholar George Lipsitz has stated about popular culture, "this ain't no sideshow."[56]

NOTES

1. While it is certainly the case that the Cuban nation has also demonstrated an interest in participating in the global economy with its establishment of joint ventures with corporate entities from foreign nations, at the same time, like many other less-developed countries, Cuba is concerned with the dangers of economic exploitation inherent in globalization. See John M. Kirk, series editor's foreword to *Afro-Cuban Voices: On Race and Identity in Contemporary Cuba*, ed. Pedro Pérez Sarduy and Jean Stubbs (Gainesville: University Press of Florida, 2000), viii: "The social distortions resulting from the demise of the Soviet Union, and from the post-1980s Special Period, as Cuba opened up rapidly to foreign investment and domestic economic reform—what Fidel Castro termed a 'pact with the devil'—have only aggravated the situation." See also Jeremy Brecher and Tim Costello, *Global Village or Global Pillage: Economic Reconstruction from the Bottom Up* (Boston: South End Press, 1994), 16, 24: criticizing globalization as leading to a decline in working and social conditions overall with an increase in prosperity only for developed nations and a small elite of underdeveloped countries.

2. George Lipsitz, *Time Passages: Collective Memory and American Popular Culture* (Minneapolis: University of Minnesota Press, 1990), vii.

3. Jocelyn Linnekin, "On the Theory and Politics of Cultural Construction in the Pacific," *Oceana* 62 (1992): 249, 251. See also Robin Moore, *Nationalizing Blackness: Afrocubanismo and Artistic Revolution in Havana, 1920–1940* (Pittsburgh: University of Pittsburgh Press, 1997), 87.

4. Richard K. Sherwin, *When Law Goes Pop: The Vanishing Line between Law and Popular Culture* (Chicago: University of Chicago Press, 2000), 8: observing that "law is both a producer and a byproduct of mainstream culture" and thus cannot "escape the forces and conflicts that play out in the culture at large."

5. Moore, *Nationalizing Blackness*, 4: "Music and dance have always been

among the most democratic of the arts in Cuba, representing forms of expression accessible to minorities that appeal to listeners across class and racial boundaries."

6. Elisa Murray, "The Sound of Son," *Seattle Weekly*, 1 April 1999, 53.

7. Heather Johnson, "'Social Club' Delivers Sassy Salsa from Forgotten Greats," *University of Virginia Cavalier Daily*, 7 September 1999, U-Wire edition.

8. David E. Thigpen, "Forget Me Not: At 72, Ibrahim Ferrer at Last Finds Fame," *Time*, 9 August 1999, 1.

9. "Those were the golden days of Cuban music, before the revolution left many of the great artists of Ferrer's generation scraping to get by." Ibid., 1.

10. Jan Fairley, "Cuba Roots," *Scotsman*, 23 October 1999, 18.

11. Ibid.

12. "In 1997 Ferrer was plucked off a Havana street by California guitarist Ry Cooder, who invited him to sing on a new album he was producing, Buena Vista Social Club." Thigpen, "Forget Me Not," 1.

13. Judy Cantor, "Isla de la Musica: The Biggest Surprise at Havana's Cubadisco '98: A Burgeoning Retinue of Americans Hoping to Cash In," *Miami New Times*, 28 May 1998, Features Section.

14. *The Newshour with Jim Lehrer*, PBS, 16 November 1999, transcript no. 6599.

15. Ibid.

16. Ibid. See also Sandra Levinson, "Talking about Cuban Culture: A Reporter's Notebook," in *The Cuba Reader: The Making of a Revolutionary Society*, ed. Phillip Brenner, William M. LeoGrande, Donna Rich, and Daniel Seigel (New York: Grove, 1989), 487, 495.

17. Yvonne Daniel, "Rumba: Social and Aesthetic Change in Cuba," in *Blackness in Latin America and the Caribbean: Social Dynamics and Cultural Transformations, Eastern South America and the Caribbean*, vol. 2, ed. Arlene Torres and Norman E. Whitten, Jr. (Bloomington: Indiana University Press, 1998), 481, 487–88: describing how the Cuban government through its Ministry of Culture provides financial, organizational, and ideological support for the promotion of the arts as part of its revolutionary agenda of national education.

18. *Newshour with Jim Lehrer*, transcript no. 6599.

19. What is especially naive about Cooder's idealized vision of Cuban music is the way in which it contrasts with Cubans' own conception of culture as inherently political and therefore part of the revolution. Indeed, music figures prominently in U.S.-Cuban relations: "intellectuals and embittered exiled artists regularly fan the flames of anticommunism by proclaiming that under Cuban socialism there is no freedom for the artists." Levinson, "Talking about Cuban Culture," 487. Furthermore, the volatile protests that greeted the Miami concert of the popular *son* group from Cuba, *Los Van Van*, exemplify the political tenor of Cuban music, just as the drama that surrounded the simple custody

dispute of Elián González exemplifies that everything about Cuba is political. Mike Clary, "Amid Protest Cuban Group Plays Miami Concert: Angry Foes of Castro and Police in Riot Gear Don't Deter More Than 2,000 from Hearing Los Van Van Perform," *Los Angeles Times*, 10 October 1999, A8; David Cole, "The 'Cuba Exception,'" *Nation*, 7 February 2000, 4. Yet it is Cooder's seeming naïveté about the political aspects of what he is viewing that also positions the documentary as an alternative perspective to the more widely disseminated conservative perspectives of anti-Castro exiles, in that the BVSC documentary grants humanity—albeit in a problematic way—to those Cubans struggling under the U.S. trade embargo.

20. Fairley, "Cuba Roots," 18.

21. Rogelio Martínez Furé, "A National Cultural Identity? Homogenizing Monomania and the Plural Heritage," in *Afro-Cuban Voices: On Race and Identity in Contemporary Cuba*, ed. Pérez Sarduy and Stubbs, 154, 159.

22. Although always present in the Cuban culture, until recently manifestations of Afro-Cuban religious beliefs, like other religions, were discouraged by the Cuban state. Today there is considerable concern among Santería adherents that Afro-Cuban religion has become a commercialized vehicle to attract tourism and the resulting foreign currency. Juan Benkomo, "Crafting the Sacred Batá Drums," in *Afro-Cuban Voices: On Race and Identity in Contemporary Cuba*, ed. Pérez Sarduy and Stubbs, 140, 142–43.

23. Ed Morales, "Dreaming in Cuba," *Village Voice*, 8 June 1999, 66.

24. Nick Gold and Nigel Williamson, *Buena Vista Social Club Compact Disc Liner Notes* (New York: Warner Music Group Company, 1997), 8.

25. Ann duCille, *Skin Trade* (Cambridge: Harvard University Press, 1996), 1–2: describing race as a "hot property."

26. Laura E. Donaldson, "On Medicine Women and White Shamans: New Age Native Americanism and Commodity Fetishism as Pop Culture Feminism," *Signs: Journal of Women in Culture and Society* 24 (spring 1999): 677, 682: describing one of the most important innovations of contemporary commodity consumption as "the rummaging through of imagined histories to envision a different life for onself . . . immune to the corrupting influences of Western society."

27. Fatimah Tobing Rony, *The Third Eye: Race, Cinema, and Ethnographic Spectacle* (Durham: Duke University Press, 1996).

28. Ibid., 194–95.

29. *Buena Vista Social Club Compact Disc Liner Notes*, 3.

30. Moore, *Nationalizing Blackness*, 89–93, 285.

31. Judy Cantor, "The New Miami Sound: It's Straight from Contemporary Cuba and It Has Taken Root in a Most Unlikely Place: Little Havana," *Miami New Times*, 20 August 1998, Features Section.

32. Paul Fisher, "Cuban Music: Revolution Heats Up Airwaves," *Japan*

Times, 13 July 1999. See also Cantor, "Isla de la Musica": contemporary Cuban musician notes that he is not pleased "by the recent glut of Cuban discs with wrinkled faces on the covers" because of its obstruction of revolutionary music.

33. Cantor, "Isla de la Musica."

34. Ibid.

35. Daniel Chang, "Reviews of New Latin Dance, Soundtrack and Rap Releases; Afro-Cuban All Stars 'Distinto, Diferente' Nonesuch," *Orange County Register,* 19 January 2000, Entertainment News Section.

36. Ibid.

37. Christopher John Farley, "Viva la Musica Cubana," *Time,* 22 June 1998.

38. Ibid.

39. Cantor, "Isla de la Musica."

40. Judy Cantor, "The Politics of Music," *Miami New Times,* 17 September 1998, Features Section. The U.S. State Department has denied Cuban music executives visas for fear that they might engage in legally prohibited transactions, such as signing Cuban artists directly to U.S. record labels.

41. Thigpen, "Forget Me Not," 1. Even for Cubans, Nat King Cole and his chemically straightened hair symbolize apolitical and nonaggressive and thus acceptable Black celebrity. Alden Knight, "Tackling Racism in Performing Arts and the Media," in *Afro-Cuban Voices: On Race and Identity in Contemporary Cuba,* ed. Pérez Sarduy and Stubbs, 108, 109: "A particular irony of Cooder's reference to Ferrer as the 'Cuban Nat King Cole' is, in fact, that Nat King Cole experienced blatant racial discrimination when he traveled to Cuba in 1951. In fact, the Hotel Nacional de Cuba has just recently issued a posthumous apology for denying Nat King Cole (and Josephine Baker) lodging at the hotel in 1951 because of his race. "Natalie Cole to Visit Cuba in November," *Granma,* 30 August 2000, available http://www.granma.cu/ingles/ago5/36cole.htm.

42. Douglas Butterworth, *The People of Buena Ventura: Relocation of Slum Dwellers in Postrevolutionary Cuba* (Urbana: University of Illinois Press, 1980), xiv.

43. *Newshour with Jim Lehrer.*

44. Debra Evenson, *Revolution in the Balance: Law and Society in Contemporary Cuba* (Boulder: Westview, 1994), 110.

45. Louis A. Pérez, Jr., *Cuba: Between Reform and Revolution,* 2d ed. (New York: Oxford University Press, 1995), 307.

46. Even though the socialist revolution has made great strides in addressing the problems of racial stratification through the operation of its economic redistribution programs, racial disparities persist today. See, e.g., Tanya K. Hernández, "An Exploration of the Efficacy of Class-Based Approaches to Racial Justice: The Cuban Context," *University of California Davis Law Review* 33, no. 4 (2000): 1142–51.

47. *Buena Vista Social Club Compact Disc Liner Notes,* 8.

48. Ibid., 27.

49. Arjun Appadurai, *Modernity at Large: Cultural Dimensions of Globalization* (Minneapolis: University of Minnesota Press, 1996), 77: describing how mass marketing creates an "imagined nostalgia for things that never were."

50. Mike Clark, "New on Video," *USA Today*, 17 December 1999, 13E: "Ry Cooder album that successfully promoted accomplished, aged Cuban musicians who had been forgotten even in their own country"; Sean Piccoli, "From Buena Vista, a New Kind of Cuba Libre," *Fort Lauderdale Sun-Sentinel*, 6 June 1999, 1D: "brilliant musicians who were practically forgotten at home."

51. Cantor, "Isla de la Musica." See also Moore, *Nationalizing Blackness*, 107–8.

52. Moore, *Nationalizing Blackness*, 97.

53. *Johnson v. M'Intosh*, 21 U.S. (8 Wheat) 543 (1823). See also Christine A. Klein, "Treaties of Conquest: Property Rights, Indian Treaties, and the Treaty of Guadalupe Hidalgo," *New Mexico Law Review* 26 (1996): 201.

54. Thomas Ross, *Just Stories: How the Law Embodies Racism and Bias* (Boston: Beacon Press, 1996), 1–18.

55. Sherwin, *When Law Goes Pop*, 5: "Culture provides the signs, images, stories, characters, metaphors, and scenarios, among other familiar materials, with which we make sense of our lives and the world around us."

56. Lipsitz, *Time Passages*, 3.

4

"Lemme Stay, I Want to Watch"

Ambivalence in Borderlands Cinema

Luz Calvo

THE MEXICO-U.S. BORDERLANDS—a physical and psychic space characterized by mixture—challenge U.S. fantasies of cultural, racial, and sexual purity. Set in these borderlands, Orson Welles's *Touch of Evil* (1958) represents U.S. cultural anxiety about sexual relationships that cross racial lines. Welles's classic film provides the student of borderlands cinema with a complex and highly ambivalent representation of desire, violence, and sexuality set along the Mexico-U.S. border.

"Ambivalence" is used in this essay to signal the coexistence of contradictory feelings and attitudes toward one object. Traditionally, psychoanalysis considers the coexistence of love and hate in the child's relation to the parents. Intense, ambivalent feelings toward one's parents are the material that psychoanalysts love to talk about. My concern, however, is slightly different: I focus on public rather than private ambivalence, in particular, ambivalence about racial and sexual difference that surfaces in U.S. popular culture texts, such as cinema.

The ambivalence I find in Welles's film is fear and anxiety on one side, and desire and fantasy on the other. Psychoanalysis teaches that ambivalence plays a structuring role in the formation of identity. Keeping in mind Stuart Hall's admonition that identity is created *through* representation (1996), I argue that ambivalence about race and sexuality is one thread that contributes to the social construction of Latino/a and Anglo identity in the U.S. Southwest. I utilize some concepts from psychoanalytic theory not to elevate Sigmund Freud's theories (1953–74) as the only or best methodological framework, but because they allow me to explore in some depth the ambivalence I find represented in this particular film.

Touch of Evil is structured by a primal scene fantasy that signals ambivalence. The "primal scene" was theorized by Freud as the child's confrontation, either in reality or fantasy, with parental sexuality. Freud found that the child, on seeing (or imagining) his or her parents engaged in sexual relations, reacted with ambivalence. On the one hand, the child feels a certain fascination. On the other, there is fear and anxiety, especially because the small child interprets the act as violence inflicted on the mother. Yet, without some understanding of the primal scene, the child would not be able to answer the question of origin: "Where did I come from?" The most literal response to that question is that "I" come from an act of sexual intercourse.

In some sense, racial identity also rests on an understanding of personal and historical origins that implies a primal scene scenario. In the case of Mexican identity, the primal scene is the historical memory of the often violent sexual relations between the Spanish colonizer and the Native woman. I call this the primal scene of colonialism. This historical reality, however, has not quietly disappeared into the past. Rather, it haunts our present as a psychic reality: as a dream (or, more accurately, a nightmare), the scene of sexual violence often appears in reversed or scrambled form in cultural productions, such as film. While some may believe the scene of violence to be a reality buried in the history books, I argue that, instead, the colonial scene of sexual and racial violence continually surfaces, albeit in distorted form, in popular culture. Of course, this is not meant to suggest that all of Mexican identity can be reduced to this historical moment. (Nor can the entire personality of an individual be reduced to their primal scene encounter; rather, this is but one aspect of a complex set of processes that constitute the subject.)

I focus on one moment in history—the primal scene of colonialism—because it provides a complex example of the way past events surface in popular culture texts. In addition, I find this one moment an important site for analysis because race and sexuality are so thoroughly embedded in the primal scene of colonialism that it becomes necessary to theorize race and sexuality together—as intersected, mutually constitutive categories.

A very direct representation of the primal scene of colonialism occurs in another film, Edward James Olmos's *American Me* (1992).[1] In this film, the protagonist, Santana (Olmos), the leader of the Mexican mafia, is serving time in prison. Structured as a flashback, the scene of the rape of Santana's mother functions as primal scene, explaining Santana's origin and identity. In June 1943, the month of the Zoot Suit Riots, Santana's mother is raped inside a tattoo parlor by a group of Anglo navy sailors. Crosscut with the scene of the rape is the de-zooting of the man who raised Santana (his father, though possibly not his biological father) and the cutting off of his ducktail—a symbolic castration of the Chicano. The symbolic equivalence of these two acts is framed by the crosscutting between the two scenes. In rapid succession the audience is confronted, alternately, with the gang rape of Santana's mother and the de-zooting of his father.

In the midst of the violence on the street outside the tattoo parlor, a man in fetal position crashes through a plate glass window: this is the symbolic birth of Santana himself. The resonance with Mexico's primal scene of colonialism is obvious: the rape of the indigenous woman by Spanish colonizers is replicated in the rape of the Chicana by Anglo servicemen. In this film, race and sexuality intersect in the primal scene that produces Santana.

Santana explains his situation in a prison letter to his female love interest: "I am two people. One was born the day I met you, the other was born in a downtown tattoo parlor." *American Me* represents the masculine-identified Chicano subject trapped by the logic of a colonial symbolic order. It is an ambivalent identity, to be sure. In Santana's words, he is not one person but two. Ultimately, however, Santana's identity is (de)formed from the remnants of the history of colonial sexual violence in the southwestern United States, even if there is another part of himself that yearns for something else.[2]

In contrast to Olmos's rather direct representation of the rape of the Chicana during the Zoot Suit Riots, Welles produced an alternate scenario that re-envisions but does not necessarily transcend the originary scene of sexual and racial violence. My point is not that Welles's film is somehow more "accurate" or "realistic" than Olmos's; on the contrary, I believe that Welles's representation of racial and sexual identities along the border is the "stuff" of fantasy. Yet, precisely because his film delves into a cultural fantasy, it is able to present a nuanced, complex, and thoroughly ambivalent representation of Mexican, Chicano, and Anglo subjectivities along the border. For this reason, I believe that Welles's film merits critical attention from scholars of Latino/a popular culture.

Originally released in 1958, *Touch of Evil* is now regarded as a classic. The famous opening sequence, filmed in a continuous long shot, sets up interlocking anxieties about crossing the border, racial mixture, and (hetero)sexuality. Here, the camera tracks two interracial couples as they negotiate their way from the streets of a Mexican border town into the United States. The first couple is an American businessman, Mr. Linnekar, on a date with a Mexican stripper named Zita. They travel in a large convertible that, unbeknownst to them, carries a time bomb hidden in the trunk. The second couple, the film's protagonists, is Miguel "Mike" Vargas (Charlton Heston), a Mexican government official, on a stroll with his new American wife, Susan (Janet Leigh). They walk arm in arm through streets filled with tourists, street vendors, and the predictable donkey.

Once on the U.S. side of the border, Susan remarks to her husband, "Do you realize this is the first time we have been together in my country?" Vargas answers, "Do you realize I haven't kissed you in over an hour?" In retrospect, we can see that the newlyweds' symbolic exchange of nationality (Susan's remark) with sexuality (Vargas's answer) is charged with danger. The couple's verbal and symbolic exchange foreshadows the ensuing explosion.

Before the newlyweds can consummate their kiss, there is a deafening blast and a sudden cut from the startled reaction of Vargas and Susan to the scene of a car exploding in flames. Linnaker and his date perish in the explosion, and the subsequent investigation draws Vargas into a detective story and away from his wife. The murders set in motion a narrative that aims to reestablish "law and order" and—with less enthusiasm—to reunite the honeymoon couple.

As the narrative unfolds, Vargas discovers that a corrupt Anglo detective, Hank Quinlan (Orson Welles), is attempting to frame the Mexican boyfriend of Linnekar's daughter for the murders. While attempting to establish the young man's innocence, Vargas leaves his young bride alone in a seedy motel. Detective Quinlan then teams up with the leader of a drug-running gang, Uncle Joe Grandi (Akim Tamiroff), in a plot to undermine Vargas. In a pivotal scene, the Grandi gang threatens and assaults Susan. While it appears to the audience that Susan is about to be raped, we later learn that the gang was just "scaring her real good." Meanwhile, Quinlan double-crosses the gang, murders Uncle Joe, and frames Susan, left drugged at the scene of the crime. Quinlan's partner, Menzies (Joseph Calleia), cooperates with

Vargas in order to surreptitiously tape Quinlan's confession and clear Susan's name.

In this essay, I focus on one critical scene: the rape of Susan by the racially mixed Grandi gang. I suggest that this "rape" functions as a primal scene. Film theorist Christian Metz suggests a convergence between the scopic regimes of the cinema and the primal scene: "Cinematic voyeurism, *unauthorized* scopophilia, is from the outset . . . strongly established . . . in direct line from the primal scene." Metz argues that "film unfolds in that simultaneously very close and definitely inaccessible 'elsewhere' in which the child *sees* the amorous play of the parental couple, who are similarly ignorant of it and leave it alone, a pure onlooker whose participation is inconceivable" (1975, 264).

If, as Metz suggests, the cinema structures itself like a primal scene, then the staging of violent sexuality on the screen would magnify this effect. The violent, aggressive, sexual scene of rape echoes that child's interpretation of sexuality as violent. The "rape" staged in *Touch of Evil* imbricates race in the primal scene. Susan is assaulted by a racially mixed gang as she waits in El Mirador, a motel located in a desolate area on the U.S. side of the border.[3] Alone in her room, Susan wears baby doll pajamas—a sartorial regression, for she has changed from the provocative lingerie she wore earlier when talking to her husband on the phone. A medium shot reveals a childlike Susan leaning against the wall, trying to hear what is going on in the adjacent room. Susan listens attentively to a woman's voice whispering to her, "You know what the boys are trying to do, don't you?" Susan, perplexed, makes no response. The voice continues, with a sexual allusion: "They are trying to get in there. They went to get the master key."

When the door to Susan's motel room begins to open, Susan has a look of fear. Enter the first member of the Grandi gang, Pancho, through the door, and Susan scrambles to the bed, clutching the sheet. The camera shifts between shots of each successive gang member shown from Susan's point of view and shots of the tremulous Susan shown from the gang members' point of view. This scene replicates the obsessive racist fantasy: the rape of the white woman by a man of color. This racist fantasy is deeply embedded in a particular cultural imaginary that associates racial mixing with sexual contamination and violence. Welles plays with this fantasy in the scene of Susan's "rape": Janet Leigh, an icon of white womanhood, is being attacked by a racially mixed gang. The anxiety about the white woman's purity is heightened further when a bulldagger (a lesbian in a 1950s butch style) enters Susan's motel room and slowly, almost sadistically, circles Susan. At the pinnacle of the rising tension, the bulldagger (Mercedes McCambridge) whispers to Pancho, "Lemme stay, I want to watch."

In her brief performance, Mercedes McCambridge as bulldagger is portrayed as masculine and most definitely "perverse": she wears a leather jacket, men's slacks, and short mannish hair. Her dramatic entrance is a queer moment, as the spectator must scramble to decipher her gender: is she a pretty boy or a rough girl? She enters with an entourage, two hard-looking femmes wearing tight sweaters. The bulldagger and her femmes intensify both the "mixed" nature and rebel status of this border gang: not only is the gang racially mixed but it seems sexually mixed as well. (Perhaps "ambiguous" would be a more apt description, as neither the sexuality nor the race of this gang is easy to read.) The presence of the girls does not bother the gang boys (who might be read as queer themselves), but does seem to increase Susan's —and, perhaps, the spectator's—panic.

James Naremore (1989) argues that this scene so excessively stresses the threat to Susan that the image of the "white woman being raped by a Mexican thug" suggests a parody of Griffith's *Birth of a Nation* (164). He insists, moreover, that in the rape sequence Susan is "forced to confront her own private demons":

> We see the beginning of the rape from the woman's point of view, as a succession of hideous, glassy-eyed faces stare down into the camera and whisper to one another. Suzy's WASPish innocence is set off against the vivid stereotypes of a racist and sado-masochist imagination, as if the film were deliberately calling up fears that a respectable marriage between the "good" characters cannot repress. (164)

A similar interpretation is posited by Terry Comito (1985), who argues that "it is as if Uncle Joe's boys were obligingly acting out Susan's own fantasies about swarthy rapists (with a leather jacketed lesbian thrown in for good measure)" (23). Like Naremore, Comito privileges the "white woman's point of view," and the fantasy is interpreted as a projection of *her* fear/desire.

The fantasy of rape of a white woman transposes the scene of colonial violence and trauma: sexual contact between the woman of color and the white colonizer. The site, history, and memory of sexual contact (often, but not always, violent) between the woman of color and the white colonizer provoke profound anxiety for all colonial subjects, both colonized and colonizer.[4] The memory of historical trauma remains unconscious in the fantasy structure, but it can be deduced from the social context of the rape fantasy's persistent circulation. Concealing the originary trauma, the syntax of the film's fantasy reveals both fascination and horror at the scene of racial mixture and its association with violence.

In setting *Touch of Evil* in a fictional border town, Welles highlights questions of racial and cultural difference by putting these differences in tension with sexual difference and sexual transgression. Similarly putting racial difference into a relationship with sexual transgression, borderlands theorist Gloria Anzaldúa (1987) describes borderlands inhabitants as "the squint-eyed, the perverse, the queer, the troublesome, the mongrel, the mulatto, the half-breed, the half dead; in short those who cross over, pass over, or go through the confines of the 'normal'" (3). The bulldagger played by Mercedes McCambridge is seen to be the quintessential border figure: she is racially and sexually ambiguous and she troubles the social symbolic by asserting her "perverse" desire.

A more recent filmic representation of such a border figure occurs in John Sayles's 1996 *Lone Star*. In this film, Pilar Cruz (Elizabeth Peña) represents the border figure who troubles the social symbolic by asserting a "perverse" desire. Pilar is the daughter of a Mexican American restaurateur (Mercedes Cruz) and an Anglo sheriff (Buddy Deeds). Yet, until the end of the film Pilar does not know the true identity of her father. Pilar, in love with Buddy's son, Sam, discovers that she is involved in a relationship with her half brother. Instead of repudiating her love for Sam, Pilar rejects the social symbolic that makes incest a taboo.

In this essay, while focusing on Welles's *Touch of Evil*, I have considered various examples of borderlands cinema that represent sexual relationships that cross racial lines; that is, sexuality between Mexicans and Anglos. In *American Me* (Olmos 1992), the rape of Santana's mother is represented unambiguously: it is the ultimate cause of Santana's tragic life. In *Touch of Evil* and *Lone Star*, interracial sexuality is much more ambivalently represented. In these films, interracial sexuality is staged to evoke both anxiety and fascination, fear and desire. As borderlands cinema, all these films demonstrate an underlying preoccupation with the past and what I have called the primal scene of colonialism as evidenced by their representation of interracial sexuality. In the primal scene, as in scenes from these films, the spectator is constituted as voyeur who watches with anxious fascination. In this sense, all three films constitute the spectator in the position of Mercedes McCambridge when she pleads, "Lemme stay, I want to watch."

NOTES

1. Another example of the representation of colonial sexual violence in borderlands cinema occurs in *Silent Tongue* (Sam Shepard 1993). Emma Pérez (1999) persuasively discusses this film in relation to my concept of the primal scene of colonialism (110–14, n. 34).

2. Unfortunately, in my view, the film itself is trapped by the logic of the colonial symbolic order. The film's obsessive anxiety with the "anal economy" of prison sexuality demonstrates its collusion with what I call the "Law of the White Father." (Film theorist Sergio de la Mora has theorized the "anal economy" of this film [1995].) The Law of the White Father exists at the level of symbolic interaction. In other words, the Law of the White Father refers to a symbolic system and not to any one father in particular. This symbolic system is white-supremacist, patriarchal, and heteronormative. *American Me* colludes with the hegemonic symbolic system to the extent that it presents anal sex as repulsive, always already violent, and sick. (In *American Me*, anal sex is everywhere, but exists only as rape.) The film implies that Santana's "sickness" can be traced back to the rape of his mother during the Zoot Suit Riots. Not only is Santana trapped by this logic, but the film is as well.

3. Susan is not actually raped; instead, she is injected with sodium pentathol and moved to a hotel room in Mexico. The female gang members take her clothes and blow marijuana smoke in her hair.

4. See Pérez (1991) for an illuminating discussion of Mexican/Chicano anxiety about the originary trauma of Mexican identity. Through her reading of Octavio Paz's "Hijos de la Malinche" in *Labyrinth of Solitude*, Pérez posits an "Oedipal-Conquest-Complex" figuring Oedipus in racial terms—the Indigenous woman as mother, the Spanish colonizer as the White Father, and the Mestizo/a child of that union (167–69).

BIBLIOGRAPHY

Anzaldúa, Gloria. *Borderlands/La Frontera: The New Mestiza*. San Francisco: Aunt Lute Books, 1987.

Comito, Terry. "Welles's Labyrinths: An Introduction to *Touch of Evil*." In *Touch of Evil*, ed. Terry Comito, 3–33. New Brunswick: Rutgers University Press, 1985.

Freud, Sigmund. "From the History of an Infantile Neurosis." In *The Standard Edition of the Complete Psychological Works of Sigmund Freud*. London: Hogarth Press, 1953–74.

Hall, Stuart. "New Ethnicities." In *Stuart Hall: Critical Dialogues in Cultural Studies*, ed. David Morley and Kuan-Hsing Chen. London: Routledge, 1996.

Metz, Christian. *The Imaginary Signifier: Psychoanalysis and the Cinema*. Bloomington: Indiana University Press, 1975.

Mora, Sergio de la. "'Giving It Away': American Men and the Defilement of Chicano Manhood." Cine Estudiantil Film Festival. San Diego: Centro Cultural de la Raza, 7–11 March 1995.

Naremore, James. *The Magic World of Orson Welles*. Dallas: Southern Methodist University Press, 1989.

Olmos, Edward James. *American Me*. Universal Pictures, 1992.

Pérez, Emma. "Sexuality and Discourse: Notes from a Chicana Survivor." In *Chicana Lesbians: The Girls Our Mothers Warned Us About*, ed. Carla Trujillo. Berkeley: Third Woman Press, 1991.

———. *The Decolonial Imaginary: Writing Chicanas into History*. Theories of Representation and Difference, series ed. Teresa de Lauretis. Bloomington: Indiana University Press, 1999.

Sayles, John. *Lone Star*. Castle Rock, 1996.

Shepard, Sam. *Silent Tongue*. Belbo Films, 1993.

Welles, Orson. *Touch of Evil*. Universal, 1958.

MUSIC

5

Encrucijadas

Rubén Blades at the Transnational Crossroads

Ana Patricia Rodríguez

Everyone carries the mark of time
Everyone carries the trace of dreams. . . .
How can we erase the distances without traveling them?
Why pretend the North is in the South, and hallucinate?
— Rubén Blades, "La Rosa de los Vientos"

RUBÉN BLADES IS best known as a Nuyorican recording artist of Latino-Caribbean music. His vast urban salsa-lore includes unforgettable figures such as Pedro Navaja, Pablo Pueblo, Juan Pachanga, Ligia Elena, and others. Blades's other genealogy, however, can be traced to a greater Central American history and diaspora, set off by U.S. interventions in the region throughout the twentieth century. In various musical compositions, Blades sings of this other (Central) America, whose history includes the secession of Panamá from Colombia in 1903, the construction and completion of the Panama Canal by the United States in 1914, and the U.S. military occupation of Panamá through 1999.[1] Indeed, Panamá and the rest of Central America share a recent history of military dictatorship and armed conflict, and perhaps a more pronounced U.S. presence than the rest of Latin America.[2] Situated within this context, Rubén Blades's latest work—especially *La Rosa de los Vientos* (1996) and *Tiempos* (1999)—contributes to the (re)constructions of national, regional, and transnational Central American identities and cultures that are taking shape today.[3]

On the eve of the twenty-first century, Panamá finally recuperated the Canal (Zone) from the United States and entered into an ambiguous "partnership," giving the U.S. government "peacekeeping" guardianship of the waterway. To commemorate the Panamanian recovery of the Canal Zone, Blades released *Tiempos* and performed in concert in Panamá on 31 December 1999. Most of the songs in *Tiempos* evoke hope for the future of the Americas, while revisiting a past of conquest, intervention, and occupation. The CD begins with an instrumental piece entitled "Mar del Sur" (South Sea), referring to the Pacific Ocean as identified by Vasco Núñez de Balboa (1475–1519) off the southern coast of Veragua (Panamá) in 1513. With Balboa's early sighting of *la mar del sur*, the isthmus became the most coveted site of imperial powers, which since then have sought to control the waterway linking worlds and peoples. *Tiempos* returns to the conquest of the isthmus in the song "Puente del Mundo" and to the invasion of Panamá by U.S. military forces in "20 de Diciembre," while the lyrics to "Encrucijada" (Crossroads) describe the tenuous state of Central America under current neoliberal rule.

In "Encrucijada," Blades explores Panamá's and Central America's quandary in the twenty-first century, when people find themselves "tratando, creyendo que no es tarde para hablar. / Tiempo de encrucijada: lucha o retirada" (trying, believing it is not too late to speak. / Time of crossroads: struggle or retreat). Blades ends the song with a painful yet poignant call to action or resignation—"O somos familia rota, o somos Nación salvada" (We are either a broken family or a saved nation). *Tiempos* marks thus the passing of the U.S. occupation of Panamá with great uncertainty for the future, yet the recording (with its melodious compilation of classical, popular, and folkloric sounds) also suggests a time for coming together, for resolving differences, and for moving forward. Both *Tiempos* and *La Rosa de los Vientos* record the calm after the long storm in Central America, which not only transformed the region, but also set afloat a great number of people who resurface in other locations (as U.S. Central American Latinos?). In these musical productions, Blades's work speaks to Central American transnational experiences and migrations, and participates in the construction of Central American Latino identities in the United States and elsewhere.

BUSCANDO (CENTRO) AMÉRICA IN BLADES'S WORK

Truth be told, Rubén Blades is rarely acknowledged as a Central American Latino artist—even though he was born and lived in the isthmus until the 1970s, ran for president of Panamá in 1994, and presently makes his home for part of the year in Casco Viejo, the colonial district of Panamá City. For the most part, Blades has been identified as a Caribbean Latino in New York, with an occasional mention of his Panamanian national origins. He has been associated with the Cuban, Puerto Rican, and largely Afro-Caribbean musical forms that he uses in his recordings. Although it is true that Panamá is part of the geopolitical Caribbean Basin and that Blades is of West Indian descent, his ties to Central America have been largely glossed over by many critics, who, for the most part, read Blades's work within a greater Latino Americanist project. José David Saldívar, for example, locates Blades at the crossroads of an inter-Americas discourse, especially in his albums *Siembra* (1978) and *Agua de Luna* (1987), the latter of which recuperates for Latin(o) American reception a partial cultural memory vis-à-vis Gabriel García Márquez's texts.[4] Frances Aparicio claims that, as cultural interpreter, Blades "speak[s] to the collective realities of Latinas/os in the United States and in Latin America," while Lisa Sánchez González situates Rubén Blades's work "within the Puerto Rican diaspora," and within a history of U.S. intervention and occupation that links Puerto Rico, Panamá, and the rest of Latin America.[5] Since the turn of the nineteenth century, Puerto Rico and Panamá have been imbricated in a common (neo)colonial history, though their political ties to the United States have differed considerably.[6] Panamá's particular history of occupation and resistance, however, is resignified as Puerto Rican when Sánchez González proposes that Blades be read in "living connection to our present."[7] Whose present?

In her reading of salsa practices in "the colonial diaspora," Sánchez González shows Willie Colón's and Rubén Blades's collaborative work to be "particularly relevant" for the construction of a U.S. Latino interpretative community. Her (mis)recognition of Blades's Panamanian colonial legacy as Puerto Rican provides a productive albeit skewed discursive space into which we may read Blades's own extended musical interventions. Although Sánchez González argues that *Amor y Control* (1992) resonates with Blades's and other Hispano-Caribbean writers' "brand of bitter irony," she suggests also that most of the songs in the

CD seem not to offer critiques of, or symbolic resolutions to, a history of (neo)colonialism.[8] In *Amor y Control*, Blades narrates stories of "death, despair and hopelessness" and "elaborates tales that evoke images of helpless victims caught in a hemispheric web of poverty and apocalyptic degeneration," but he does not take into account "the historical roots of racism, poverty and Caribbean maldevelopment."[9] At least this is the case for Sánchez González in her readings of "Adán García" (Adam García), "El Apagón" (The Power Failure), and other songs from *Amor y Control*. A Panamanian/Central American narrative of resistance, however, might be recuperated from these songs, thus enabling a reading of Blades's work within the extensive corpus of Central American social protest discourses and genres, which include anti-occupation novels, anti-imperialist literature, and testimonial narratives.[10]

Read in light of Central American resistance literature, Blades's "El Apagón" is not about defeated histories (as Sánchez González claims) but a critique of the extended power networks and the particular responses they elicit in the isthmus. In "El Apagón," Blades uses the image of a "power failure" to highlight, not efface, a chain of abuses, which, by the 1980s, had become commonplace in many Latin American countries—"la tortura de un subversivo" (the torture of a subversive) and "los gritos de víctima y de victimario" (the screams of victim and victimizer). The power failure provides an ironic twist to the macabre life of the "sub-D[eveloped] world." Because of the power outage, a tortured man gets a slight reprieve, a robber goes about his business, churchgoers continue in the dark, TV watchers miss a local beauty pageant, and others argue over who is to blame for *el apagón*. In the song, the power failure is metonymically linked to the conquest beginning in 1492—"Quinientos años de cotorreo. Se fue la luz, y sigue el saqueo!" (Five hundred years of loose talk. The lights went off, and the looting continues!). The song "Adán García" does not tell just any story of "death, despair and hopelessness," but chronicles the last day in the life of an unemployed Panamanian, who is driven to rob a bank armed with his son's water gun and who is subsequently killed by the Panamanian police on the Avenida Central. Adán—the would-be bank robber and defender of his family—is killed by (policing) forces of the global economy, right in the heart of the commercial district of the City of Panamá and in one of the busiest duty-free zones of the world.

In *Amor y Control*, Blades exposes thus the internal and local conflicts of Panamanian society under U.S. military, political, and economic rule. Among other things, the U.S. brought "Gold and Silver Roll" to Panamá, the system by which U.S. white laborers in the Canal Zone were paid in gold (dollars) and nonwhite laborers (Panamanian nationals included) were paid in silver (local) currency. The institution of "Gold and Silver Roll" enforced Jim Crow law in the Canal Zone and intensified racial stratification in the country.[11] In the song "West Indian Man," Blades weaves family and national history, telling of his grandfather, who

> [c]ame from the sea, to Panamá,
> to work in the jungle and build the Canal.
> He got paid in silver, the white man in
> gold, and the yellow fever took
> everyone's soul.
> Grandaddy was a West Indian Man,
> y vivió y murió en Panamá.
>
> .   .   .   .
> That is where the Blades come from.
> From St. Lucy, he came down.[12]

Reading Blades and his work strictly and exclusively as Nuyorican erases, I believe, the particular legacy of colonialism and imperialism in Panamá. To ignore this Central American history is to render Rubén Blades without significant *antecedentes*, or historical records. In Spanish, the term *antecedentes* refers not only to those who came before (the ancestors), but also to the *papeles*—the documents, credentials, and records—that "prove" or legitimize a person's identity. Fittingly, in his 1988 album entitled *Antecedente*, Blades declares his history in "Born of You" ("Nacer de Ti"):

> I come from the ocean and the straits,
> from the crossroads of highways
> and afternoons.
> I come behind human footprints and the steps of seagulls
> traveling counter-light like. . . .
> I am from the Terminal ports, from the dark
> ocean depths, from the impossible to count
> multitude. . . .
> I was a rebellion, a slave's uprising, a tower bell

of fragile cities. I was the fever and the gold
that came and left.[13]

Using evocative metaphors associated with Panamá and Central America, "Born of You" recapitulates the history of Panamá, which becomes a land of boom and bust for local populations with the arrival of European and U.S. imperialism. It seems imperative then (at least to me as a U.S. Central American Latina), to situate Blades's transnational political and cultural work within a Central American framework, and to examine his recent repositioning as a U.S. Central American Latino. In Bakhtinian terms, in the defamiliarization of the Nuyorican artist, as we know him, crucial Central American narratives and identities can be recovered in Blades's work.

Throughout his work, Blades has produced a critique of U.S. intervention in Central America and has advocated in favor of hemispheric solidarity with Central Americans. In 1984 he composed the soundtrack for the testimonial film *When the Mountains Tremble*, based on the life of Nobel Peace laureate Rigoberta Menchú and her struggle for the rights of her people, the Maya Quiché of Guatemala.[14] In "El Padre Antonio y el Monaguillo Andrés," from *Buscando América* (1984), Blades alludes to the assassination of the Salvadoran Archbishop Oscar Arnulfo Romero, offering a valuation of liberation theology and an exposé of repression in the Americas.[15] In "Salvador," a reggae sequel to "El Padre Antonio," Blades describes the escalating violence in the country, concluding that "[n]o one can protect your life in Salvador."[16] His albums *Antecedente* (1988) and *Amor y Control* (1992) also offer a historical record of Panamá intervened. And it is no secret that because of Blades's closing line, "Nicaragua without Somoza," at the end of the song "Plástico," the album *Siembra* (1978) was banned in that country by the Anastasio Somoza Debayle regime.[17] More recently, Blades's political commentary and artistic practice of solidarity with Central America have culminated in his sequel recordings, *La Rosa de los Vientos* (1996) and *Tiempos* (1999), which were produced on-site and in collaboration with Central American artists. Music of the times, these eclectic recordings navigate old and new Blades fans in a sea of themes, musical forms and artists of Central America. Appropriately, the title of the first installment in this series, "La Rosa de los Vientos," refers to the navigational instrument (a type of compass) that was used by early European explorers to ride the trade winds and to find their way in the oceans of the Western Hemisphere.

Blades's collaborative work with Central American musicians in *La Rosa de los Vientos* and *Tiempos* records a contemporary moment, an *encrucijada*, in Central America when military warfare has given way to the violence of global capital and neoliberal rule in the region. After the civil wars, the winners in Central America were not Central Americans per se, but global capital, which gained access to a region of vast human and natural wealth—Central American people, flora, and fauna, all afloat amid the *vendavales* of economic forces. Jonathan R. Barton, in *A Political Geography of Latin America* (1997), notes that "[w]ithin the globalized context of neocolonialism, the manipulation of armed force is being replaced gradually by the manipulation of market force."[18] In the 1990s Central America (and other "developing" regions of the world) became an arena where global corporate forces compete violently for labor markets. Amorphous and long-distance organizations such as the World Bank and the International Monetary Fund (IMF) now determine domestic policies in specific countries. Within this regimentation of capital and appropriation of resources, Central America (re)gains its place among the impoverished states of the South, of which Latin America is a "key region."[19] Today Central Americans find themselves asking, how did crisis lead to crisis, how did we get to where we are, how (to quote an old Central American proverb) did we go from *guatemala* to *guatepeor*?

CULTURAL REALIGNMENTS: WHY PRETEND THE NORTH IS IN THE SOUTH?

In 1996 Blades released *La Rosa de los Vientos* within the larger context of the electoral defeat of the Sandinistas in Nicaragua (1989), the U.S. invasion of Panamá (1989), the signing of the peace accords in El Salvador (1992), the peace negotiations in Guatemala (1996), the infiltration of neoliberal economic forces, and the emigration of a great number of Central Americans. In the decades of political, military, and socioeconomic crisis, many Central Americans were forced to migrate within the confines of their own countries, or to immigrate across national borders throughout the isthmus and over wide expanses, to the United States, Mexico, Canada, Australia, and Europe. The emigration of Central Americans reached its peak in the 1980s during the so-called lost decade of Latin America and the decade of the Hispanic in the United

States. Between 1978 and 1993 over 5 percent of the population of Central America was displaced by local military and economic crises.[20] Studies show that during the 1970s and 1980s, Central Americans crossed each other's borders in numbers large enough to produce what historian Edelberto Torres-Rivas has identified as an international demographic shift in Central America.[21] In 1985 the United Nations High Commission for Refugees (UNHCR) registered the migrations and permanent resettlements of Central Americans throughout the hemisphere.[22] As many as 1.5 million Central Americans migrated throughout the isthmus, and by the early 1990s more than 1.3 million Central Americans had immigrated to the United States.[23] The isthmus became, once again, a corridor of migrations, as Carolyn Hall wrote in 1985, "el corredor entre las dos Américas grandes" (the corridor between the two great Americas). According to Hall, the isthmus, a late land formation that joined the two landmasses to the north and south, has always served as an intercontinental bridge for dispersion of animals, plants, humans, and cultures, and as an interoceanic commerce and transport route later in its history.[24] Now, it serves as the gateway of new migratory flows, the *encrucijada* of Rubén Blades's new *Tiempos*.

For some time, migration scholars have studied material ties, such as financial remittances and communication networks, that Central American transnational border crossers institute across vast physical and affective separations.[25] These material connections reenact the porous boundaries of global capital, shuffling human and economic capital back and forth, northward and southward. Embodying human excess in the depleted economies of the South and human capital in the labor market of the North, Central American immigrants not only maintain their countries' economies solvent, but they also intervene in the politics of their countries, implementing new practices of citizenship. In fact, Central American immigrants living in between countries exercise what Benedict Anderson has called a "long-distance nationalism," often resulting in ambiguous political consequences in their countries of origin.[26] At the same time, Central American immigrants and their migrating cultures are being shaped by (and are shaping) the conditions of living at a distance (*lejanía*),[27] or what Homi Bhabha calls dwelling "in the 'beyond'"[28] of national borders and extended across transnational locations.

Finally, in *Traspatio florecido: Tendencias de la dinámica de la cultura en Centroamérica (1979–1990)*, Rafael Cuevas Molina concludes that "[t]he profound crisis that Central American society encountered during that period [of the 1980s] produced modifications in the cultural field that changed the face of Central America."[29] Although Cuevas Molina does not study Central American cultures in their diaspora, his work suggests that there is much room for analysis of Central American cultural production outside the isthmus.[30] Heavily interpellated by the regional crises of the 1980s, Central Americans living outside the isthmus embody Central American Latino subjectivities as they are taking shape in various locations. Informed by this context, Rubén Blades's corpus of musical work also speaks to a history of turmoil, devastation, and (im)migration produced by (neo)colonial, imperialist, and lately neoliberal forces in the isthmus. His most recent political and cultural interventions in Central America not only reference Central American history, but also enact the workings of larger (transnational) cultural circuits, resulting from the migrations and relocations of Latin American populations to other spaces.

"LA ROSA DE LOS VIENTOS": BUILDING TRANSNATIONAL INTERDISCURSIVE COMMUNITIES

The song "La Rosa de los Vientos" stages an imagined southward return to Central America, its history, and its legacies. The song, from the CD of the same name, was produced and recorded on location in Panamá in 1996 by Rubén Blades in collaboration with Panamanian composers, musicians, and technicians. The project, according to Blades, was a multipurpose attempt to draw from the wealth of creativity in Central America ("el aporte local"), to defend its culture ("defend[er] nuestra cultura"), and to open new roads for the future ("nuevos caminos hacia el futuro"), which he initiated by running for president of Panamá in 1994.[31] Retiring from the music industry temporarily and returning to Panamá indefinitely, Blades campaigned as the presidential candidate for the independent, nationalist, and pan-Caribbean party Papá Egoró ("'Mother Earth' in the indigenous Embará language"),[32] which he founded as a progressive alternative to existing coalitions and traditional political parties in Panamá.[33] In the election, Blades received 17.1 percent of the votes against the 33.3 percent secured by the winner, Ernesto Pérez Balladares of the Democratic Revolutionary Party (PRD), which was founded by General Omar

Torrijos in 1978 and which was General Manuel Noriega's party during the 1980s.[34]

The song "La Rosa de los Vientos" represents, hence, a return of sorts to Central America by a U.S. Latino who is part of a larger Central American community living at a distance. The song also articulates a critique of the effects of global capital and politics in Central America: Why should we imagine that the North is in Central America? What alternative endings and images can be constructed for the isthmus? The lyrics of "La Rosa de los Vientos," which follow below, give testimony to the predicaments faced by many Central American nations and people as they enter the twenty-first century. A few key stanzas deliberate reflectively over the fate of the region.

> *Who says we (are) lost, if in our worries lives Panamá?*
>
> *Who believes there is no better ending to our history?*
> *Let's keep breathing, also for the rest,*
> *because the cause is worthy, I am not tired of trying.*
>
> . . . .
>
> *I am from the place where the rose of the winds is born;*
> *the winds lash at it, but it grows within!*[35]

In "La Rosa de los Vientos," Blades offers the poignant image of a single rose standing firmly, despite being battered by strong winds. The rose, a most traditional poetic conceit with unlimited connotative potential, has learned to grow into itself, into its own, protecting itself against the outside forces that would beat it down. The speaker/narrator in the song is someone from that place upon which the rose stands firmly and resiliently: "I am from the place where the rose of the winds is born; / the winds lash at it, but it grows within!"

The rose and the speaker, it is suggested here, represent subjects of the South, or Central America, and the song is an allegory of the resiliency of the South, as the lyrics make clear. The rose/speaker locate themselves in a place that is in decline, from which young people are forced to flee, where people's dreams have been almost extinguished, where people have been almost forgotten, where there is little hope for some, where the final word for many is *never* (*el jamás*), and where pathways (to the future) have been all but foreclosed. Despite all this, the rose stands firm, weathering the forces of its time. In short, "La Rosa de los Vientos" (and the *cantautor* who tells her story here)[36] resists and rejects the representation of Central America as a site of disorder, decline, and violence, or what Stephen Benz has identified as the *tropicalization* of Central America by various agents in the media, politics, and general public.[37] In the song, each line is resemanticized, as naturalized statements and assumptions about Central America are successively turned into charged interrogatives and critiques.

In this poem/song, written and scored by the Panamanian Rómulo Castro and sung by U.S. Panamanian Rubén Blades, the collective of U.S. and Panamanian artists (per)forms the role of the enunciating transnational subject. Rather than assuming generalizations and stereotypes of the region and its people, this subject voices incited/excited questions, or the kinds of excitable speech acts that Judith Butler discusses in her book *Excitable Speech: A Politics of the Performative* (1997).[38] The questions articulated in "La Rosa de los Vientos" challenge the injurious, degrading language that has been used to produce *tropicalized* images of Central America and to justify all sorts of violent assaults on the region. The statements expressed in the dominant discourse on Central America are turned into interrogatives that perform a kind of verbal confrontation. The lines in the song dare responses to questions: *"¿Quién dijo?" "¿Quién dice?"* (*"Who said?" "Who says?"*). The lyrics of the song enumerate and challenge fixed ideas in/about Central America: Who says all its youth must emigrate? Who says our dreams must be extinguished? Who says we have been forgotten, or that we have been vanquished? Who says that there are roads foreclosed ("imposible de encontrar")? Who says we are lost if we (Panamá, and the rest) persist? Who says we cannot construct better/other endings to our history? Who said our lives are (pre)determined, that we must live by lies, and forget to love? How can we erase the distances without moving forward? Finally, the song asks, Why believe that the North is in the South, and hallucinate? In asking *why* repeatedly and forcefully, the enunciating subject of the excited discourse of the song disarticulates the *definitive* narrative produced of Central America, namely, its image of "generalized public squalor."[39]

"La Rosa de los Vientos" thus deconstructs the prevalent images of Central America as a place from which people must flee, where all dreams for a better future and alternative solutions have been abandoned, and where all hope has been lost. It defies the notion that Central America is *lost*, only because the rest of the world has forgotten it.

Identified with Panamá and by extension with the rest of Central America, Blades's song offers the rose, battered by (yet withstanding) the circumstances around it, as a sign of Central American resiliency, itself a form of resistance and the refusal to recede into hegemonic narratives. The song gives tribute to the endurance of a region and people who continue to weather the powerful forces, *el vendaval*, of political and military violence embedded in a long history of expropriation of regional goods. Despite its history, the weathered rose in the song has grown amid the intemperate economic, political, and cultural landscape of Central America. In Blades's anthem of the South, the trail of history tapers into two lines that express the collective hope of Central Americans. In Blades's rendition of Central America, each person carries the mark of time (local and larger histories) and the trace of dreams (visions, agendas, and plans for the future). "La Rosa de los Vientos" reminds the listener that history has far from ended in this part of the developing world, despite the prognosis of the North. With words to the South, the *cantautor* sings out, "Let's keep breathing, also for the rest, / because the cause is worthy, I am not tired of trying."

La Rosa de los Vientos and *Tiempos* participate hence in the construction of a transnational *interdiscursive community*, spanning the South and the North, as Magda Zavala and Seidy Araya propose in their work that calls for a revision and expansion of Central American cultural and discursive spaces.[40] Blades's project further expands the dimensions of a regional Central American cultural field by supplementing a Central American Latino voice to the mix of local Panamanian (Central American) artists. In addition to promoting the exposure of local artists, Blades's work contributes to the construction of a Central American Latino discursive space in the South, in Panamá. He returns to Panamá to interpolate Central American Latino identities and voices into the local scene. In particular, the song "La Rosa de los Vientos" becomes the site of a common enunciation between local/national artists and other/national artists; that is, between Panamanians in the South and Panamanians from the extended Central American community (loosely borrowing from the expression sometimes used by Cubans in Cuba to refer to Cubans living elsewhere). Subjects occupying vastly different locations, South and North, these speak from a common *location* of interests and extended affiliated identities produced inside and outside Central America.

Finally, the North/South paradigm, which generates the idea that "technology and information overwhelmingly flow from north to south,"[41] and that human (labor) capital moves from south to north, is shown to be part of a more complex dynamic in Blades's transnational musical practices. As Jean Franco claims, "Present-day writers [and others] in . . . Central America have also inherited the traumatic aftermath of repressive military governments and civil war, followed by a new era of modernization under the aegis of neoliberalism that has mixed extreme poverty with rapid technological development."[42] The greater Central American cultural field (in which Blades participates) represents an expansive *location of material and symbolic culture,* to use further the phrase from Homi K. Bhabha. Although not strictly and exclusively situated in the geographical South or North, this discursive field is bound to a whole system of historically produced economic, political, and social relations and conditions of living that may be shared by Latin American and Latino subjects across the spaces they occupy. Within this uneven transnational circuitry of material and cultural capital, Central American Latino subjects have elaborated significant points of contact. While Blades travels and mediates between U.S. and Central American cultures, his CDs perform a transnational exchange of cultural capital. Along the way, Blades's musical interventions offer alternative narratives of peace and hope for Central America, or the construction of "un mejor final," better endings to the dominant narratives of Central America, as Blades suggests in his song.

"La Rosa de los Vientos," hence, challenges the inscription of the South in Central America as a site of decline and disempowerment, and the North as the source of power and domination. But rather than stopping at protest, Blades and company's "La Rosa de los Vientos" performs another script for Central America—the linking up of Central American Latino subjects across divides and separations induced by global forces. The song, moreover, becomes a discursive site for enacting transnational linkages between Central Americans (in the South) and Central American Latinos (in the North). It voices an appeal for building extended Central American Latino identities and alliances; for developing strategies for reading the South as its own entity—the self-standing and self-sustaining rose; and for resisting the tropicalization of Central America and its attendant appropriation of economic, cultural, and human capital from the region.

NOTES

1. See Walter LaFeber, *The Panama Canal: The Crisis in Historical Perspective* (New York: Oxford University Press, 1989); John Weeks and Phil Gunson, *Panama: Made in the USA* (London: Latin American Bureau, 1991); Héctor Pérez-Brignoli, *A Brief History of Central America*, trans. Ricardo B. Sawrey A. and Susana Stettri de Sawrey (Berkeley: University of California Press, 1989).

2. For an analysis of U.S. military, political, and economic intervention in Central America during the last decades of the twentieth century, see James Dunkerley, *The Pacification of Central America: Political Change in the Isthmus, 1987–1993* (London: Verso, 1994).

3. Rubén Blades, *La Rosa de los Vientos*, Sony Music International, 1996, CDT-81992/485061-2; *Tiempos*, Sony Music International, 1999, TRK 83184 2-494410.

4. José David Saldívar, *The Dialectics of Our America: Genealogy, Cultural Critique, and Literary History* (Durham: Duke University Press, 1991).

5. Frances R. Aparicio, *Listening to Salsa: Gender, Latin Popular Music, and Puerto Rican Cultures* (Hanover, NH: University Press of New England, 1998). Lisa Sánchez González, "Reclaiming Salsa," *Cultural Studies* 13, no. 2 (1999): 237–50.

6. The Jones Act of 1917 imposed U.S. rule and citizenship upon Puerto Ricans, opening for them a legal migratory route to the United States that was (is) not open to other Latin American populations. In 1903 Panamá seceded from Colombia only to become a virtual protectorate of the United States. An extended U.S. military base in the Caribbean, the Panamanian Canal Zone was subject to U.S. law until the treaties of 1977 authorized the return of U.S.-occupied territory to Panamá in 1999.

7. Sánchez González, "Reclaiming Salsa," 237.

8. Rubén Blades, *Amor y Control: Rubén Blades con Son del Solar*, Sony Music International, 1992, CDZ 80839 471643-2. Sánchez González identifies irony as a Caribbean sensibility, which is shared by writers such as Ana Lydia Vega, Luis Rafael Sánchez, Alejo Carpentier, Gabriel García Márquez, Rubén Blades, and others. Sánchez González, "Reclaiming Salsa," 243.

9. See Sánchez González, "Reclaiming Salsa," 243.

10. See Barbara Harlow, *Resistance Literature* (New York: Methuen, 1987). Harlow claims that resistance narratives "propose historically specific analyses of the ideological and material conditions out of which they are generated," and are intertextually linked to local and larger political struggles (116).

11. For a brief discussion of racial politics and labor migration in Panamá, see LaFeber, *The Panama Canal*.

12. Rubén Blades, "West Indian Man," *Amor y Control*. English translation is provided by the artist.

13. Rubén Blades y Son del Solar, "Born of You" ("Nacer de Ti"), *Antecedente*, Elektra/Asylum Records, 1988, Elektra 60795-2. English translation is provided by the artist.

14. Rubén Blades, orig. music, *When the Mountains Tremble*, dir. Pamela Yates and Thomas Sigel, Skylight Pictures, 1984.

15. Rubén Blades y Seis del Solar, *Buscando América*, Elektra/Asylum Records, 1984, Elektra/Asylum Records 60352-2.

16. Rubén Blades, *Nothing But the Truth*, Elektra/Asylum Records, 1988, Elektra 60754-2.

17. Enrique Lopetegui, "Interview: From Pop to Populism," *Los Angeles Times*, 12 September 1993, Sunday home edition: calendar, p. 5.

18. Jonathan R. Barton, *A Political Geography of Latin America* (New York: Routledge, 1997), 3.

19. Ibid.

20. Dunkerley, *The Pacification of Central America*, 46.

21. Edelberto Torres-Rivas, "La sociedad: La dinámica poblacional, efectos sociales de la crisis, aspectos culturales y étnicos," in *Historia general de Centroamérica*, 6 vols., ed. Edelberto Torres-Rivas (Madrid: FLACSO, 1993), 6:165.

22. Universidad para la Paz/Universidad Nacional, *Los refugiados centroamericanos* (Heredia, Costa Rica: Universidad Nacional, 1987), 186.

23. For a brief history of and statistics on Central American immigration to the United States, see Raquel Pinderhughes, Carlos Córdova, and Jorge del Pino, "Our Multicultural Heritage: A Guide to America's Principal Ethnic Groups," available http://bss.sfsu.edu/~urbstu/rp/arti/art3.htm (5 October 2001).

24. Carolyn Hall, "América Central como región geográfica," *Anuario de Estudios Centroamericanos* 7, no. 2 (1985): 6–7.

25. See Carlos B. Córdova, "Undocumented El Salvadoreans in the San Francisco Bay Area: Migration and Adaptation Dynamics," *Journal of La Raza Studies* 1, no. 1 (1987), 9–37; Sarah J. Mahler, *Salvadorans in Suburbia: Symbiosis and Conflict* (Boston: Allyn and Bacon, 1995); Sarah J. Mahler, *American Dreaming: Immigrant Life on the Margins* (Princeton: Princeton University Press, 1995); Terry A. Repak, *Waiting on Washington: Central American Workers in the Nation's Capital* (Philadelphia: Temple University Press, 1995); Nora Hamilton and Norma Stoltz Chinchilla, "Central American Migration: A Framework for Analysis," in *Challenging Fronteras: Structuring Latina and Latino Lives in the U.S.*, ed. Mary Romero, Pierrette Hondagneu-Sotelo, and Vilma Ortiz (New York: Routledge, 1997), 81–100; Olivia Cadaval, *Creating a Latino Identity in the Nation's Capital: The Latino Festival* (New York: Garland, 1998); Thomas Winschun, *¿Por qué se van? La emigración de salvadoreños a los Estados Unidos* (San Salvador: Fundación Heinrich Böll, 1999); and Cecilia Menjívar, *Fragmented Ties: Salvadoran Immigrant Networks in America* (Berkeley: University of California Press, 2000).

26. Benedict Anderson, "Exodus," *Critical Inquiry* 20, no. 2 (1994): 314–27. According to Anderson, (im)migrants participate in the (re)construction of a nation from other locations through various mediations and networks: "positioned in the First World, he [*sic*] can send money and guns, circulate propaganda, and build intercontinental computer information circuits, all of which can have incalculable consequences in the zones of their ultimate destinations" (327).

27. An interesting and relevant case is that of Salvadoran immigrants, or the *hermanos lejanos* (the distant brothers and sisters), to whom a monument is dedicated in San Salvador. In addition, *La Prensa Gráfica*, one of the country's main newspapers, uses the term "Departamento 15" (Department 15) to refer to the extended community of Salvadorans residing outside El Salvador. (There are fourteen departments or provinces in El Salvador, the fifteenth representing the Salvadoran diaspora.) The newspaper also publishes daily a section entitled "Departamento 15" in print form and at the Internet Web site of *La Prensa Gráfica*, available http://www.laprensa.com.sv/ (5 October 2001).

28. Homi K. Bhabha, "Introduction: Locations of Culture," in *The Location of Culture* (New York: Routledge, 1994), 7.

29. Rafael Cuevas Molina, *Traspatio florecido: Tendencias de la dinámica de la cultura en Centroamérica (1979–1990)* (Heredia, Costa Rica: Editorial de la Universidad Nacional, 1993), 15. Translations from the original text in Spanish into English are mine.

30. Ibid., 16–17.

31. Blades, *La Rosa de los Vientos,* insert.

32. George Priestley, "Elections: The Opposition Returns to Power," *NACLA* 28, no. 2 (1994): 13.

33. Ibid., 11–14; Dunkerley, *The Pacification of Central America,* 36.

34. Marco Gandásegui, "Panamá: Años decisivos," *Nueva Sociedad* 132 (1994): 4; Priestley, "Elections," 13. The PRD follows a neoliberal agenda and cooperates with the United States, Priestley, "Elections," 11–14.

35. The translation of "La Rosa de los Vientos" into English is mine. The original text in Spanish is as follows: "¿Quién dice que perdimos, si entre las angustias sigue Panamá? / ¿Quién cree que no hay manera de dar a su historia un mejor final? / Sigamos respirando, también por los demás, / porque la causa es buena, no me canso de tratar. . . . / ¡Yo soy de donde nace la Rosa de los Vientos; / la azota el vendaval pero crece por dentro!"

36. Throughout Latino America, *cantautores* (song-authors such as the practitioners of the Cuban "new song," Silvio Rodríguez and Pablo Milanés, and more contemporary musicians such as Ricardo Arjona, Rubén Blades, Willie Colón, Juan Luis Guerra, and others) produce songs of quotidian struggle, political resonance, and historical significance.

37. See Stephen Benz, "Through the Tropical Looking Glass: The Motif of

Resistance in U.S. Literature on Central America," in *Tropicalizations: Transcultural Representations of Latinidad,* ed. Frances R. Aparicio and Susana Chávez-Silverman (Hanover, NH: University Press of New England, 1997), 59. Benz explains that the isthmus is imagined as a "deadly, diseased, disorderly, dissolute, and decadent" region, which must be brought to order by outside forces.

38. Judith Butler, *Excitable Speech: A Politics of the Performative* (New York: Routledge, 1997).

39. Dunkerley, *The Pacification of Central America,* 17.

40. Magda Zavala and Seidy Araya, *La historiografía literaria en América Central (1957–1987)* (San José, Costa Rica: Universidad Nacional, 1995).

41. Jean Franco, "What's Left of the Intelligentsia? The Uncertain Future of the Printed Word," *NACLA* 28, no. 2 (1994): 16.

42. Ibid., 18.

6

"The Sun Never Sets on MTV"

Tijuana NO! and the Border of Music Video

Josh Kun

IN SEPTEMBER 1997 the news was made official. MTV International—the conglomerate body of MTV affiliates outside the United States. (MTV Europe, MTV Mandarin, MTV India, MTV Latin America, MTV Australia, MTV Japan, MTV New Zealand, MTV Brazil, MTV Asia)—had conquered the world. The announcement was given extra fanfare and advertising hype by *Billboard*, the music industry's principal trade magazine of record, and it was done in precisely those terms. By engineering planetary conquest, MTV International had found its way into 300 million households across the world and become what *Billboard* called "the world's first global network."[1]

The feature article headline summed up the package's logic the best by cutting straight to the Euro-imperialist chase: "The Sun Never Sets on MTV." On the page opposite to the article was a full-page advertisement from the record label EMI that depicted a graphic of the planet Earth viewed from somewhere in outer space, but instead of conventional topographical formations (shapes of continents, intimations of islands), the landmass on the Earth was in the shape of the MTV logo. On the next page was another ad, from Sony Music International, with a galaxy view of Earth with MTV flags planted in points across the world so that the entire planet appears to be claimed in the name of MTV (a knowing flashback to the company's original promo spots: an astronaut sticking an MTV flag into the surface of the moon). The ad copy from Sony gave an even clearer voice to the image of an MTV-colonized Earth: "No tanks, no planes, no ships, no bombs, no battles, no bloodshed. Not a bad way to conquer the world." No wonder the article's author, Marilyn

Gillen, calls the birth of MTV in 1981 "M day," when "victory was still not assured . . . global domination was not yet on the agenda."[2]

I want to resist simply arguing against this position. Instead, I want to step inside it and inhabit the logic and experience of global corporate networking in order to better understand how artists who circulate and produce their work within it—namely, the U.S.-Mexico border band Tijuana NO!—use it to think about the kinds of interventions they wish to make. The music videos of Tijuana NO! urge us to develop a new grammar of globalization that disarticulates dominant ideology from technical systems of material production, one that properly accounts for the way musicians and videomakers are manipulating mass media against their will as modes of emergent citizenship and tools for social change, while denouncing and dismantling the prescribed models of citizenship and the structures of racism, imperialism, and colonialism that these tools are packaged in.

ACTING LOCAL

Since the founding of MTV International as an entity separate from the U.S. MTV channel in 1987, it has gone out of its way to disavow and reject accusations of cultural imperialism by proclaiming that its broadcast strategy relies on the celebration of local markets and local music. The point made by MTV executives is that their "Think Globally, Act Locally" motto works in opposition to (and is consequently more culturally progressive than) what they call the "one world, one feed logic" of global networking that merely envelops and subsumes all world cultures under the specter of U.S. media encroachment.

MTV International emphasizes that it does the opposite: it employs multiple regional and local feeds that are directed very specifically at local and regional markets and tastes and it uses local musicians, producers, celebrities, and VJs in order to, in the words of MTV International chairman Bill Roedy, "tap into the local people who know the most and know the music culture." He claims, "It's not like McDonald's or one size fits all. It's the antithesis of homogeneity."[3]

For all the obvious contradictions in the *Billboard* advertising special—the global network that denies its colonialism and imperialism while celebrating it—the fact remains that the amount of locally produced music videos airing on the international affiliate networks has risen considerably over the past five years, causing one executive to connect it to "the shift from Anglo-American dominance in the music industry."[4] Read any interview with an MTV International executive and you'll hear talk about the importance of the local, the way MTV Latin America, for example, began as a "pan-Latin" network based in Miami in 1993 serving all of Latin America with roughly the same programming, and then in 1996 switched to a regional format with a hub in Mexico City serving Mexico, Central America, and the Caribbean, and one in Buenos Aires serving South America.

Yet the contradictions continue when we remember that this "shift" is being supported and made possible by a U.S. company owned by Viacom International (the same company that owns VH1, Nickelodeon, Comedy Central, Madison Square Garden, Paramount, and Blockbuster). That the end of Anglo cultural domination is being allegedly facilitated in the name of a U.S. company that controls the very local markets it simultaneously taps into, disseminates, and exploits receives no attention by MTV executives. Much of their rhetoric always returns to how MTV is helping the world to be the world; how MTV, by going global, is giving voice to the local when previous globalizers had kept it silent.

STOLEN AT VIDEOPOINT

What remains unvoiced here is what the music has to say about all this. The MTV International advertising celebration presents the international music videoscape as a one-way network of top-down corporate control and management. While this impetus toward coercive media indexing is no doubt crucial to follow and track, it is I believe equally crucial not to let the discourse of empire that the ads and articles use control the direction of the discourse itself. That is, just because MTV International says it has conquered the world does not mean that it has.

A few weeks after the issue of *Billboard* was released, I was in Tijuana researching an article on rock *en español* for *Rolling Stone* magazine and visiting Alex Zuñiga, a friend who plays drums in a band called Tijuana NO!. Born and nurtured within the Tijuana–San Diego borderlands, Tijuana NO! concocts antigovernment, anti-U.S., anti-imperialist, anti-PRI, antiracist, anti-NAFTA, pro-immigrant, pro-Zapatista, pro-anarchy punk explosives and throws them at anyone who might, on the off chance, have anything to do with power. It is also a band signed to the German-owned multinational record label BMG International, one of the labels that offered congratulations to MTV for its recent conquest. The band's videos—shot, produced, and directed in Tijuana and Mexico City—have also screened intermittently on MTV Latin America, which was launched in 1993 as MTV Latino and now serves 7.3 million households in nineteen countries.

If you adhere to a traditional Marxian critique, then Tijuana NO!'s place on MTV Latin America and its signing to BMG would be seen as not only highly contradictory but politically and ideologically incongruous and disingenuous. On record and in live performance, the band is vocally opposed to the very discourses of conquest, control, and corporate expansionism that the network and their label embody. On its three records to date, the band has taken on U.S. imperialism, racism, and xenophobia at nearly every turn.

On its latest release, *Contra Revolución Ave*—the band's first bilingual English and Spanish collection of songs—is a transfrontera duet with East Los Angeles Chicano rapper Frost entitled "Stolen at Gunpoint," in which together they demand the reconquest of Mexican land "stolen at gunpoint" by the United States after the U.S.-Mexico war ended in 1848 with the signing of the Treaty of Guadalupe Hidalgo. They join with a Chicano rapper to launch a postcolonial attack on the territorial residue of the very cultural imperialism that created the divide between Chicanos/as and Mexicanos/as in the first place.[5] It is, as Ruben Guevara so rightly notes, part of rock *en español*'s *reconquista* of the Americas in the name of the subaltern: indios, mestizos, africanos.[6]

The video for the song begins with this 1848 act of imperialist annexation, with a slow pan of Section X from the text of the Treaty of Guadalupe Hidalgo, and then cuts to images of the contemporary musical subversives who plan to reverse history: simulated mug shots of Tijuana NO! and Frost as wanted-by-the-FBI outlaws and cultural terrorists. Coupled with the song's chorus, which name-checks all the states "stolen at gunpoint" by the U.S. government in the name of Manifest Destiny and an expanding slaveocracy, are shots of each band member leaping through animated reproductions of each state's map. As their bodies crash through, the maps shatter into shards, the holism of the U.S. state fractured into postnational bits.

The band extends the notion of reconquering or, as it puts it in the song, "getting back" the land that once belonged to Mexico by placing the video's central narrative in the more contemporary political moment of 1994 and the passage of Proposition 187 in California. While images of Mexican revolutionary figures Emiliano Zapata and Pancho Villa flicker across the screen, the band members position themselves as neo-revolutionaries on the hunt for Proposition 187's most prominent booster, ex-California governor Pete Wilson. By video's end, Tijuana NO! and Frost hunt Wilson down, capture him, and then eventually murder him. "Stolen" is a fantasy of violent retribution for political injustice, in which the make-believe murder of Pete Wilson hyperbolically stands in for a desired end to legislatively sanctioned nativism and xenophobia.

The prime objective of "Stolen"'s reconnaissance mission is not Wilson's murder but the reterritorializing and resettling of once-Mexican landholdings. Its prime significance is Frost and Tijuana NO!'s alliance toward making this happen—a Mexican band that calls the border home and a Chicano rapper from East L.A. now living in Arizona who has recorded both the brown pride anthem "La Raza" and the noirish escape scenario "Mexican Border." The collaboration is significant not only because it marks an increasing trend of Chicano and Mexicano artists working together in the face of a long history of misunderstandings and cultural dissonance between the two communities, but also because by performing together they use music video to expose the lie of border division. Wilson and Proposition 187 threaten Tijuana NO! as much as Frost.

This linked borderlands oppositionality is accentuated by the video's splicing together of archival images from both the Mexican revolution and the Chicano movement, most notably clips of the 1970 Chicano moratorium where unarmed Chicanos/as are seen being bludgeoned by LAPD billy clubs. The video's director edits the smash of the police baton so it lands in time with the song's drum crash. Frost and Tijuana NO! suggest the urgency of transnational community coalition building through musical partnership—a transnational politics of audio-resistance—and the urgency of recognizing that anti-immigrant legislation in California is part of a white supremacist continuum of cyclical occupation and domination that extends back to 1848, when Tijuana was first separated from the Port of San Diego.

The locality of the "Stolen at Gunpoint" video, then, is not one that rests comfortably in the marketplace of a globalization that imagines fixed national units dissolving into an internationalized economic whole. Tijuana NO! and Frost come together in the name of a "local" that neither MTV U.S. nor MTV Latin America recognizes or has access to, a local that is already more than local, one that extends beyond the maps and limits of national belonging drawn by the coercion of imperial conquest and cultural segmentation. Despite the band's wishes, "Stolen" never aired on MTV Latin America because of its violent content. If it had, it would have interfered with the logic of a media network that requires specifically moored coordinates of the local in order to most profitably construct and imagine the global it wishes to promote.

THE LAST STREET OF TIJUANA

Instead of seeing Tijuana NO!'s relationship to music video as a grand contradiction, I want to see it as a strategy, a tactic of refusal launched from within the very circuits of commerce itself. After all, Tijuana NO! does not see itself as operating outside MTV and BMG; it does not suffer from delusions of "underground" resistance.

Tijuana NO!'s music video reel now contains four videos the band has made over the course of three albums, all of which (save for "Stolen at Gunpoint") have been aired at some point, on different rotation cycles, on MTV Latin America. Thus, when MTV Latin America executives brag about the fact that currently 95 percent of all the stations' programming is done locally and roughly 50 percent of all videos shown come from various Latin American countries, Tijuana NO! is one of the bands who play the role of "the local" in the drama of the global network. Yet, to reference the work of Jacques Attali, Tijuana NO! may be part of the global network of MTV Latin America, but its performances operate as "subversive noise," noise that disrupts the order of the system it is produced within by generating interference that prophecies the coming of a potential new order.[7] As information systems theory and cybernetic theory remind us, noise is also what disrupts a circuit of communication and data transmission; when noise enters a network, the network is disrupted. The flow of data gets stopped, confused, scrambled.

Tijuana NO! does this in a number of ways. First, as a band from the Tijuana–San Diego border, it confuses the figure of the local itself. In MTV's discourse, the local must be a fixed term in order to properly fit into the marketing maps of globalism. Yet Tijuana NO! met at a Black

Flag concert in downtown San Diego. Like most "local" Tijuanenses (40 percent of whom cross the border at least once during any given week), the members of Tijuana NO! spend large portions of every week crossing back and forth across the border into San Diego. They don't identify as a Mexican band; they identify as a border band.

Ever since the 1907 construction of the Tijuana and Tecate railroad—which connected Tijuana to the United States, not Mexico City—Tijuana has been a city more directly in dialogue with the United States than southern Mexico.[8] As a result, the identity of Tijuana NO!—which draws musical inspiration as much from U.S. punk bands as from local Tijuana crews—is not nationally constructed; as *fronterizos*, citizens of the border, they have a relationship to Mexico and for that matter to the United States that is highly ambivalent. To borrow a framework from Zygmunt Bauman, this ambivalence makes them strangers to national unities. The border becomes another of Bauman's figures of modern ambivalence. Like the Platonic pharmakon that is both remedy and poison and the Derridean supplement that is both addition and replacement, the border is an "undecidable"; it is not either/or but simultaneously both/and.[9] This undecidability of the border makes it especially well equipped to interfere in and frustrate discussions of the local and the global, the national and the transnational.

Indeed, no matter how many times the border has wreaked its very real, material violence on the bodies of Tijuana NO!'s band members, they still talk of the border as something that is just *in the way* of everyday life, something that no matter how it pretends to be present, is actually a figment of the U.S.-Mexico political imagination. So what is local in the space of the border? Is Tijuana NO! even eligible for MTV Latin America status? Is it Latin American? Is it a San Diego band as much as a Tijuana band? If it identifies as much with San Diego as it does with Tijuana, shouldn't you be able to see its videos in San Diego, and not just once you cross the border into a Tijuana living room?

Part of what we encounter in the videos of Tijuana NO! is that these local and national ambivalences actually help turn Tijuana into a site of political and cultural transformation accessible to artists looking to define and design their role in a global economic system determined to lock them out. In Saskia Sassen's terms, Tijuana is a prime example of a "global city," a city central to the grid of globalization that is doubly claimed "by both global capital which uses the city as an 'organizational commodity,' but also by disadvantaged sectors of the urban population, which in large cities are frequently as internationalized a presence as capital."[10] Sassen's focus on the global city as a vital manifestation of place within the placelessness of globalization is meant to replace defeatist notions of the "futility of resistance" under globalized economic conditions with a renewed sense of possibility that views cities as "terrain for a politics of engagement." In its videos, Tijuana NO! treats Tijuana precisely in this way, as a global city that has become a commodity under globalization and yet still is a site of political and cultural possibility—"a strategic site for disempowered actors" that affords new modes of presence and new modes of subjectivity.[11]

Tijuana NO! band members position themselves as actors and agents within the global city by emphasizing their identity as *fronterizos*, as politicized border citizens who refute the policing and militarization of the U.S.-Mexico border through videos shown on MTV Latin America. I suggest that we view these videos as a means of gaining access to the national and cultural citizenship that Tijuana NO!—and the Tijuanenses and Chicanos/as they sing about—is denied in the dominant sphere. The musicians of Tijuana NO! make videos, in part, to exercise control over the representation of their citizenship within the visual landscape of the global economy. The videos rewrite their scripts of citizenship to better articulate their experiences as Tijuana artists living in the policed national battlefields of the borderlands. Because of their status as *fronterizos*, living between and moving across national affiliations, Tijuana NO! members access and enact what May Joseph has termed "nomadic citizenship," citizenship that instead of obeying the rules and demands of strictly mapped national formations, gets performed across *and* within national boundaries.[12]

As a result it is a citizenship imagined outside and yet in oppositional relationship to the modes of citizenship offered and catalogued by dominant culture. In this way, nomadic citizenship is both a condition imposed by the institutions and ideologies of the state and a strategy of negotiation with these very forces. Joseph's formulation works particularly well for Tijuana NO! and other artists living in the borderlands because of the extent to which the border region is on the one hand produced and maintained through U.S. military imperialism and on the other, is a zone of possibility and emergence that never fully answers the call of the national. Music video—as just one of many possible artistic responses to this doubleness—becomes a way of occupying this middle ground of nomadic citizenship and working it as a stage of

invention—an audiovisual medium that sounds and sights formula-
tions of citizenship not beholden to either national legacies or the ideological dictates of global economic restructuring. Tijuana NO!'s videos
envision "the incomplete, ambivalent, and uneasy spaces of everyday
life through which migrant communities must forge affiliations with
majority constituencies."[13]

Consider the video for "La Esquina del Mundo," a song that translates as "The Corner of the World" and was cowritten by Tijuana NO!
and Fermin Muguruza, the leader of Negu Gorriak, a Basque separatist
punk band. The song itself is laden with anti-imperialist noise, a blaz-
ing Spanish-language punk shout that describes the border as "the last
street of Latin America / the line that marks us from outside / the limit
between stone and village." Inspired by Eduardo Galeano's political
history, *Open Veins of Latin America*, Tijuana NO! calls for open borders
in the face of militarized and legislated closure ("open doors / that's the
only way"), casting the border as a war zone and calling for armed
struggle: ."38 special / well-aimed bullet / bars and stars are at war."[14]

The band's call—which couples "open doors" with "open veins"—
could not have been made at a more politically charged moment. 1994
was the same year that U.S. politicians like Pete Wilson and vigilante
groups like Light Up the Border were attempting to close the border
through organized and well-funded campaigns of force and terror:
Wilson through Proposition 187, which cut off all health and educational benefits to undocumented Mexican immigrants, and the "community" watchdog group Light Up the Border through the nighttime
deployment of headlight-blaring cars and trucks to the border fence in
a reactionary effort to assist the Border Patrol in spotting and catching
"illegals."[15]

The song was written while Muguruza and Tijuana NO! were
standing on the beach in Playas, the coastal Tijuana neighborhood
where the rusting border wall runs out of land and opens up into the
sea—the last corner of Latin America's terrestrial world. In the video,
which was shot in 1994 by Mexico City director Angel Flores, the band
performs live on the sand in front of this coastal portion of the wall—a
remnant of another episode of U.S. imperialism, a landing strip used in
the Persian Gulf invasion—and in view of both the ocean and the empty
stretch of U.S. territory waiting on the other side. Camera shots peer
through the wall's openings, and tracking shots let us clearly see the
band performing on the Mexico side of the line. By performing the song

live directly in front of the border wall with the hot sand for a stage, they turn this site of conquest and imperialism saturated with the historical residue of both 1848 and Desert Storm into a site of insurgent perform- ance, a televised performance of antiauthoritarian and antinational rage that takes place within yards of roaming border patrol trucks.

"La Esquina del Mundo" both lyrically theorizes the political and artistic realities contained within the site-specificity of the U.S.-Mexico border and musically performs these realities by colliding punk, rock, and ska styles birthed and reformatted across the Americas. This is not simply a song that just happened to be recorded *at* or *near* the border, not simply a song by a band that just happened to be *from* the border, not simply a song that may pretend to be *about* the border. This is a song—a collection of words and chords and beats and guitar crunches and bass wallops and vocal howls—that *is* the border, that renders the border in sound, that makes the border and all its experiences and his- tories and political narratives audible.[16]

One of the visual manifestations of this punk border aesthetic is a series of frames that depict a friend of the band trying to jump the wall and run across to the other side. The way it's shot emphasizes the extent to which, as Guillermo Gómez-Peña has argued, the border can func- tion as a Möbius strip, a twisting line that always doubles back on itself in a prism of mirrored reflections.[17] When the band's friend scales the wall and takes off along the beach, we lose sight of which side he is on; the camera dizzily pans down the length of the wall in a stream of bi- national disorientation so that his running body is silhouetted against a rushing whir of the wall's pillars. Tijuana NO! performs (and thereby allows us to see) what Aida Mancillas has described as "the sensible border . . . an organic membrane, permeable in both directions, through which people, materials, ideas, and culture pass, combine, split, give off energy, and recombine in innumerable variation."[18]

Set as a backdrop to the wall in this scene of flight/return is a Ti- juana mural that depicts a hemispheric map of America composed of tortured faces screaming silent screams of anger and violence that the band's music makes audible. Huddled figures painted to look like an- droids and extraterrestrials are seen being marched off by INS agents; faceless, nameless aliens are intercepted mid-invasion, before recolo- nizing the California earth.

In short, what the video for "La Esquina del Mundo" gives us is a band from Tijuana, along with painters and videomakers from Tijuana and Mexico City, who actively and wittingly use a media network that articulates itself through the language of U.S. imperialism to critique U.S. imperialism itself. Or put another way, the video is a mass-mediated meta-critique: contesting histories of U.S. imperialism by launching offensives of political and cultural interference within imperialist networks of global control.

VIDEO HA-HA

Tijuana NO! works this angle of music video meta-critique even more explicitly in another video that has also aired on MTV Latin America, the title track from its second album, "Transgresores de la Ley." The entire "Transgresores" video, like the song it is based on, is a tribute to the EZLN, the Ejército Zapatista de Liberación Nacional. Led by the black ski-masked Subcomandante Marcos, the EZLN emerged out of the Lacandón Jungle in Chiapas in 1994 and issued a Declaration of War against the Mexican government. In the lyrics to "Transgresores," Tijuana NO! repeats one of the EZLN's principal slogans, itself on loan from the revolutionary discourse of Emiliano Zapata: "land and liberty." The song offers a blistering homage to Zapata, who "lives and continues fighting / only a handful of men are ready to die in order to continue the revolution," as well as a tribute to the EZLN's revival of *zapatismo*: "the peasant farmers who never rest / waiting in the jungle as if in a rebel trench."[19]

Unlike "Stolen at Gunpoint," Tijuana NO!'s video for "Transgresores" is not an actual duet between the band and a fellow cultural conspirator, but a virtual one—a video duet between the band and a televised image of Subcomandante Marcos. The video is framed by scenes of the band members seated in a dark room watching flickering black-and-white broadcast tape of Marcos. In the final shot of the video, after the song itself has ended, the band members are again gathered in front of the television, transfixed like worshipers, absorbing and studying every one of Marcos's words. To call this a collaboration between Tijuana NO! and Marcos—a collaboration that Tijuana NO! initiates, stages, and enacts using Marcos as a malleable audiovisual icon and media actor—makes sense considering Marcos's own history of involvement with musical acts (there have been numerous EZLN tribute albums and Marcos has even recorded a record of his own).

On February 20, 1999, Marcos sent an e-mail communiqué out to "Musicians of the World" who have in different ways—benefits, protests, tribute albums—helped the cause of the Zapatista movement (he even includes the lighting crew and ticket sellers). "Music holds roads that only the knowledgeable know how to walk," Marcos wrote, citing Viejo Antonio, "Together with dance, [it] builds bridges that bring closer worlds that otherwise you wouldn't even dream about."[20] When Tijuana NO! played a concert in Mexico City with Los Angeles agit-punk band Rage Against the Machine in 1999, the show began with a prerecorded message from Marcos in which he pledged his admiration for both bands and addressed their relevance not only to the struggle of *zapatismo* but also to the recent university student strikes at Universidad Nacional Autónoma de México (UNAM).

The remainder of "Transgresores" is more of a traditional performance video with quick-cut shots of the band in live performance in front of swirling mosh pits crammed with slam-dancing *rockeros/as*. Significantly, one of the performances used in the video is taken from a Zapatista benefit concert the band participated in on a stage set directly in front of the National Palace in Mexico City. In "Esquina," the site of performance is the rusting border wall, a symbol of national ambivalence, of the success and failure of policing the borderline between the United States and Mexico. In "Transgresores," the site of live performance is the National Palace in the nation's capital during an activist concert designed to interrogate Mexican nationalism. In both videos, Tijuana NO! chooses performance sites that trouble the national-local, sites that resonate with national crisis not national confidence, where the meanings thought to be bound to conceptions of the "national" and "local" suddenly emerge as unreliable and unstable.

The EZLN debuted its revolution on the same day that the North American Free Trade Agreement went into effect ("Transgresores" debuted later that year). It was a high-tech event: Marcos released the Declaration of War on radio and national TV, and faxed it to the international press. There were also Web sites that broadcast up-to-the-minute accounts of Zapatista movement and philosophy to worldwide audiences (now with much of the armed revolution in a political deadlock, the EZLN's largest political offensive continues on the Internet through lists, postings, and sites).[21] And yet Marcos continued to critique the First Worldization of Mexico through neoliberal reform. He wanted his revolution to show "the real Mexico," the starving, tortured, indigenous

Mexico living without basic resources and without recourse to social justice.[22]

MTV may claim to help national culture hold steady against globalization, but this is not the national culture it bargained for—Tijuana NO! and Marcos give it national crisis, national ambivalence. They give it Mexican nationalism as a corrupt, weak face hiding behind a mask of U.S.-financed lies. They give it a nation of campesinos who pledge allegiance to a transnational, global network of their own, the worldwide movement for indigenous rights and revolution. The 1994 march shown in the "Transgresores" video included the cheer "First World Ha Ha Ha!" mocking the destructive ideologies of progress and development associated with First World intervention in Latin America—the very things NAFTA was meant to promote, the very things at the center of MTV International discourse.

The end result is that Tijuana NO! uses a music video aired on MTV Latin America to give face and voice to "the one without faces, the one without voices."[23] And as viewers, we become part of this cycle of technological hijacking and media interference: we watch the band members watch televised images of Marcos; we watch people—musicians and videomakers on the one hand, indigenous revolutionary leaders on the other—using technology and media that were never meant for them to attack the very systems and institutions and economies that provide the tools that make their performances possible. The video becomes part of the EZLN's virtual revolution and once it hits MTV, Tijuana NO! and Subcomandante Marcos have pulled a fast one on MTV's love affair with the local. Instead of local flavor or local exoticism, they get local anger.

WATER'S EDGE

When I was visiting with Alex, Tijuana NO!'s drummer, in 1997 just weeks after MTV reached its 300 millionth home, we sat on the sand of the beach at Playas, where the video for "Esquina" was shot. To our right was the same rusting border wall in the video, to our left were a handful of families and *cholos* waiting their turn to squeeze through the gaps in the wall and make a dash to the other side. Through the wall you could see migra trucks similar to the ones in the video, casually lurking, daring the waiting Tijuanenses to cross. But ahead of us was that expanse of ocean and we could see exactly the point where the wall ends, where the wall simply stops and mile after mile of water begins. "The wall is going to fall someday," Alex said to me. "The water is gonna just wash it away." A few hours later, we were back at his house, plopped on the couch watching MTV, eager to catch a glimpse of a Tijuana NO! video slipping through the rotation cracks, eager to hear the empire striking back, in Spanish, just one more time.

NOTES

This essay grew from lectures I delivered at Colby College, New York University, and University of California, San Diego. I thank Pam Toma, José Muñoz, and George Lipsitz for making that possible. Cecilia Bastida saved the essay from many inaccuracies and Jorge Ignacio Cortiñas offered valuable suggestions.

1. Special advertising insert, "MTV International, 300 Million Households and Growing: A Billboard Tribute to the World's First Global Network," *Billboard* 109 (13 September 1997): 49.

2. Marilyn Gillen, "The Sun Never Sets on MTV," *Billboard* 109 (13 September 1997): 50.

3. Ibid., 50–52.

4. Ibid., 50. For example, during MTV Asia's first year, only one Asian video aired; now the percentage is nearing 40 percent.

5. Tijuana NO!, "Stolen at Gunpoint," *Contra-Revolución Ave* (BMG, 1998).

6. Ruben Guevara, liner notes essay, *Reconquista! The Latin Rock Invasion* (Los Angeles: Rhino/Zyanya, 1997).

7. Jacques Attali, *Noise: The Political Economy of Music* (Minneapolis: University of Minnesota Press, 1985), 3.

8. Debra Castillo, "Borderlining: An Introduction," in *Tijuana: Stories on the Border,* ed. Federico Campbell (Berkeley: University of California Press, 1995), 4.

9. Zygmunt Bauman, "Modernity and Ambivalence," *Theory, Culture, and Society: Explorations in Critical Social Science* 7, nos. 2–3 (1990): 145.

10. Saskia Sassen, *Globalization and Its Discontents: Essays on the New Mobility of People and Money* (New York: New Press, 1999), xx.

11. Ibid., xxviii.

12. May Joseph, *Nomadic Identities: The Performance of Citizenship* (Minneapolis: University of Minnesota Press, 1999), 2–3.

13. Ibid., 17.

14. Tijuana NO!, "La Esquina del Mundo," *Transgresores de la Ley* (BMG, 1994).

15. On Proposition 187, see George Lipsitz, *The Possessive Investment in*

Whiteness: How White People Profit from Identity Politics (Philadelphia: Temple University Press, 1998); and for an examination of *Light Up the Border*, see Jesse Lerner and Scott Sterling's documentary *Natives: Immigrant Bashing on the Border* (1991), available through Filmmakers Library Distribution.

16. For more on the border as a field of sound, see Josh Kun, "The Aural Border," *Theatre Journal* 52, no. 1 (2000): 1–22.

17. Guillermo Gómez-Peña, *Warrior for Gringostroika* (St. Paul: Graywolf, 1993); and Josh Kun, "Border Warrior," *San Francisco Bay Guardian*, 31, no. 41 (July 1997).

18. Aida Mancillas, Ruth Wallen, and Marguerite R. Waller, "Making Art, Making Citizens: Las Comadres and Postnational Aesthetics," in *With Other Eyes: Looking at Race and Gender in Visual Culture*, ed. Lisa Bloom (Minneapolis: University of Minnesota Press, 1999), 110.

19. Tijuana NO!, "Transgresores de la Ley," *Transgresores de la Ley*.

20. Subcomandante Marcos, "To Musicians of the World," unpublished e-mail communiqué (20 February 1999).

21. Josh Kun, "Chihuahuas, Rockeros, and Zoot Suits: A Conversation with Guillermo Gómez-Peña," in *Dangerous Border-Crossers: The Artist Talks Back*, ed. Guillermo Gómez-Peña (New York: Routledge, 2000).

22. Medea Benjamin, "Interview: Subcomandante Marcos," in *First World Ha, Ha, Ha! The Zapatista Challenge*, ed. Elaine Katzenberger (San Francisco: City Lights Books, 1995).

23. Elaine Katzenberger, Introduction to *First World Ha, Ha, Ha!* i.

7

Bidi Bidi Bom Bom

Selena and Tejano Music in the Making of Tejas

Deborah R. Vargas

> Tejano . . . it's not just music . . . it's a way of life.
>
> —T-shirt slogan

THE MAKING OF *TEJAS*

At the 1995 Houston Livestock Show and Rodeo, Selena broke attendance records for all artists performing that year, outselling Vince Gill and Trisha Yearwood, some of country-western's biggest performers.[1] Selena's heavily Texas-Mexican and Mexicano fan base displaced the Anglo-Texan population of East Texas usually drawn to the Houston rodeo. In arguably the most notable concert performance of her career, Selena's opening set of songs provides one of the examples in this essay of the way she transformed the "place" representative of Tejano music, performing the discursive landscape of "third space" culture. Instead of beginning the show with her biggest Tejano hits, a country-western tune appropriate to the rodeo, or the English-language pop songs she had been working on for her future CD, Selena began with a disco medley, harking back to influential music of her childhood.[2]

Selena performed her Tejana subjectivity by drawing from a legacy of African American music production. In this case she draws from disco and the particular influences of African American women such as Gloria Gaynor and Donna Summer. Metaphorically, the medley brings together three different sets of histories and populations, Anglo-Texans, Tejanas/os, and African Americans, into a public culture where such a collaboration rarely occurs.

A closer exploration of Selena's opening medley of many of disco's signature tunes provides an insightful example for exploration:

> (Gloria Gaynor's "I Will Survive") Oh not I / I will survive / As long as I know how to love / I know I will survive ... hey ... hey ... todos de pie vamonos todo mundo. (Lipps Inc.'s "Funky Town") Talk about talk about talk about mo-oo-v 'in / Won't you take me to.... Funky-town ... let me hear you Houston, Tejas ... México.... (Donna Summer's "Last Dance") ... (Van McCoy's "The Hustle") Do the hustle ... (instrumental medley) ... bring it down y'all ... let me hear some gritos ... (at this moment the instrumental medley of "The Hustle" is interrupted by a Latin instrumental percussion beat) ... (music moves back to disco medley with "The Last Dance") someone found a letter you wrote me on the radio.[3]

Throughout the opening medley Selena addresses the audience in Spanish and English, calling out to the public from Houston and across the border into Mexico, while a Latin percussion beat interjects as transition between the various disco songs.

Tejas is both the discursive and geopolitical "place" representative of Texas-Mexican cultural production, in particular, Tejano music.[4] *Tejas* is a site of "third space" cultural production that emerges in conversation with the discourses of Anglo-Texas colonialism and Mexicano nationalism. "The making of *Tejas*" represents a community that comes into being through the productions of music and its associated cultural practices, including Tex-Mex language, racialized working-class aesthetics, and counterhegemonic historical narratives. If, as Lipsitz (1994) contends, music is a possible site for the construction of "place," then Tejano music is a site for the construction of *Tejas*. Moreover, based on conjunto/Tejano music's unique relationship to this geopolitical landscape, the music itself comes to represent a discursive mechanism for Tejano subjectivities. As one T-shirt slogan states, "Tejano ... it's not just music ... it's a way of life."

Selena's performance of the disco medley and her call-and-response engagement with her Tejano public merge the contemporary global economy of music genres with bodies, cultures, and regional histories through her interpretation of "third space" culture. Selena's moves and Tejano "sound"—crossing and mixing border-altering beats—reimagine a transformative "place" for her Tejano public. In this performance and other aspects of her career highlighted in this essay, Selena exemplified the complexity of her cultural work in "the making of *Tejas*." She engendered a unique vision for Tejana/o subjectivities that spoke to possibilities for transnational conversations between Mexican Americans and Latina/os south of the border, crisscrossing cultural influences among African American women and Chicanas, and the production of subversive racialized sexualities. This brief analysis of Selena foregrounds Selena's aesthetic and music productions. My analysis of Selena, a working-class, dark-skinned, big-hipped, third-generation, primarily English-speaking Tejana, and her music, insists upon exploring the link between her music and the conceptualized "third space" of *Tejas*.

Chicana feminist theorists have articulated the discursive "third space" as symbolized by the "in-between" socially constructed territory north of the Río Bravo (Anzaldúa 1987; Fregoso 1998; Pérez 1999). Moreover, I utilize Pérez's (1999) articulation of "third space performative acts" to explore the ways Tejana singers, like Selena, negotiate gender, race, class, and sexuality in their cultural work within both an Anglo-Texan colonial imaginary and Tejano masculinity. Thus, if we situate Selena within this "third space" cultural production of Tejano music, we must also reckon with how her presence destabilized the normative masculinized subjectivity circulating within the production, performance, and representation of the music. My critical assessment of Selena's music provides key examples of how and where she accomplished this intervention into and transformation of Tejano music, while representing an alternative subjectivity within a music industry strongly dominated by its patriarchal legacy.

Selena persistently affiliated with the "place" of Tejano music in the way she self-identified as a public figure, even though her unique "sound" was establishing a different direction from other singers of Tejano music. This, I argue, exemplifies how Selena drew from aspects outside the normative influences of the music in order to succeed within it. For example, media critics have often read the glitzy glittery aspects of Selena's self-made aesthetics through the lens of "hyper-Latina sexuality." I contend that the sexuality performed by Selena (i.e., prominently emphasized by glitter, rhinestones, and so on) reveals her musical influences from disco, funk, glam, and new wave. Selena's music called forth particular moments and music genres outside Tejano music. These "outside" influences were arenas where gay men and women of color utilized public (music) sites for gender and sexuality liberation and subversion, particularly evident in the disco era.[5]

Selena's Tejano "sound" was always a challenge to contain within the confines of music labels. For example, early on, Selena y Los Dinos were described by U.S. radio personalities as "Tejano plus Top 40 . . . they were doing a lot of Rocio Durcal tunes they turned into polkas . . . that was one of the singers Selena looked up to. Tejano music just took a Mexican tune and *Americanized* it" (Patoski 1996, 64).[6] Selena further affirmed that the band's goal was to "'Chicano-ize' [the music] with a popular fusion of Mexican, rock, and pop" (Patoski 1996, 57). Selena's coordination of different musical influences, as well as material culture and dance performance, demonstrates well the kinds of "third space performative acts" Tejanas deploy as cultural workers and music makers in *Tejas*.

TEJAS IN THE AMÉRICAS

Some of the immediate media attention given to Selena upon her death was dismissed as sensationalized hype surrounding any popular figure who dies young (e.g., Janis Joplin, Richie Valens, Buddy Holly). Yet I contend that a great deal of the public mourning for Selena around the United States and different parts of Latin America was symptomatic of the extent to which Selena's music and persona made inroads into new regional and Latin American music markets, markets where Tejano music had not traveled before. Selena's musical accomplishments were marked by numerous awards won in Mexican and Latin American popular music festivals and sales higher than that of any Tejano music artist before her.

Selena's representation as Tejana in some ways made her a cultural emissary of *Tejas* into uncharted Latin/o music markets. Whereas some may argue that Selena's music deflated the traditional sound of Tejano music, I argue that Selena's music allowed Tejano music to persist rather than collapse within the broader contemporary marketing project of pan-Latino or "Latin" music. Moreover, Selena's music and racialized representation as an English-speaking brown woman from the United States introduced audiences in Latin America to the cultural, historical, and political context of *Tejas,* and thus a different racialization of "Mexicana" or "Latina." Cristina Castrellon, spokesperson for Representaciones Artisticas Apodaca, noted Selena's significance within Tejano music and the broader landscape of the Latin/o American music market. Castrellon stated that Selena was unlike most Tejano/conjunto performers, having taken this regionally based music beyond the northern Mexican region; "[Selena] was one of the few performers to totally fill the Teatro del Pueblo in Monterey."[7]

Selena's musical and aesthetic interventions propelled her to become the foremost representative of Tejano music in contemporary time not only by translating the sound of Tejano music that spoke to a new generation of Texas-Mexicans but by translocating the music as well. Selena introduced Tejano music to the Central American and Puerto Rican public. Selena accomplished this unprecedented feat by stepping boldly. To stand within the ranks of Tejano music required her to disrupt the male-privileging order of the Tejano music industry. Selena symbolically embodied Tejano music and initiated its travel beyond its regional public and places. As such, Selena validated a uniquely gendered working-class racialized aesthetic for Tejano music, a cultural sensibility that came to stand for Mexican American experience in Texas to an audience unfamiliar with it.[8]

At the time of her death, Selena was making inroads into Central America, she played Guatemala in mid-1994, and there were plans for a tour of South America later in 1995.[9] In 1994 "Amor Prohibido" went to number 1 on the Latin International Chart. Selena's music was popular in various parts of Latin/o America, particularly Mexico, El Salvador, and Puerto Rico. As such, the history and culture that mark the music of *Tejas* discursively engaged the histories and cultures of new populations.[10] This was quite evident in the musical duets and group material Selena was recording with well-known artists, including the Puerto Rican (Nuyorican) hip hop group the Barrio Boyz and Honduran pop singer Alvaro Torres. In fact, Selena inserted these "Latin" music collaborative projects into *Tejas* as well. On two separate occasions she invited both the Barrio Boyz and Alvaro Torres to perform with her on the Tejano Music Awards in San Antonio, Texas, the home of Tejano music.

EL SONIDO Y IMAGINARIO DE TEJAS (THE SOUND AND IMAGINARY OF *TEJAS*)

Selena created a new and informative "sound" for Tejanas/os at the end of the twentieth century. Her "sound" and representation consistently pushed against the racial, language, gender, and generational borders of the music. Selena created a "place" for her fans to come "home" to. In fact, Selena described the unique project around establishing her Tejano music "sound" as "[conjunto] polka, a little bit of country, and a little bit of jazz." She added, "Fuse all those types of music together, I think that's where you get Tejano."[11]

Selena's music, sound, lyrics, and movement came to discursively (per)form the music beat of *Tejas, el sonido de Tejas,* a sound that resonated with her public and represented the unique social location of Texas-Mexicans. Like Selena, generations before her have inserted their own creative sound into the music. As Peña (1999) reminds us, although Texas-Mexican music encompasses several genres and styles such as *orquesta,* Tex-Mex, *conjunto,* and contemporary Tejano music, "they all share one fundamental characteristic: they are all homegrown, and they all speak after their own fashion to fundamental social processes shaping Texas-Mexican society" (xi).

Selena's unique brand of Tejano music "raised the stakes" of Texas-Mexican cultural production to encompass other articulations of gender and sexuality. For example, the beat and catchy phrase of her hit single "Bidi Bidi Bom Bom" shook up the "place" of Tejano music that historically relegated nonnormative genders and sexualities to the symbolic periphery of the dance floor. The "simplicity" of the song's music beat made explicit the ways body movement and music beats converge to establish a powerful relationship in people's connections and investments in a music's pleasure. Moreover, "Bidi Bidi Bom Bom," the song most often associated with Selena, is a prime example of how Selena's music and lyrics foreground women's focus on their own body, emotions, and feelings in songs about love and sexual attraction. "Me tiemblan hasta las piernas. . . . Cuando escucho esta cancíon, mi corazón quiere cantar así" (even my legs tremble. . . . When I hear this song, my heart wants to sing like this).

Selena's "third space performative act" was "making music" through a combination of body movement, lyrics, music beat, fashion aesthetics, and dance. A differently racialized/gendered/sexualized singing subject of Tejano music, Selena inscribed "her own female body onto the hegemonic male-centered narrative" discursively circulating in Tejano music (Chabram-Dernersesian 1993). Selena's cultural work included the utilization of cultural aesthetics in ways that uniquely merged fashion and style with the performance of her music, reinserting and reconfiguring working-class Chicana aesthetics that resonated with her public.[12] Her purple pantsuit—like other costumes Selena designed herself, including the rhinestone bustier and the Carmen Miranda–like tropical dress—conjures up influences of Latin/o Caribbean style that brilliantly (re)appropriate dominant racialized Latina representations such as Miranda, as well as other traditional Spanish flamenco and mariachi influences. Selena's self-fashioned and self-made Chicana/Tejana cultural aesthetic spoke to her Tejana generation's "conversation" with the increased circulation of "Latin/o" culture.

Selena's investments in self-designed style acknowledge her agency, like those of other working-class women of color who negotiate with fabric, texture, color, and accessories to (re)configure their own bodies, sexuality, and racialized representations. In fact, if we understand the color of Selena's brown skin to be the corporal signifier for the racist/sexist violence imposed on Mexicana bodies throughout the legacy of Texas, then perhaps the purple pantsuit—the costume most prominently associated with Selena—resituates her racialized body in *Tejas* in the color of royalty and high status. The purple pantsuit then becomes a metaphoric reminder to her Tejano/Texas public that, even if for a brief moment, she did indeed reign as the queen (la *reina*) of *Tejas*.

Selena's music captured the underexplored cultural dialogue between Mexican American and African American communities and the challenges for Mexican American popular music traveling south of the U.S.-Mexico border. Likewise, her self-initiated fashion documents the unique aspects of working-class Chicana aesthetics as well as the resilience of Texas-Mexican cultural production within an increasingly pan-Latino identity formation. Selena's music and aesthetics mark the agency and history of Tejanas/os within a differently manifested but still brutally racist Anglo-Texas culture, a racially imbued culture that reminds Tejanas/os that they indeed cannot forget the Alamo.

Selena's unique contributions to Tejano music made explicit the politics of desire, cultural authenticity, and sexual agency that converge when marginalized women's bodies intersect with the making of innovative music. Selena wove her sexuality through her bold fashion

creations, producing an aesthetic that countered the patriarchal definition of "place" and recovered the Chicana/Tejana's body. As Rosa
Linda Fregoso has reminded me, Selena's performances and music
making disrupted the problematic patriarchal and heterosexual definitions of "home" especially as configured for Tejanas.[13] She resonated
with the inhabitants of *Tejas,* the dark, working-class, Tex-Mex, Spang-
lish-speaking, third (plus)-generation Tejanos and especially Tejanas.
In this way, Selena's cultural work was a form of "representin'" and
she profoundly reminds us still that the arena where "war" is waged is
often the terrain of cultural production.

Even at the beginning of the twenty-first century, some six years
since her death, Selena's music is still heard on the radio and her tunes
are among the favorites at Tejano dance halls, her visual representation
still circulates, and young girls still imitate her dance moves. Selena represents an indentation on the discursive psyche of Anglo-Texas colonialism as well as on the masculinized embodiment of Tejano music,
and in that way, her cultural work still encourages third space performativity in the "making of *Tejas.*"

NOTES

I would like to acknowledge the feedback I received on this essay from my col-
leagues Maylei Blackwell, Luz Calvo, Gina Díaz, Catriona Esquibel, and Sherrie Tucker. I also thank my faculty mentors who have heard and read various
versions of my work on Selena: Angie Chabram-Dernersesian, Rosa Linda
Fregoso, Herman Gray (dissertation chair), Michelle Habell-Pallán, Emma
Pérez, Mary Romero and Patricia Zerella. This essay is dedicated to my parents,
whose stories about "growing up Tejano" taught me a great deal about the politics of "place" for Mexican Americans in Texas.

1. My dissertation work includes Tejana singers/musicians throughout
the twentieth century who, like Selena, have been vital cultural producers in the
"making of *Tejas.*" Some of these include Rita Vidaurri, Eva Garza, Chelo Silva,
Rosita Fernandez, Beatriz Llamas, Laura Canales, Eva Ybarra, Shelly Lares, and
Elida Reyna.

2. Gregory Nava, director of the movie *Selena* utilizes the reenactment of
Selena's concert to reinforce the movie's American "assimilationist" narrative.
The movie opens with Selena singing a disco medley, the viewer's first impres-
sion. The scene represents the climax of her career, attaining success right before

her death, thereby reinforcing a linear trajectory from her singing in Spanish to English, the marker of "success."

3. Transcription of *Selena* soundtrack medley, *Selena, The Original Motion Picture Soundtrack*. Song title: "Disco Medley Parts I and II: I will survive/Funkytown/Last Dance/The Hustle/On the radio" (©EMI Latin and Q Productions, 1997).

4. I draw from Lipsitz's (1994) notions of discursive "space" and literal "place" for understanding this regional musical production; The articulation of a discursive formation of *Tejas* is literally marked by a geographical landscape, socially constructed borders, racialized language politics, a history of colonization, in conversation with the unique emergence of Tejano music.

5. The influence of African American music on Selena's sound and aesthetics, such as disco, is an area that has been underexplored. Selena specifically mentioned Donna Summer as one of her favorite music influences. This is an area of analysis I elaborate further on in my broader dissertation work.

6. I have added italics to stress how "Americanized" makes reference to Tejano music being situated within the geopolitical space on "this side" of the border.

7. Carmina Danini, "In Mexico Singer's Fans Mourn Loss," *San Antonio Express News*, 1 April 1995, 12A.

8. Even today much of the general public recognizes Tejano music only through Selena's. For example, on a conference trip in Mexico City I often spoke to cab drivers about the popular music scene in the city, and followed up by asking whether they were familiar with Tejano music. Consistently there was a response such as (translated): "Oh yeah . . . that's the music Selena sang." What would always follow was commentary connecting me to that "place."

9. Danini, 12A.

10. After her death, a CD was released entitled *Recordando a Selena*, recorded by Familia RMM, a group of Puerto Rican salseros including Celia Cruz, Manny Manuel, and Yolanda Dukes. The CD was a compilation of Selena's hit singles redone in salsa and merengue The CD included a song specifically written for Selena, honoring her for her music contributions to the Puerto Rican and Latino community.

11. Selena in 1994 newspaper interview. Sandra Gonzales and Kathleen Donnelly, "Rising Tejano Singing Star Slain in Texas—Grammy Winner Selena Likened to Madonna," *San Jose Mercury News*, 1 April 1995, 1A.

12. On a trip to Selena's recording studio (Q Productions), I was given a tour of the numerous costumes she wore at various performances. During the tour, I noticed that the room next to the recording booth seemed under renovation, so I asked what was being built there. I was told that the room was one of Selena's fashion studios, where she drew, designed, and sewed her own

costumes. The wall dividing this room from the recording booth was being torn down to extend the space for recording.

13. Personal conversation with Fregoso about the gender and sexuality politics for Tejanas of "going home."

BIBLIOGRAPHY

Anzaldúa, Gloria. *Borderlands/La Frontera: The New Mestiza.* San Francisco: Aunt Lute Books, 1987.

Chabram-Dernersesian, Angie. "And Yes . . . the Earth Did Part: On the Splitting of Chicana/o Subjectivity." In *Building with Our Hands: New Directions in Chicana Studies,* ed. Adela De La Torre and Beatriz Pesquera. Berkeley: University of California Press, 1993.

Fregoso, Rosa Linda. "Recycling Colonialist Fantasies on the Texas Borderlands." In *Home, Exile, Homeland: Film, Media and the Politics of Place,* ed. Hamid Naficy. New York: Routledge, 1998.

Lipsitz, George. *Dangerous Crossroads: Popular Music, Postmodernism and the Poetics of Place.* New York: Verso, 1994.

Patoski, Joe Nick. *Selena: Como la Flor.* Boston: Little Brown, 1996.

Peña, Manuel. *Música Tejana.* College Station: Texas AandM University Press, 1999.

Pérez, Emma. *The Decolonial Imaginary: Writing Chicanas into History.* Theories of Representation and Difference series, ed. Teresa de Lauretis. Bloomington: Indiana University Press, 1999.

8

Hip Hop and New York Puerto Ricans

Raquel Rivera

As a Puerto Rican living in Sunset [Park], hip-hop music and culture
has been part of me as much as salsa and colonialism have.
—Edward Rodríguez, "Sunset Style"

No nací en Puerto Rico. Puerto Rico nació en mí.
—Mariposa, "Ode to the Diasporican"

WHY DID NEW YORK'S principal Spanish-language newspaper, *El
Diario*, "El campeón de los Hispanos" (The champion of Hispanics),
wait until platinum-selling Puerto Rican rap artist Big Punisher
(Christopher Ríos) passed away to celebrate his achievements?[1] For the
same reason that Jessie Ramírez (2000), columnist for *El Diario*, draws a
simplistic distinction between "American" and "Tropical" rap. He
imagines the first category to be solely populated by African Americans
and the second only to include Latino artists whose rhymes are mostly
in Spanish. Thus, Ramírez completely neglects the existence of Latino
rap artists like Big Pun whose lyrics are written mostly in English. Since
these artists don't fit easily into the currently acceptable mold of "Latinidad," they have been virtually ignored by most Latino-oriented
media.[2] Ironically, mainstream media outlets have in the last few years
largely accepted and even capitalized on the notion that "Black and
Latino" creativities are the epicenter of U.S. rap music and the larger hip
hop culture of which rap is part.[3]

New York–raised Puerto Ricans have been an integral part of U.S.
hip hop culture since its first stirrings in the early 1970s (Flores 1988;

127

Hager 1984; Rose 1994; Toop 1992). Hip hop is as vernacular to them as the culture of their parents and grandparents. Big Punisher (Big Pun) described hip hop creative experiences as being among his most ordinary childhood experiences:

> For me, growing up in the Bronx, I mean, I was surrounded by hip-hop. It was all around me. I was living hip-hop before I knew it was hip-hop. 'Cause graffiti, and dancing and music . . . that was just "playing outside" to me, y'know what'm sayin'? But that was hip-hop culture. And that was my natural life, so I lived it . . . naturally. (Rodríguez 1998)

Big Pun's experience is far from an exception. He is only the most famous among those New York Ricans that Valentín (2000) describes as having "gr[own] up on Hip Hop like kids grow up on Similac." Yet, though hip hop is a vernacular culture shared by young New York Latinos and African Americans, in the case of the former their participation is often presumed to be a defection from Latinidad into the African American camp. Nothing could be further from the truth. Second- and third-generation Latinos have simply stretched the boundaries of Latinidad. They refuse to abide by prescribed notions of Latino aesthetics, particularly when these ignore the experiences of young New York Ricans and are posed as disconnected from African American creative practices.

THE HIP HOP ZONE

Hip hop is one of the most vibrant and profitable products of late-twentieth-century youth culture. Participants most often define its core art forms to be MCing (rapping), DJing, breaking ("breakdancing"), and graffiti art, but it can be argued that there are also hip hop–specific takes on fashion, poetry/spoken word, fiction, video/film making, and language. Hip hop began during the first half of the 1970s in New York City and was most notably cultivated by African Americans, Puerto Ricans, and other young people of Caribbean parentage in marginalized areas such as the South Bronx, Harlem, and the Lower East Side. New York Puerto Ricans have been key participants, as producers and consumers of culture, in hip hop art forms since those very beginnings.

The hip hop musical zone—in terms of Puerto Rican engagement—is currently split into two related, but distinct, subzones. I will dub the first a Boricua/Latino–centric rap scene and the second a "core" New York hip hop music scene. The Boricua/Latino–centric rap scene in New York is closely affiliated with the rap and reggae music being produced in Puerto Rico. Its most popular exponents have been raised in the Island and the great majority are based there.[4] Nevertheless, New York–based Puerto Rican (and, increasingly, Dominican) artists also abound in this sector of the hip hop zone.[5] Most artists who participate in the Island-style rap and reggae circuit are Spanish-dominant and have either been raised primarily in the Island or spent substantial periods of their lives there.

In terms of musical and verbal aesthetics, these artists are much more closely tied to the rap and reggae music of Puerto Rico than to the "core" New York hip hop music scene. Granted, establishing the "core" and "fringes" of New York hip hop is a subjective and potentially sticky endeavor. But an argument can be made for the existence of a "core" New York hip hop music scene, where African Americans are the most commercially visible group but which has included the substantial participation of West Indians and Caribbean Latinos (particularly Puerto Ricans), and to a lesser extent, other ethno-racial groups. This "core" is regarded as such within most hip hop emic discourses, given its importance and impact on the larger, translocal hip hop zone.[6] The Puerto Ricans who have participated in this "core" New York hip hop music scene have largely been English-dominant youth of the one-and-a-half, second, and third generations.[7] I focus my observations on this "core" New York hip hop subzone, for this is the realm whose Latino participants have been most glaringly ignored and/or misunderstood. It is they who pose the most overt challenges to traditional notions of Latinidad.

The borders between the New York hip hop "core" and Island-style rap and reggae zones are porous. DJ Tony Touch, for example, is one of the few hip hop artists who comfortably weave in and out of these two zones. His mixed tapes are popular among both audiences. Though U.S.-raised and currently Brooklyn-based, he travels frequently to Puerto Rico to spin at musical events and clubs. Tony Touch also works regularly at New York clubs that feature hip hop music, at times for mostly Latino audiences, at times for mostly African American audiences, at times for "mixed audiences." *Boricua Guerrero* (1997) is another example of the porosity of these two hip hop zones. This commercially successful album, though directed largely toward a Spanish-speaking audience (Stephenson 1997), attempted to bridge the gap between these zones by pairing popular rappers from the New York "core" scene with artists from the Island. It included collaborations between Nas and Daddy Yankee, Q-Tip and Chezina, Fat Joe and Mexicano, and Big Punisher and Jahvia. Its executive producers were Stanley "Cash" Stephenson, a New York African American, and Elías de León, a Puerto Rican raised in Puerto Rico and presently residing in New York.

Though *Boricua Guerrero* contributors Fat Joe (Joseph Cartagena) and Big Punisher share the bond of Puerto Rican identity with their Island-based counterparts, their creative production is most comfortably lodged within the "core" hip hop music scene of New York. In this album that—as stated amid gunfire in the "Intro"—seeks to bring together "two nations, two languages, one race," Fat Joe and Big Punisher aesthetically stand closer to the New York African American artists than to the Island-based rappers.

Within the New York "core" hip hop realm, some Puerto Rican hip hoppers do highlight their ethno-racial identity, but others do not. Some often include mention of it in their lyrics, while others rarely do. Some hang out, dance, and/or make music mainly with Puerto Ricans or other Latinos; others may be the only Puerto Ricans in an otherwise all African American crew.

Unlike the Island-based rap and reggae scene, where the participants are mostly Puerto Rican and almost exclusively Latino, the physical spaces where Puerto Ricans participate in "core" hip hop tend not to be ethno-racially segregated in the same way. At times, the majority of the participants in these spaces are African American. Other times, Latinos (mostly Puerto Rican) and African Americans make up the majority of the participants, with smaller proportions of "whites" and Asians.

For the Puerto Rican hip hoppers who participate in "core" New York hip hop, ethno-racial or national-origin identities are not necessarily foregrounded in their hip hop–related activities. Neighborhood, borough, city, coastal, gender, sexual, and class identities often take precedence as categories of affiliation within the hip hop zone. One of the reasons for this has been that stressing Puerto Rican identity "too much" can leave Puerto Ricans out of the hip hop common-cultural territory shared with African Americans. For example, the Arsonists are an all-Latino (mostly Puerto Ricans) rap crew, but their debut album *As the World Burns* (1999) makes no effort toward ethno-racial identification. There are no music samples, phrases, or references that point toward it—or if there are, they must be well hidden, because I could not identify any. Group member Q-Unique (Anthony Quiles) actually objects to being boxed into a "Latinos in hip hop" category because it "funnels" Latinos together while separating them from African Americans (Q-Unique 1995). Freestyle (Robert Wallace), former Arsonist crew member, though also wary of the Latino hip hop category, allows that it can be useful as long as it is only a description of the ethnicity of the artists involved: "The label makes sense if it means Latino guys doing it, but not if it means there's a Latino way of doing hip hop" (Freestyle 1998).

Another example can be found in Big Punisher's formula for commercial success, which rapper B-Real (a Chicano and member of the popular Los Angeles group Cypress Hill) describes in the following manner: "he left a good impression on people, because he didn't capitalize on the fact that he was Latin and capitalize on that market. He was just an overall hip-hop head who happened to be Latin" (MTV News Gallery 2000). Though Big Punisher, when compared to the Arsonists, infused his music much more with commonly recognizable Puerto Rican ethno-racial markers, his primary aesthetic devotion was still to the multiethnic "core" New York hip hop realm where African Americans and Puerto Ricans are central characters. I will elaborate this point further in the section that follows.

AN MC FIRST

Big Punisher does not inhabit Christopher Ríos's body any longer. The news of his death on February 7, 2000, hit the rap music scene like a bomb made from depleted uranium (like those the U.S. navy has covertly used for practice in Vieques, Puerto Rico). Big Pun was one of the most popular and innovative rap artists of the late 1990s. His first album, *Capital Punishment* (Big Punisher 1998), debuted at number 1 on *Billboard*'s R&B and rap charts and at number 5 on its pop charts; it was greeted by raving reviews and heavy rotation on radio stations and music video TV shows. A popular figure for the wider and multiethnic rap audience, Pun holds particular significance for Latinos in general and Puerto Ricans most specifically. This South Bronx Puerto Rican was the first Latino solo rap artist to achieve platinum sales.

Earlier Latino rap artists like Kid Frost, Mellow Man Ace, Latin Empire, and Gerardo had been largely perceived as marginal novelties with average artistic skills who catered almost exclusively to Latino audiences. Pun, however, managed the tricky balancing act of infusing his music with Puerto Rican culturally specific elements but still being perceived as having excellent and innovative artistic skills, holding on to hip hop authenticity among African Americans and Latinos and having wide commercial appeal.[8] His Puerto Rican idiosyncrasies were perceived to be not marginal to hip hop but part of a cultural force that has been enriching it since its earliest times. The delicate balance between street authenticity, cultural specificity, and commercial success achieved by Pun has been often explained by fans and critics as a result of his having been, first and foremost, an MC and, second, an MC who happened to be Latino. Pun himself alluded to this when he described himself and other artists who took a similar approach: "What makes us special, is that we're Latino, not Latino Rappers. We mastered Black music—Hip Hop—not the Latino style of Hip Hop" (Valentín 2000).

Above all, Pun remained loyal to a cultural realm where the ever-evolving rules of legitimacy are set by a collective that includes Puerto Ricans and Latinos, but transcends them. His primary creative sources and references arose from an urban youth culture that has been fundamentally informed by both Latino and African American practices, but whose commercial dimension has been dominated by and, thus, identified with African Americans. Pun has been lauded within hip hop for being true to himself and his Puerto Rican roots, but his primary loyalty was to hip hop aesthetics. For the most part, he worked with manifestations of his Puerto Ricanness that the African American contingent of his core audience would find familiar, and in certain cases maybe even intriguing or challenging—but never so challenging that they could feel excluded. The key was his maintaining a foothold on the common cultural ground, in other words, the vernacular culture shared by young African Americans and Latinos in U.S. urban centers from which hip hop art forms have drawn their most basic drive.

Beware of branding him a "Latin hip hop" artist. Pun considered himself an MC first, and then came that Latino twist. As Pun himself put it in his hit "100%" from the posthumously released album *Yeeeah*

. . . *Baby!* (Big Punisher 2000): "I'm like G Rap, Pac, Master P all balled up with a twist of Marc Anthony."[9]

"BORIQUAS ON THE SET"

Frankie Cutlass's "Boriquas on the Set"—featuring Doo Wop, Fat Joe, Ray Boogie, and True God—is a self-affirming ode to New York Puerto Ricans from the early 1990s. New York Puerto Ricanness is praised and defined through a class-, generation-, and gender-specific experience. Class identity, ethno-racial affiliation, and ethno-racial solidarities are constructed with respect to each other, as evidenced by Fat Joe and Ray Boogie offsetting their respective identities against "downtown white boys" and "Caucasian[s]," as well as Ray Boogie praising the "street" and the "ghetto" while he draws connections between himself and African American, Puerto Rican, and Mexican ghetto dwellers.

> *See True and Boogie kicking street facts*
> *Headcracks for the Blacks and the Arawaks*
> *My Aztec roughnecks get love too*
> *And if you ain't from the ghetto, then muthafuck you*

Ray Boogie employs "Arawaks" as a stand-in for Puerto Ricans, an often used strategy—which extends way beyond hip hop—of defining the Puerto Rican experience in terms of Native American ancestry, particularly in order to distinguish Puerto Ricanness from the U.S. Black experience.[10] Puerto Ricans and Chicanos, the two Latino groups invoked by Boogie, are thus linked by an appeal to a shared indigenous American connection, adding yet another bond to the "ghetto" connection they share with each other as well as with African Americans.

"Boriquas on the Set" is a manifestation of Puerto Rican second- and third-generation cultural practices. These MCs employ an English-dominant, New York Puerto Rican style—an approach to language that is much indebted to the New York African American vernacular of their peers, as well as to the Puerto Rican Spanish of their parents (Flores 1993; Pedraza 1987; Urciuoli 1996; Zentella 1997). In this particular song, language is an identity badge, but it has more to do with the way English is used and less with the faint sprinklings of Spanish through these rhymes. Spanish usage is limited to Doo Wop's mention of "eat[ing] cuchifrito every time I get booted," Fat Joe's taunting an opponent to "mámame el bicho," and a sample from African American rapper Method Man in which he declares "you ain't got no ends in mi casa." Even the spelling of "Boriqua" in the song's title tells a story as it neglects Spanish orthographic rules but is faithful to popular usage among English-dominant young people.

This celebratory classic honoring hip hop's Boricua presence employs minimal Spanish and no musical sources commonly identified as Latino—its mid-range bassline and high-pitched synthesizer melody almost make it sound like an elaboration on a video game's musical background. The Boricua experience is celebrated through English-dominant rhyme skills and the flaunting of heterosexual male prowess, as well as ghetto street knowledge—coded as the "nigga" experience.

> *My nigga Joe, good looking, check it*
> *My title never got tooken*
> *From San Juan to Brooklyn*
> *I am the undefeated, undisputed*
> *eat cuchifrito every time I get booted*
> *Sex Corona, with Mona, bitch from Iona*
> *Didn't bone her, because she was a blood donor*
> *(Doo Wop)*
>
> *Yeah! Guess who comes out the camp*
> *The undisputed heavyweight Bronx champ*
> *Niggas know the time, niggas know the deal*
> *Niggas know that nigga Fat Joe is mad real . . .*
> *It's the illest nigga from the Boogie Down*
> *Represent every day with the 4 pound*
> *Rap aggressor, MC stresser*
> *Whenever horny I'm fucking bitches on my dresser.*
> *(Fat Joe)[11]*

Nigga-ness, as evidenced in Fat Joe's rhyme, defines the self as well as those around him whose respect he commands. Identity may be linked to a Boricua Arawak past, but the Boricua New York inner-city experience is coded as a "nigga" present. According to Edward Rodríguez,

The word "nigga," particularly, is a clear instance where ghetto Black and Latino youth address themselves particularly. . . . The usage of words like "nigga" and even "minority" show our rebellious mentality in realizing the collective perception our social and economic class gives us, and the lack of power we have despite our large populations. (1996)

BORICUA NIGGAS IN THE "AGE OF THE EBONIC PLAGUE"

Language plays no small role in the construction of a niggafied Puerto Rican experience. "Niggas know who niggas are" (Bravo 1998), partly through language use, particularly within the hip hop realm. "Ebonics slingin'"—to paraphrase (Jee 1998)—is a primary communicative "nigga" practice, MCing being one of its principal poetic methods.

"You may think I'm Black by the way I'm speaking," said old-school legend Rubie Dee in an early 1980s rhyme. "My verbal Ebonics get you more higher than chronic," said Hurricane Gee (Gloria Rodríguez) nearly two decades later in the late 1990s. Around the same time, the Cru released a track titled "The Ebonic Plague," featuring African American rap artist Ras Kass, the hook to which declared,

It's all about me for you and you for me
And player if you do for two, we do for three
If you think its 'bout the cash, the cars and jewelry
We living in the Age of the Ebonic Plague

"The Ebonic Plague" proposes language as a realm where community consciousness is built as well as manifested. No ethno-racial distinctions are made between the African American and Puerto Rican artists who contributed to this song; they are all part of the "we" building and living the Age of the Ebonic Plague. Linguistic manifestations of New York Caribbean Latinidad are incorporated into the "Ebonic" community realm: The trilling "r" of the word "three" in the looping statement "mike check the one, the mike check three"—which is in linguistic debt to New York Puerto Rican English; the effortless integration of "México," pronounced in Spanish, into an otherwise all-English rhyme; the opening of the last verse with a reference to the Arsonists' "The Session" (1999).

Punks pop shit we Joe Pesce 'em, no question
Cru Session, no time for second guessing

The way in which this track is imprinted by New York Caribbean Latinidad may be lost to the casual observer who is not familiar with urban Afro-diasporic youth culture. The linguistic and other markings that signify Latinidad for the second and third Caribbean-Latino generations and for their African American peers are very specific to the Black-matrixed youth culture they share.

One key misconception that needs to be cleared up is that Puerto Rican contributions to the "core" New York hip hop expressivity will only present themselves as elements readily and commonly identifiable as Puerto Rican, such as the sampling of musical sources by Latino or Latin American musicians, or the incorporation of Spanish (or other cultural markers) into rap lyrics. Sometimes Puerto Rican contributions have been readily identifiable, as in the case of the incorporation of rumba steps into uprocking during the late 1960s, the heavy use of timbales and congas in breakbeat music of the 1970s, DJ Charlie Chase's "sneaking" Bobby Valentín basslines into the music he played at jams during the 1980s, and, most recently, Big Punisher's use of Spanish words and phrases in his lyrics.[12] But most often, Puerto Rican contributions can remain obscured if we remain fixed on thinking of Puerto Ricanness as defined by markers that do not incorporate the full range of experiences and identities of second- and third-generation New York Latinos.

Edward Rodríguez (1996) describes MCs as "ghetto poets" who "have mastered their masters' language better than the masters themselves." His comments have certain parallels to Frances Aparicio's characterization of the literature written entirely or almost entirely in English by Latinos: "writing the self using the tools of the Master and, in the process, infusing those signifiers with the cultural meanings, values and ideologies of the subaltern sector" (1997, 202).

But Aparicio, contrary to Rodríguez, analyzes these literary practices through a Latin Americanist/tropicalist perspective where the "sub-versive signifiers" are tied to the underlying presence of Spanish. Thus, she neglects the urban Afro-diasporic context, which is crucial in the reappropriation of the "tools of the master" for many Latino writers, particularly those from New York. For hip hop lyricists as well as for other writers, the subversion of the "master's" language in the New York context owes as much to "linguistic tropicalization" (Aparicio 1997) through Spanish as it does to linguistic Afro-diasporization through the influence of African American oral and literary practices.

In terms of Afro-diasporic sources and approaches to creative expression, the practice of writing rap rhymes and MCing by Puerto Ricans has much in common with the school of Nuyorican poetry, which includes poets such as Sandra María Esteves, Tato Laviera, and Pedro Pietri. In the words of another Nuyorican poet, Louis Reyes Rivera, "what is referred to as Nuyorican poetry is as much rooted in African-U.S. urban poetry as it is an attempt to redefine or reclaim the Puerto Rican culture" (Hernández 1997, 129). This rootedness of Nuyorican artistic expression within an urban Afro-diasporic context, however, frequently goes unacknowledged. Anglo/Latino and master/subaltern dichotomies are most frequently privileged in discussions of U.S.-based Puerto Rican creative expression, and the tensions and connections between African Americans and Puerto Ricans are neglected. Aparicio's arguments regarding "linguistic tropicalization" are a case in point. Santiago (1994) presents another example through his erroneous description of bugalú as a mix of Afro-Antillean and Anglo-Saxon musical traditions, when it is Afro-Antillean and African American musical sources that are being blended in this genre (Flores 2000; Salazar 1992). A similar assumption is made when Puerto Rican and other Latino rappers' heavy use of English in their rhymes is criticized as being indicative of "Anglocentrism" (Morales 1991).

If Latino rappers use English in their rhymes it is because rap is an Afro-diasporic oral/musical form of expression that originated in the United States among English-dominant Afro-diasporic youth (a population that includes Caribbean Latinos). The assumption that the use of English by Latino rappers equals Anglocentrism whereas the use of Spanish or bilingualism signals some kind of adherence to Latinidad points to severe conceptual problems. Equating the use of English with Anglocentrism negates the appropriation and transformation of the colonizers' language by Afro-diasporic people. Besides, not only are Latinos following rap's Afro-diasporic English-based orality, but their use of English also derives from their most immediate communicative experience as young people raised in the United

States. Many New York–raised Puerto Ricans (and other Latinos) express themselves more comfortably in English than in Spanish. As Fat
Joe says, even though—by virtue of being Puerto Rican—promoters
expected him to rhyme in Spanish, "I can't really kick it in Spanish, I
couldn't really feel the vibe, so I'm not even gonna try and make myself look stupid" (del Barco 1996, 82). Furthermore, as Edward Rodríguez explains, "MC's don't wanna come out as exclusively Spanish
'cause they don't wanna exclude people. Black people are their people" (Rodríguez 1995).

Another problem with these charges of Anglocentrism is that they
assume that a language equals a culture. Flores, Attinasi, and Pedraza
(Flores 1993) and Urciuoli (1996) challenge the notion that the use of
English or Spanish indicates how much "assimilation" there is. Puerto
Ricans, as well as other Latinos, frequently assert their cultural identity
through their particular way of speaking English.

Language choices by New York Puerto Rican MCs run the spectrum
of linguistic codes that include multiple variants of English and Spanish. Zentella (1997, 41) has identified some of these variants (which, she
says, tend to overlap) as Popular Puerto Rican Spanish, Standard
Puerto Rican Spanish, English-dominant Spanish, Puerto Rican English, African American Vernacular English, Hispanicized English and
Standard New York City English. Significantly, within the hip hop zone,
the absence of Spanish is not taken to be necessarily related to ethno-
cultural identity. Thirstin' Howell III's all-English rhymes in *Lyricists
Lounge* (1998) have no bearing on his Puerto Ricanness; Hurricane Gee
is not considered any more in touch with her Puerto Ricanness than he
because she skillfully switches back and forth between English and
Spanish in her solo album, *All Woman* (1997).

Hip hop is a cultural realm where the Afro-diasporicity of second-
and third-generation Caribbean Latinos is affirmed and celebrated,
partly through the linguistic practices they share with African Americans. These linguistic practices are largely English-based, and at times
include the use of certain Spanish terms and phrases as common territory (Zentella 1997). Since the late 1990s, it has actually even become
common for popular African American rappers to incorporate Spanish
into their lyrics. However, the Caribbean Latinidad of New York Puerto
Ricans involved in hip hop culture is not necessarily defined through
the use of Spanish or other cultural markers commonly coded as "truly"
Latino.

CONCLUSION

Second- and third-generation Puerto Ricans in New York have a distinct cultural identity that cannot be accurately described as "assimilated"—not into African American culture and even less so into "mainstream" U.S. culture. Their identity is distinct from that of their African American peers, that of first-generation Puerto Ricans, and that of their Island–Puerto Rican peers. According to Flores,

> as Nuyorican modes of expression come to intermingle with others and thus distinguish themselves from those of the Island legacy, it is not accurate to speak of assimilation. Rather than being subsumed and repressed, Puerto Rican culture contributes, on its own terms and as an extension of its own traditions, to a new amalgam of human expression. (1993, 192)

Hip hop, as a zone of creative expression, is a three-decade testimony of common urban, class-based, and ethno-racialized identities shared by African American, Puerto Rican, and other Caribbean youth in New York City.[13] For a substantial number of New York–raised Puerto Ricans, hip hop is not the "Other's" culture. It cannot be accurately described as having been "adopted"[14] by or serving as a "disguise"[15] for them, or as being indicative of their "assimilation" into African American culture. New York Puerto Ricans have been willful, skillful, and enthusiastic co-originators, as well as key participants, of this culture. Hip hop is part of a celebration and vindication of the creativity of young New York Puerto Ricans who have been excluded from stifling traditional definitions of Puerto Ricanness and Latinidad that don't adequately take them into account. Hip hop is, for them, a vernacular realm of expression and—as Edward Rodríguez well says—as much a part of their experience as "salsa and colonialism."

NOTES

This essay is an excerpt from "New York Ricans from the Hip Hop Zone: Between Blackness and Latinidad" (Ph.D. diss., Graduate Center of the City University of New York, 2000).

1. Big Punisher passed away on February 7, 2000, due to a heart attack induced by his massive body weight.

2. *Urban Latino Magazine* is one notable exception.

3. Examples include Burke (1997), Millner (1998), Parker (1998), Valdéz (1998), and the New York Channel 11 TV special "Viva! Hip Hop Nation" (1999).

4. For example, El Mexicano, DJ Adams, Daddy Yankee, Ivy Queen, Chezina, Glori, and Vico C.

5. For example, Mafa, a Dominican DJ who has released two albums; Enemigo, a Bronx-based Puerto Rican rapper who did a guest appearance on RandB singer Corinne's debut single (produced by rap star and impresario Wyclef Jean of the Fugees') and released his first album in the summer of 2000; Don Gato, who traveled to Puerto Rico to appear as a guest artist in albums by DJ Adams and Coo-Kee; and numerous other commercially aspiring artists and crews like BWP (Boricuas With Pride), Patota y Al Callao Underground, and Gotti.

6. New York has been regarded as a hip hop hot spot, not only because of its place in hip hop history, but also because of its continuous creative contributions to this cultural zone.

7. Among the better-known are DJ Charlie Chase of the Cold Crush Brothers, Master OC and Devastating Tito of the Fearless Four, as well as Ruby Dee and Prince Whipper Whip of the Fantastic Five. All three music groups were popular crews of the early 1980s and are widely acknowledged as pioneers of rap music's early commercial era. The Fat Boy's Prince Markie Dee Morales and the Real Roxanne are two New York Puerto Ricans who attained commercial popularity in the mid-1980s. Iván "Doc" Morales is a key music producer and engineer of the later 1980s, the man behind the popular sounds of Erik B. and Rakim's *Paid in Full* and BDP's *Criminal Minded* and *By Any Means Necessary,* among many other "classic" hip hop albums. Among New York "core" hip hop Puerto Rican artists of the 1990s are MCs like Hurricane Gee, Power Rule, Kurious Jorge, Fat Joe, Big Punisher, Thirstin' Howell III, A-Butta and Building Block, and DJs and producers like Frankie Cutlass, DJ Tony Touch, Doo Wop, G-Bo the Pro, Double R, Lazy K, DJ Enuff, and Bobbito the Barber a.k.a. Cucumber Slice.

8. The only other Latino artists who had previously managed a similar feat were Sen Dog (Senen Reyes, a Cuban) and B-Real (Louis Freeze, a Chicano) of Cypress Hill.

9. Kool G. Rap, Tupac Shakur, and Master P are three popular African American rappers.

10. Other examples in hip hop include Krazy Taíno's (of the duo Latin Empire) choice of artistic name; DJ Tony Touch frequently referring to himself as the Taíno Turntable Terrorist; Mr. Wiggles declaring in DJ Tony Touch's mixtape #49 that he is "coming like an Arawak to spear shit up."

11. See Guevara (1996), Morgan (1996), and Rose (1994) for analyses of gender power dynamics and the sexualization of women within hip hop culture.

12. Uprocking (originally known as rocking) is a dance style that emerged in the late 1960s in Brooklyn and later became a source for the hip hop dance form known as breaking. See García (1996) and Valentín (1996).

13. However, that common identity does in no way contradict ethnic differentiations. That is why young New Yorkers still make distinctions between "Boricua niggas" and other "Latino niggas" vis-à-vis "nigga niggas."

14. According to Peter Manuel (1995, 92), "Among English-speaking Newyoricans in the 1980s who were growing up with ghetto blacks and inundated with hip hop culture, there developed a widespread tendency to adopt contemporary Afro-American dress, mannerisms, and music." The rich history of African American–Puerto Rican cultural cross-fertilization is absent from this account. New York Puerto Rican hip hoppers are portrayed as having been "inundated" by this "Afro-American" culture, when in fact they were hip hop's co-originators.

15. Lipsitz (1994, 71) argues that New York Puerto Rican hip hop artists display a "strategic anti-essentialism" by "bring[ing] to the surface important aspects of who they are by playing at something they are not."

BIBLIOGRAPHY

Aparicio, Frances R. "On Sub-versive Signifiers: Tropicalizing Language in the United States." In *Tropicalizations: Transcultural Representations of Latinidad,* ed. Frances R. Aparicio and Susana Chávez-Silverman, 194–212. Hanover, NH: University Press of New England, 1997.

Arsonists. *As the World Burns.* Matador OLE 343-2. Compact disc, 1999.

Big Punisher. *Yeeeah . . . Baby.* Loud Records CK 63843. Compact disc, 2000.

———. *Capital Punishment.* Loud/RCA 07863 67512-2. Compact disc, 1998.

Bravo, Vee. "Moves and News." *Stress,* no. 12 (March–April 1998): 12.

Burke, Miguel. "Puerto Rico . . . Ho!!! Frankie Cutlass." *Source,* no. 90 (March 1997): 60.

Cru. *Da Dirty 30.* Violator 314 537 607-2. Compact disc, 1997.

del Barco, Mandalit. "Rap's Latino Sabor." In *Droppin' Science: Critical Essays on Rap Music and Hip Hop Culture,* ed. William Eric Perkins, 63–84. Philadelphia: Temple University Press, 1996.

Flores, Juan. *From Bomba to Hip Hop.* New York: Columbia University Press, 2000.

———. *Divided Borders: Essays on Puerto Rican Identity.* Houston: Arte Público, 1993.

———. "Rappin', Writin' and Breakin'." *Centro* 2, no. 3 (1988): 34–41.

Freestyle (Robert Wallace), rapper and member of the Arsonists. Phone interview by author, 30 July 1998. Transcription.

García, Bobbito. "Breakin' in the Boys' Bathroom: Uprocking Will Consume You." *Rap Pages* 5 (8 September 1996): 12.

Guevara, Nancy. "Women Writin', Rappin', Breakin'." In *Droppin' Science: Critical Essays on Rap Music and Hip Hop Culture,* ed. William Eric Perkins, 49–62. Philadelphia: Temple University Press, 1996.

Hager, David. *Hip Hop: The Illustrated History of Break Dancing, Rap Music and Graffiti.* New York: St. Martin's, 1984.

Hernández, Carmen Dolores. *Puerto Rican Voices in English: Interviews with Writers.* Westport, CT: Praeger, 1997.

Jee. "Broken Language." *Stress* 15 (1998): 22.

Lipsitz, George. *Dangerous Crossroads: Popular Music, Postmodernism and the Poetics of Place.* New York: Verso, 1994.

Manuel, Peter. *Caribbean Currents: Caribbean Music from Rumba to Reggae.* Philadelphia: Temple University Press, 1995.

Millner, Denene. "Hip Hop Heads: Ready-for-Rhyme-Time Players." *Daily News,* 11 August 1998, 45–46.

Morales, Ed. "How Ya Like Nosotros Now?" *Village Voice,* 26 November 1991, 91.

Morgan, Joan. "Fly-Girls, Bitches and Hoes: Notes of a Hip Hop Feminist." *Elementary* 1 (summer 1996): 16–20.

MTV News Gallery. "Lopez, Fat Joe, Others React to Big Pun's Death." MTV News Gallery, 8 February 2000 (online). Available at http://www.mtv .com/sendme.tin?page=http://www.mtv.com/news/articles/1425724/ 20000208/lopez_jennifer.jhtml?paid=508574 (14 May 2000).

Parker, Mr. "Hip Hop 101: Fantastic Five." *Source,* no. 106 (July 1998): 64.

Pedraza, Pedro. "An Ethnographic Analysis of Language Use in the Puerto Rican Community of East Harlem." Centro de Estudios Puertorriqueños Working Paper Series, Hunter College, New York, 1987.

Q-Unique (Anthony Quiles), b-boy and rapper, member of the Rock Steady Crew and the Arsonists. Interview by author, 13 October 1995, Lower East Side, New York. Tape recording.

Ramírez, Jessie. "Juventud, violencia y música. . . ." *El Diario,* 30 June 2000, 41.

Rodríguez, Carlito. "The Young Guns of Hip-Hop." *Source,* no. 105 (June 1998): 146–49.

Rodríguez, Edward. Interview by author, Hunter College, New York, 1995. Tape recording.

———. "Sunset Style." *Ticker,* 8 May 1996, 26.

Rose, Tricia. *Black Noise: Rap Music and Black Culture in Contemporary America.* Hanover, NH: Wesleyan University Press, University Press of New England, 1994.

Salazar, Max. "Afro-American Latinized Rhythms." In *Salsiology: Afro-Cuban Music and the Evolution of Salsa in New York City,* ed. Vernon Boggs. New York: Greenwood, 1992.

Santiago, Javier. *Nueva ola portoricensis: La revolucíon musical que vivió Puerto Rico en la decada del 60.* San Juan: Publicaciones del Patio, 1994.

Stephenson, Stan "Cash," rap music producer. Interview by author, Power Play Studios, Long Island City, New York, 1997.

Toop, David. *Rap Attack: African Rap to Global Hip Hop.* Baltimore: Serpent's Tail, 1992.

Urciuoli, Bonnie. *Exposing Prejudice: Puerto Rican Experiences of Language, Race and Class.* Boulder: Westview, 1996.

Valdés, Mimi. "Pound for Pound: Big Pun and Fat Joe Are More Than Big Poppas." *Vibe* 6, no. 6 (August 1998): 108–11.

Valentín, Clyde. "Big Pun: Puerto Rock Style with a Twist of Black and I'm Proud." *Stress* 23 (2000): 41–56.

Valentín, Clyde, and Kwikstep. "Up Rockin': Hardrocks, Props and No Glocks." *Stress* 4 (fall 1996): 44–47.

WB11/WPIX. "Viva! Hip Hop Nation" (WB11/WPIX, 1999).

Zentella, Ana Celia. *Growing Up Bilingual: Puerto Rican Children in New York.* Malden, MA: Blackwell, 1997.

THEATER AND ART

9

Paul Simon's *The Capeman*

The Staging of Puerto Rican National Identity as Spectacle and Commodity on Broadway

Alberto Sandoval-Sánchez

WHEN IN 1997 the news was out that Paul Simon had in the works a new musical about a Puerto Rican teenager, Salvador Agrón, who killed two young white men in 1959, the memory of *West Side Story* was resurrected.[1] I immediately responded with perplexity: why revisit the late fifties and once again stage the stereotypical image of Puerto Ricans as gang members and criminals? Why put back into circulation the dominant paradigm of Puerto Rico as a country with a culture of poverty and violence? Yet, as the months passed, my interest in the musical grew after reading that Simon was creating a "real-life" story of redemption, and that the music would be "authentic." He even selected Nobel Prize winning poet Derek Walcott as his cowriter to assure that the musical showed "Caribbean sensibility." (Is it that easy to essentialize Caribbean identities and experience?) As I awaited the opening with great anticipation and anxiety, rumors and bad news started to plague the production. The opening, which had been scheduled for January 8, 1998, finally took place on the 29th. The word was out: *The Capeman* was an $11 million flop sinking into the deeply troubled waters of the Great White Way.

THE CRITICS: *AQUÍ Y ALLÁ*

Who was to blame for the biggest flop ever in Broadway history, Paul Simon or the critics? I was not surprised to read the scathing reviews.

Cover of Playbill for *The Capeman*. Used by permission of Playbill, Inc. All rights reserved.

Their savage and devastating comments went right to the point. *The Capeman* was "sadly inept," "flat," "incoherent," "inert," "benumbed," "boring," "erratic," "disjointed," "disappointing," and so on. The wisest and most wicked critique was a headline in the *Village Voice*: "Simon Says Flop" (Feingold 1998). It is fascinating to see how critics captured the immensity of Simon's theatrical disaster with powerful and hyperbolic images: "It's like watching a mortally wounded animal" (Brantley

1998). "[E]veryone had been shackled to a beast whose destiny they could no longer control" (Klinkenborg 1998).

While Broadway critics concentrated on the artistic failure, the Puerto Rican critics embraced the "authenticity" of the story and accused Broadway critics of racism.[2] The musical production became living proof of Puerto Rican pride and national identity affirmation. The production became an "authentic" testament of Caribbean political experience. It staged its history of imperial violence, colonialism, and diaspora. Hence, Simon became an adoptive son of Puerto Rico. The curtain itself, which reproduced the colors and design of the Puerto Rican flag, was taken immediately as an equivalent materialized representation of Puerto Rican nationhood per se. One critic asserted that the curtain "is in itself the flag of our *patria*" (Cidoncha 1998, my translation). This "patriotic" decor provided a space of/for identification in such a persuasive manner that attending the musical validated Puerto Rican national identity per se.[3] *The Capeman* was seen as an act of subversion that opened the doors (on Broadway) for Puerto Rican actors. Most important, from a Puerto Rican nationalist point of view, *The Capeman* was an authentic piece when compared to *West Side Story*.

It cannot be dismissed that there are racist practices and institutional racism on Broadway. Just think about who has access to Broadway. Whose culture and stories are staged? Who is represented and how? When do bodies of color take center stage? It is only when we take into consideration how Latino Otherness is registered within the Anglo sociocultural imaginary that the issue of racism can be fairly tackled in Simon's musical. In view of this fact, it must be taken into account a priori that when Anglo critics refer to *The Capeman* as a "wounded animal" and as a "beast," these are strong images overloaded with innumerable connotations that connect with the criminality of Puerto Rican delinquents, like Agrón, in the United States. Undoubtedly, in the surface structure of the story, the beast is Agrón, a wounded animal who cannot escape his destiny. The same applies to the deep structure of the text, where a series of associations emerge: the Capeman = Salvador Agrón = criminal = gang member = juvenile delinquent = Puerto Rican immigrant = people of color. This unconscious chain of submerged meanings, framed by racist practices, offers an unavoidable critical reading: Puerto Rican immigrants are the wounded animals, the beasts. In this sense, Puerto Rican migration is emblematized in the image and likeness of the beast: it is dangerous, ir-

Publicity poster for Ednita Nazario's record *Corazon* (in
Puerto Rico).

rational, savage, primitive. Indeed, that wounded animal, that beast,
echoes the representation of Puerto Ricans in *West Side Story*: the
Sharks, like Agrón, are barbaric, cannibalistic, uncivilized, impas-
sioned, and bloodthirsty. In *The Capeman*, the Sharks become the Vampires, embodying violence, abjection, and monstrosity: always driven
by blood and ready to kill in cold blood.

Given that it is common practice in the United States to perceive
Puerto Ricans as Blacks, as people of color, Puerto Rican bodies on
Broadway cannot escape racialization. Blackface is always at hand to
convey a touch of racial authenticity. This is applicable and visible in

Ednita Nazario's impersonation of a Puerto Rican immigrant in her role of Agrón's mother. The pop star, who is white-skinned, blue-eyed, and blonde, dyed her hair in order to authenticate Puerto Ricanness on the stage. Thereupon, up to what point did Ednita become an accomplice in racist constructions of Latinos/as within the hegemonic politics of representation of the Other? And how did she react when she saw Al Hirschfeld's caricature of her in the *New York Times* (1998) as a Black woman resembling Diana Ross? Truly, Hirschfeld's depiction of Ednita mirroring Diana Ross exposes how racial difference is stereotypically fashioned and how racist practices determine Puerto Rican identity in the United States. No need to explain what stereotypes were at work in his reception of a musical about Puerto Ricans. The caricature speaks for itself.

According to the previous interrogative and ex-centric reading, there is not enough room in *The Capeman* for subversion, transgression, and denunciation, as the Puerto Rican critics argued. Although Simon opted for redemption—acting as a good liberal in good faith by turning an antihero into a hero—the story is deeply imprinted in hegemonic stereotypical stories that perpetuate dominant negative images of Puerto Ricans and Latinos/as in the United States. Nor is *The Capeman* a political manifest denouncing imperialism. On the contrary, by making a spectacle of Agrón's life on Broadway, Simon exoticizes and glamorizes the history of Puerto Rican migration. As cultural critic Frances Negrón-Muntaner has correctly observed: "[The musical] confirmed that Puerto Ricans are criminals, liberals are inept, and Latinos can very well play their own stereotypes in other people's [Simon's] childhood recollections" (2000).

VIVA PUERTO RICO

The fundamental factor that led Puerto Ricans and Latinos/as to identify *The Capeman* as a Latino project was the enormous Latin American/Latino popularity and fame of its cast. Not only did Rubén Blades, Ednita Nazario, and Marc Anthony attract Latino audiences because of their celebrity, but their bodily presence added the necessary reality effect to convince audiences of the authenticity of the musical. Simon succeeded in casting an international Panamanian, a native Puerto Rican, and a Nuyorican, with whom audiences could identify according to their own ethnic/national identities and migratory experiences. Those audiences also responded positively to an advertising campaign that strategically targeted Puerto Ricans and Latinos.

The first advertisement in the *New York Times* on August 10, 1997, announcing the opening of the box office was a call on Puerto Rican patriotism, even if it really was meant to sell tickets. In red, white, and blue, the colors of the Puerto Rican flag were transformed into a *casita*— a wooden house of the poor painted in bright colors in the countryside of Puerto Rico—and at the advertisement's center was a black and white photo of a boy taken in the late forties or early fifties.[4] The advertisement awoke feelings of nationalism and home(land)sickness since the picture of the boy evoked memories and marked in black and white with an aura of nostalgia the pivotal era of the Puerto Rican diaspora. The image of the flag and the *casita* guaranteed for Puerto Rican audiences the long-awaited rewriting of *West Side Story*. The photo of the boy as well as the life-size photos of Rubén Blades, Ednita, and Marc Anthony at the entrance of the theater and a huge Kodak billboard on the facade of the Marquis Theatre with a larger-than-life photo of the three of them evidenced the historical accuracy and confirmed the authenticity of the musical. For a nation that has been a U.S. colony for a century and is continuously depicted in negative and stereotypical terms, this advertisement awoke an ultimate sense of personal honor and national pride. As a whole, *The Capeman* gave long overdue recognition to the neglected Puerto Rican presence in New York City, especially in the Anglo cultural and theatrical arena. This was no *West Side Story*. Paul Simon became a hero for daring to wave the Puerto Rican flag on Broadway. In a way, it was as if the Puerto Rican parade had moved to Broadway. Literally, it did. The parade was staged in one of the final scenes when Agrón returns home. Moreover, the nation, the homeland, and the *casita* were housed at the Marquis Theatre, on Broadway, in Times Square, at the center of *la capital del mundo*.

For Puerto Rican, U.S. Puerto Rican, and Latino audiences, being there meant many things: for some it meant appropriating a dominant cultural space. They had crossed over along with the show's stars. For Puerto Ricans from the Island, it signified prestige upon returning to the Island. For young Latinas, it was ecstasy. Their idols were there *en carne y hueso*. As a whole, no matter how incongruent the musical was, Broadway is Broadway. The spectacle of the musical must have been breathtaking and exhilarating for those who had no previous or mini-

Publicity billboard for *The Capeman* at the Marriott Theatre in Times Square. The Kodak photo center stages the Latino cast: Marc Anthony, Ednita Nazario, and Ruben Blades. Photograph by Manuela Rivera Sánchez de Ramos.

mal exposure to the Great White Way. At the end of each performance, with a raving standing ovation and a spirit of celebration, Latinos/as confirmed their affinity, solidarity, pride, and Latinidad. They were making history.

THE REAL THING

Dios sabe how many times I heard "mira, mira" and "oye, oye" during the performance. Each time a cultural icon was exhibited, or a Spanish word was said, or any recognizable melody or beat was played, or when Ednita or Marc Anthony sang their lines, the Puerto Rican audience could not control their euphoria and true passionate response. For a Latino audience, thirsty for positive images of their people, hungry for self-representations, starving for their own stories, dying for a Latino cultural and ethnic presence in the hegemonic Anglo cultural domain, no matter if stereotypes were at work, for them, *The Capeman* could not get more real and authentic. As a Puerto Rican critic affirmed, "This is the first ever authentic Puerto Rican theatrical work, since *West Side Story* was not boricua in its nature" (Cidoncha 1998, my translation). Like most of the critics on the Island, both pop superstars and audiences were convinced about the authenticity of the musical.

Particularly Cristina—the Oprah Winfrey of the Spanish-speaking world—enthusiastically promoted the musical on her Univisión talk show (1998) and called on all Latinos to support Simon's effort. Most significant, as guests on her program, Ednita and Marc Anthony stated their belief that *The Capeman* was as authentic as it could get. For Ednita the show was genuine: when referring to the music she stated in total conviction, "There is aguinaldo . . . bomba and plena, danza and salsa. It is authentic, the aguinaldo is the aguinaldo. . . . There are Puerto Rican musicians, arrangers and instruments in *The Capeman*. It is for real. I sang an aguinaldo, the fact is that it is sung in English" (my translation). Marc Anthony entirely agreed with her: "Just imagine it, a salsa or an aguinaldo with Simon's melody and lyrics. . . . But it is authentic." If English is the language of the new world order, there is no reason for English *unauthenticating* Puerto Rican culture—definitely, globalization is at work here. Or is English irrelevant because Puerto Ricans are more assimilated and becoming more bilingual? After all, for sure, singing an aguinaldo in English without losing its authenticity is only one minor contradiction among many for a colonial nation like Puerto Rico.

Another contradiction that surfaced in Cristina's show was Ednita's affirmation that *The Capeman* was a real and authentic story unlike *West Side Story*. Given that the musical was based on a historical character, the representation of Agrón was taken as authentic. In contraposition, *West Side Story* was categorized as fiction. The confusion in distinguishing between what is real and what is not in the theatrical arena resulted from the lack of recognition that within the Anglo hegemonic imaginary, Puerto Ricans are mostly negatively depicted and stereotyped. In this manner, the production was misleading. Both the stars and Latino audiences failed to realize how stereotypical as cultural fiction *The Capeman* was. The musical was not a documentary, but it mimicked a historical moment at the peak of Puerto Rican migration to New York City with much accuracy, particularly in displaying a repertoire of Puerto Rican ethnic artifacts treasured by immigrants and islanders. No matter how well intentioned Simon was as he tried to rectify and rewrite the Puerto Rican history of migration, the musical itself, through its claim of authenticity and use of history, biography, news-reels, and slides, ended up recycling the same old stereotypes of Puerto Rican Otherness. Furthermore, the danger of authenticity is that it an-chors culture in ahistorical and apolitical domains, opening the door to stereotypes, perpetuating the notion of cultural purity, and discarding the ongoing historical process and negotiations of cultural creativity and social change. In order to undo the mythification of authenticity, we must see authenticity as a social and cultural construction in the mod-ern Western world.[5]

The Capeman constituted a fragmented and "made-in-America" in-ventory of Puerto Rican migrant history, culture, folklore, music, tradi-tions, and Hispanic heritage. It all came back to memory on Broadway, in the most sacred theatrical space of the imperial United States of America. As this Puerto Rican inventory was paraded on stage, it be-came more authentic because it had never been seen there before, and now it appeared as an accurate construction. This reality effect was molded and obviously mediated by nostalgia, as if culture stays frozen and unchangeable through time. Paul Simon had done his job magnifi-cently in *replicating* the Puerto Rican reality and order of things. How could they have questioned its authenticity when 85 percent of the pro-duction team were Latinos/as, two of the stars were Puerto Ricans, the music was the "real thing" but in English, and the whole package was completed with references in the lyrics to Puerto Rican culture and the experience of migration? Once the spectators entered the theater, *The Capeman* provided the occasion for a collective "authentic" and "nostal-gic" cultural experience. In this way, the musical marketed as the "real thing," as is Coca-Cola, managed to put on the stage an ethnographic exhibit turning cultural difference into a spectacle and commodity.

THE CAPEMAN: A POSTMODERN SPECTACLE

Was *The Capeman* about Puerto Ricans, about their music and culture? Or was it about Paul Simon and his music? When we consider that Simon's primary interest was in the music, we see that *The Capeman* was really about Simon himself and his music. Agrón's story, under these circumstances, was a pretext. Trapped in the hegemonic stereotypical discursive construction of Puerto Ricans, Simon acted in complicity with the stereotypes of *West Side Story*. When we realize that his main concern was not in dramatic structure, plot development, or the creation of believable characters, then we can see that his main intention in redeeming Agrón was one idea that lacked a careful consideration of the dramatis personae. All this is confirmed with Simon's release of the album Paul Simon/*Songs from The Capeman*, where he is lead singer. These songs did not narrate the story; instead they attested to Simon's authorial power and egocentric undertaking. They fragmented the story line and showed no concern for the dramatic structure of the musical. One more time, the protagonist and the story were a pretext, making it clear that *The Capeman* was really about Simon's music, his songs, his voice, his talent. It is no surprise that the cast had minimal cameo appearances in his album release. They were extras, like the African voices in his sensational success with *Graceland* (1986).[6] In these terms, Simon's co-opting of Puerto Rican music and musical self-enhancement place him in a position to speak for the Other, therein authorizing him to proclaim, "I was born in Puerto Rico," a song of the same title. The issue is not that he passes as a Puerto Rican, rather, that he takes the place of the Other and writes the Other's own history. Such a blatant act of cultural appropriation is more explicit in *The Capeman* than in his previous co-options of African and Brazilian music (*Graceland* [1986] and *Rhythm of the Saints* [1990], respectively).[7] In this case, it gets more complicated because *The Capeman* was not only about music, it was about the politics of representation in the theatrical domain. A musical is not only to be heard as a song, but also to be staged with real "ethnic and racialized" bodies and materialized cultural and ethnic markers imprinted in the props, costumes, and scenery.

In *The Capeman* (as in his previous releases) Simon, who has always been consciously and continually searching for "foreign" rhythms, has become a sort of musical ethnographer. It cannot be ignored that the relationship between the anthropologist and the ethnic Other is a relationship of power.[8] In this sense, Simon's touristic musical ventures position him in an authoritative location that replicates relations of power between the imperial gaze and hearing practices and the colonial subject, resulting in the native's lack of agency. From a privileged position, he is the one who decides what is going to be removed and relocated to the Anglo cultural imaginary. Certainly, the cultural exchange is one-sided and determined by power relations through which a dominant capitalist and imperialist sector in the music industry controls the culture of the subaltern, and accommodates it to specific agendas and ways of seeing—indeed, entertainment and exoticism play a key role in redefining the music of the Other in the global musical market. This is a process of transl(oc)ation where the native rhythms, instruments, and music become dislocated, mediated, and resignified as they are incorporated in a new symbolic order in given cultural models and ideological formations. Simon's decision to remove the music of Africa, Brazil, and Puerto Rico from its cultural, social, and political habitat will always be located in given hegemonic (global and imperialist) discursive constructions, where the culture of the subaltern circulates in mainstream culture as commodity in the entertainment business.

My point is that at work in *The Capeman* are imperialist practices that are not the product/production of transculturation. *The Capeman* is not a bilingual or Spanglish piece. Its dominant language is English, and the Spanish words included are minimal. Although these words have affective and patriotic connotations functioning within specific structures of feeling for a Puerto Rican audience, their usage is not immediate linguistic exchange in a given cultural specificity for the process of communication to take place between Latino and Anglo peoples. In Simon's hands, these words are linguistic and cultural tokens that transmit and affirm a sense of foreignness, ironically signaling at the same time for the Latino audiences a sense of authenticity for what has been co-opted.

Transculturation is not a list of words or a cluster of floating cultural and ideological paradigms, or fleeting ethnic and national symbols and icons. It is a dialectical process that takes place in given discursive positionings as transcultural subjects oscillate, and even collide, between languages and cultures. Transculturation is that liminal and interstitial location where culture, language, and identities are in continual and processual exchange, inconsistent dynamic fusion, constant dislocations, disidentifications and negotiations and partial accommodations.[9] This is not the case with *The Capeman*. Nor was it the case with *Graceland* or *Rhythm of the Saints*; and may I say, it wasn't the case with Carmen Miranda in the forties or Ricky Martin in the new millennium either. In these three albums, the exclusive composer is Paul Simon, who does not sing in the native language of the subaltern, although he belligerently appropriates their music. No wonder that he has been accused of being a "cultural rapist" and a "musical carpetbagger" (*New York Times Magazine,* 9 November 1997). It must be emphasized and understood that his musical appropriations are not solely about rhythm and melody. They are about the incorporation, representation, and appropriation of the culture of the subaltern in a global economy from a dominant point of view.

Simon's musical albums register how the local is appropriated in a new global capitalist economy still under the burden of imperialism. Although it is claimed that the technological superhighway has brought down national borders, still, whose culture is represented and how it is represented, who gets to sing and in what language, and even which themes are embedded in the songs are issues determined by imperial capitalist relations of power in the music industry, which could be camouflaged as a new politics of diversity, difference, and multiculturalism. In this new world order, with constant flows of cultural capital and peoples, everything/everyone can be a spectacle, transnationalized and consumed.

The Capeman succeeded because, in a postmodern world saturated with simulacra, authenticity is rooted in the artificial *replication* of the image, which, once translated into pure spectacle, surfaces as authentic in a consumer culture. As such, *The Capeman* became a referendum on Puerto Rican national identity and revealed that English is not an issue to Puerto Ricans in affairs of cultural authenticity. In respect to Puerto Rico's colonial status, at center stage the following decisive political propositions were in place: Is Puerto Rican culture still Puerto Rican after a hundred years of colonialism? Is Puerto Rican identity still Puerto Rican after migration? Are Puerto Rican identity and culture still Puerto Rican after being a spectacle on Broadway? The vote was in, and it was a landslide at the Broadway polls. In their ecstatic reception and unconditional consumption of *The Capeman,* Puerto Rican and Latino audiences reaffirmed that Puerto Rico is still Puerto Rico and Puerto Ricans are still Puerto Ricans wherever they are. What amazes me is how *The Capeman* spectacularized Puerto Rican culture and history, how it openly pirated Puerto Rican folkloric music, how it represented Puerto Ricans within the hegemonic and stereotypical discursive domains of the ethnic and racial Other and, after all that, it was taken as authentic. In reality, the postmodern condition can work wonders in the nationalist arena once transnationalism operates under the forces of spectacle and commodification.

NOTES

In memory of Manuela Rivera Sánchez de Ramos, siempre estarás en mi corazón.

1. *The Capeman* is based on the homicide that took place in New York City in 1959 in a clash between Anglo and Puerto Rican gangs. The tragedy garnered national attention because of its display of urban juvenile delinquency. Two Puerto Ricans, Salvador Agrón and Tony Hernández, members of a gang known as the Vampires, were arrested after hiding for three days from the police. The manhunt became a media event. Agrón was sentenced to die in the electric chair until Governor Nelson Rockefeller commuted his death sentence to life in prison. Hernández was paroled in 1968. The musical follows the story of Agrón's life from Puerto Rico, to his teenage years in New York City, through his imprisonment and his redemption. Agrón was paroled in 1979 and died of a heart attack in 1986 at the age of forty-two.

2. See particularly J. M. García Passalacqua's article *"Capeman* Too Strong for Anglo Reviewers" (1998) and Ileana Cidoncha's "Requiém para un campeón" (1998).

3. This process of identification shows how nation and authenticity conflate, as historian Jeffrey M. Pilcher has observed: "The supreme test for any expression of national culture is neither beauty nor sophistication, but authenticity. A 'genuine' work of art, however humble, demonstrates a nation's cultural autonomy, and this distinctiveness in turn justifies its claims to political sovereignty. As a result, definitions of authenticity evolve to suit national programs" (1998, 156). The irony is that Puerto Rico is a colony of the United States.

4. *Casitas* have a distinct meaning for New York Puerto Ricans. Since the eighties, in the barrios of New York City, the Puerto Rican communities have been constructing their own *casitas* on vacant lots. *Casitas*, painted with vivid and bright Caribbean colors, are not only the embodiment of nostalgia for days gone by and for a culture left behind, they have become community archives and performance centers for the preservation and transmission of Puerto Rican culture, thus representing an act of intervention and resistance. They are repositories of memory for the losses and chaotic life after migration. Cultural critic Luis Aponte-Parés has lucidly interpreted the prime function of *casitas*: "the *casita*, like the ubiquitous Puerto Rican flag, becomes a vehicle through which their builders articulate and defend their national identity, their imagined community, their innate essence determining who they are in the urban milieu" (1998, 274). *"Casitas* become places to displaced people" (275).

5. See Richard Handler's essay "Authenticity" (1986), where he centers on the social construction of authenticity in the Western world and its genealogy in the anthropological field.

6. See Veit Erlmann's analysis of *Graceland* in *Music, Modernity, and the*

Global Imagination (1999) for an excellent critical reading of Simon's musical role in a postcolonial world and the politics of difference in the global entertainment industry. I am very grateful to Charlotte Canning for providing me with this reference.

7. For theoretical studies on cultural appropriation, see Deborah Root's *Cannibal Culture* (1996) and Coco Fusco's *English Is Broken Here* (1995).

8. On this matter of relations of power in the anthropological field, see James Clifford's "Traveling Cultures," 17–46, in *Routes* (1997).

9. On transculturation, see Alberto Sandoval-Sánchez and Nancy Saporta Sternbach's *Stages of Life: Transcultural Performance and Identity in U.S. Latina Theatre.*

BIBLIOGRAPHY

Aponte-Parés, Luis. "What's Yellow and White and Has Land All Around It? Appropriating Place in Puerto Rican Barrios." In *The Latino Studies Reader: Culture, Economy, and Society,* ed. Antonia Darder and Rodolfo D. Torres, 271–80. Malden, MA: Blackwell, 1998.

Brantley, Ben. "The Lure of Gang Violence to a Latin Beat." *New York Times,* 30 January 1998, review, E1, E27.

Canby, Vincent. "*Capeman* Doesn't Fly, Despite the Music." *New York Times,* 8 February 1998, 4, 14.

The Capeman. Playbill program, 98, no. 2 (February 1998).

Cidoncha, Ileana. "Requiém para un campeón." *El Nuevo Día,* 27 March 1998, review, 82.

Clifford, James. *Routes: Travel and Translation in the Late Twentieth Century.* Cambridge: Harvard University Press, 1997.

Cristina. *El Show de Cristina.* Univisión, 1998.

Dubner, Stephen J. "The Pop Perfectionist on a Crowded Stage." *New York Times Magazine,* 9 November 1997.

Erlmann, Veit. *Music, Modernity, and the Global Imagination: South Africa and the West.* New York: Oxford University Press, 1999.

Feingold, Michael. "*The Capeman*: Simon Says Flop." *Village Voice,* 4–10 February 1998, review, 125.

Fusco, Coco. *English Is Broken Here: Notes on Cultural Fusion in the Americas.* New York: New Press, 1995.

García Passalacqua, J. M. "*Capeman* Too Strong for Anglo Reviewers." *San Juan Star,* 8 February 1998, review, V3.

Handler, Richard. "Authenticity." *Anthropology Today* 2 (1986): 2–4.

Hirschfield, Al. "Story of a Life." *New York Times,* 8 February 1998, caricature, 4.

Klinkenborg, Verlyn. Editorial. *New York Times,* 12 February 1998, A34.

Negrón-Muntaner, Frances. "Feeling Pretty: *West Side Story* and Puerto Rican Identity Discourses." *Social Text* 63, no. 2 (2000): 83–106.

Pilcher, Jeffrey M. *¡Que Vivan los Tamales! Food and the Making of Mexican Identity.* Albuquerque: University of New Mexico Press, 1998.

Root, Deborah. *Cannibal Culture: Art, Appropriation, and the Commodification of Difference.* Boulder: Westview, 1996.

Sandoval-Sánchez, Alberto, and Nancy Saporta Sternbach. *Stages of Life: Transcultural Performance and Identity in U.S. Latina Theatre.* Tucson: University of Arizona Press, forthcoming 2001.

Simon, Paul. *Graceland.* New York: Warner Bros. Records, 1986.

———. *Rhythm of the Saints.* New York: Warner Bros. Records, 1990.

———. *Songs from* The Capeman. New York: Warner Bros. Records, 1997.

10

Gender Bending in Latino Theater

Johnny Diego, The His-panic Zone, *and*
Deporting the Divas *by Guillermo Reyes*

Melissa A. Fitch

DRAMATIST GUILLERMO REYES was born in Chile in 1962 and im-migrated to the United States in 1971. Recently he has received a con-siderable amount of critical acclaim. His two works relating to the gay Latino immigrant experience, *Men on the Verge of a His-panic Breakdown* and *Deporting the Divas*, have met with the greatest success. *Men*, in par-ticular, won two Ovation awards in Los Angeles in 1994 and received enthusiastic reviews during its run off Broadway in 1997.

The purpose of this essay is to examine how alternative sexualities are presented in three plays written by the Chilean American play-wright: *Deporting the Divas* (1996), *The Seductions of Johnny Diego* (1997), and *The His-panic Zone* (1997). *Deporting* had successful runs in San Francisco and Tucson in 1996. *The Seductions of Johnny Diego* had its world premiere in March 1998 in the Lyceum Theater at Arizona State University, where Reyes is an assistant professor of theater. *The His-panic Zone* was presented in workshop form at Arizona State University in December 1997. I will briefly identify some of the complexities of writing and staging Latino theater that touches upon the theme of al-ternative sexualities; then I will concentrate specifically on the central male characters of these three works.

The inherent theatricality and performative nature of sexuality (un-derstood as the manner in which verbal, visual, auditory, body, and ges-tural signs configure "gender" for an audience) as well as the transfor-mative nature of dramatic characters and staging will be underscored in the case of the two full productions staged, *Deporting the Divas* and *The Seductions of Johnny Diego*. This study will discuss how Reyes intentionally creates characters who gender bend in order to disrupt both the heterosexual and homosexual gender/sexuality paradigms. His characters, by and large, reject limitations imposed by the labels "gay" and "straight" and thus present a sexual identity that is fluid.

Reyes's plays offer a parodic Latino self-tropicalization (to use the term coined by Susana Chávez-Silverman and Frances Aparicio) in the form of high camp, melodrama, and humor. Such reworkings of the stereotypical Latino/Latin American in the U.S. cultural imaginary have become commonplace in contemporary Latino queer theater. Recently, in addition to Reyes, other Latino/a queer playwrights such as Cherríe Moraga, Luis Alfaro, Monica Palacios, and Beto Araiza and performance artists such as Carmelita Tropicana (Alina Troyano) and Marga Gómez have also recycled and played with these dominant fictions of the Latino other, a landscape up until now populated by Carmen Miranda, Ricky Ricardo, "hot" Latinas, and more recently, the Taco Bell chihuahua and Ricky Martin's bom bom. Concurrent with the rise in theatrical productions and performance pieces that focus on queer identity, there has been an upsurge in academic research on the topic, most notably by David Román and Alberto Sandoval (1997) and Antonio Prieto Stambaugh (1996). Caridad Svich and María Teresa Marrero (2000) have seen this growing interest as the logical result of the new current of Latino theater, which is "bold, frank, uncompromising," and unafraid to treat subjects traditionally viewed as taboos within the Latino community (ix).

It is important to clarify here with regard to sexuality that Latinos are working within two distinct systems in which homosexuality is defined. The system of naming based on the Anglo-American paradigm is one in which any homoerotic experience is enough to call into question a man's masculinity and/or dominant sexual practices. The mechanisms used to prevent arousing the suspicion of any such "deviant" behavior are what form the basis for Sedgwick's "epistemology of the closet" and contribute to the practice of compulsory heterosexuality (1990).

In contrast, within the Latin American tradition, in many cases, there is not the underlying sexual suspicion that characterizes the Anglo model. The prevalent view is that the "homosexual" is the man being penetrated. Furthermore, the penetrator maintains or even enhances his machismo by virtue of the encounter. The question then becomes, how do Latino plays negotiating such themes handle this fundamental contradiction between the two systems? Furthermore, how can a dramatist such as Reyes write plays that incorporate gay or bisexual Latino characters in a world in which to be gay is almost universally perceived as a transgression? The dramatist's treatment of alternative sexualities enacts the multiplicities and contradictions of living within multiple marginal subjectivities in the United States.

Antonio Prieto Stambaugh (1996) has affirmed that it is important to examine Latino theater that allows for characters with alternative sexualities because "Las ideas que tienen otros sobre un individuo o una comunidad son la fuerza con la cual y en contra de la cual ese individuo o esa comunidad forjará un concepto de sí mismo/a y una proyección al exterior" (The ideas that others have about an individual or a community are the force with which, and against which, this individual or this community will forge a concept of itself and/or a projection to the exterior) (290). It is by way of this projection, in the form of performance, that images are circulated and visibility is increased. Thus, representations of gays, lesbians, and bisexuals in Latino theater affirm their existence and can also have an impact on the collective identity of the Latino community.

The characters that populate Reyes's plays are South Americans fleeing dictatorships, Mexicans, Cubans, Puerto Ricans, and Central Americans. They are first- and second-generation Latinos in the United States, some of whom speak only Spanish, while others can barely pronounce their Spanish surnames, and still others speak in a hybrid of the two languages. The plays emphasize in a comical manner the vast differences that separate Latinos while stressing the need for solidarity among them. Reyes underscores the need to feel pride in one's heritage, and this message is conveyed in a humorous and often poignant fashion. His funny and thought-provoking style was best summed up by an audience member at the matinee performance of *The Seductions of Johnny Diego* on April 4, 1998, who was overheard to remark, "You are laughing so hard you barely notice that there is a knife going through your heart."

Reyes's plays often revolve around the literal and metaphorical borders that separate individuals and fragment identities. As a dramatist living in the Southwest, he creates plays that are flavored by the peculiarities, increased tensions, and volatility of border life and death.

Over the last six years in Arizona there has been increased militarization of the zone as the number of agents sent to curtail the illegal immigration has quadrupled. Walls have been built and more sophisticated
weaponry has been sent to the forces in the region. The policies and
practices of the federal government, ironically named "Operation Safe-
guard" in Arizona, have led immigrants to attempt to cross into the
United States in the most desolate terrain of the border, leading to death
by heat stroke, hypothermia, dehydration, and other exposure-related
causes as the desert temperatures soar in the summer. At the same time,
also in Arizona, violent vigilante groups have sprung up to "protect"
their land and round up entrants. Meanwhile, there has been an alarm-
ing increase of deaths due to the high-speed pursuit by border agents of
vans carrying suspected illegal aliens, many times filled beyond a safe
capacity. Immigrants who make it to the United States are subjected to
exploitation by employers and are unable to partake of the most basic
of human services, such as the ability to report a crime that has been
committed against them. Finally, within the United States, Mexican
Americans born here as well as resident aliens routinely have their own
civil rights circumscribed by overzealous border agents who subject
them to searches during traffic stops along southern Arizona highways.

It is important to provide both the context for the reception of
Reyes's work in theater and the playwright's own sexual/ethnic/geo-
graphic locations because cultural production is always rooted in its so-
ciohistorical moment and geography.[1] It is only in this particular context that an audience is able to relate to the series of "in" jokes told at the
expense of politicians and public figures. Yet an additional layer of context relates to Reyes's particular generation, with cues and popular culture markers specific to those raised in the 1970s and 1980s.

Deporting the Divas, the first play to be examined here, was originally presented in San Francisco by Teatro Rinoceros and El Teatro de la
Esperanza in 1996 and directed by Jorge Huerta. It recounts the love
and fantasies of Miguel/Michael Gonzalez, played by actor Rubén
Islas. Gonzalez is a Chicano who is part of the Border Patrol in San
Diego. Miguel's primary objective is to find and deport illegal aliens for
the INS. One night he encounters a gay wedding taking place at an
abandoned ranch. He is fascinated by the scene of the lovers celebrating
that night and dancing the *quebradita*, and this fascination causes him to
reevaluate his life. He is the married father of two and yet he has always
been attracted to men and has dreamed specifically of the "divas," the

fabulous transvestites based on the style of the great feminine icons such as Carmen Miranda, Eva Perón, or Judy Garland. In the play, Miguel/Michael takes a Spanish class entitled "Spanish for Pochos," where he meets and falls in love with Sedicio, an illegal alien.

Reyes plays with the concept of the border on multiple levels. His central character is both bicultural and bisexual and he is referred to at various times throughout the play as both Miguel and Michael. Among the divas about whom he dreams are Miss Fresno, a Guatemalan of German descent living illegally in the United States and about to compete in the Miss America contest, and Sirena, a sultry Argentine tango singer. Sirena comes onto the scene in all of her "grande dame" splendor and turns Michael on with her sultry "Qué tal, che?" She is the femme fatal in Miguel's hard-boiled detective story fantasy, a direct import from the classic movies of the 1940s in the United States. Sirena is part of Michael/Miguel's lively fantasy life, and her presence in the play adds to what is already a constant sense of unreality that permeates the piece, in which exaggerated music and lighting cues call attention to the construction of gender that the diva represents. *Deporting the Divas* deals with what it means to be on the border in virtually every sense of the term, a theme that is also carried into *The His-panic Zone*, most especially in the monologue entitled "Campus Borders."

The subtitle for the monologue, one of the many vignettes that form the basis of Reyes's *The His-panic Zone*, is "A hysteria-driven monologue." A somewhat nerdy young man is addressing the "Campus Committee on Correct/Incorrect Activities." He becomes progressively more agitated throughout the monologue, telling the committee of all the difficulties he has encountered fitting in as a bisexual, half-Spanish young man on a campus in which everyone is forced to constantly "perform" their ideological, sexual, religious, and ethnic identities. He arrives at college and is promptly placed in the gay Chicano dorm, heralded as the representative of two victimized groups. The student, however, makes the mistake of falling in love with a feminist Italian American and is forced to hide his heterosexual tendencies from the campus identity police. At the end of his speech he summarizes his confusion eloquently:

> All I can tell them is that I am both Spaniard and Indian, I am straight and gay, I am here and there. I straddle fences and borders, correct and incorrect, I want to make love to the Columbus' female descendant,

and my genitals are not necessarily meant to rape and plunder an entire continent when at this point in my youth I would be satisfied with
one sexual encounter, and I came to campus to openly explore the universe without being accused of being a traitor to my people. (Reyes
1997, 21)

As in *Deporting the Divas*, in this monologue from *The His-panic
Zone* Reyes underscores the performative nature of all identity. Identities are fluid and all may be changed according to the moment and the
particular needs of the individual. What is interesting in the monologue is how it tweaks the notion of "passing" by showing characters
who are all trying to pass not for Anglos or heterosexuals, but for minorities or gays in an effort to fit in, to be "cool," to be affiliated with
a group, be it ethnic, religious, or sexual in orientation. This is a parodic reworking of the norm at large, mostly white college campuses
where students will often strive to fit in by erasing their ethnic or sexual identities.

As Bradley Boney has said, "To understand the passing/not passing dynamic requires some overview of the forces and conditions that
make passing both possible and necessary" (1996, 54). Racism, clas-
sism, homophobia, and the very real consequences these may have related to housing, education, and employment opportunities all demonstrate the reasons one might find passing desirable. Boney points out
that passing is also a way of erasing one's identity and that such behavior leads, at best, to confusion and at worst to self-loathing (54).
Reyes demonstrates that the tyranny of identity politics may be felt
from both sides, that there is a certain "exotic" glamour as well as sense
of belonging that may be found in adhering oneself to the struggle of
any oppressed group.

The characters in Reyes's plays are fighting the imperative that they
"out" themselves politically, sexually, or ethnically. His characters are
tragic in that they feel persecuted not merely by the Anglo mainstream
but by militant campus Latinos with whom it is expected, even required, that they become activists.

In this same vein one may see how Reyes approaches the topic of
choice and deftly incorporates it in a nonthreatening manner in his play
The Seductions of Johnny Diego. Probably one of the most remarkable aspects of *Johnny Diego* is precisely how unremarkable the presentation of
alternative sexual lifestyles is. One never doubts the fundamental love

that exists among members of the Zeveda family, who manage to put the "fun" into their dysfunction.

In the play, directed by Joseph Megel and staged in Tempe at the Lyceum Theater in the spring of 1998, the Irish Mexican Zeveda family has succeeded in its pursuit of the American dream. They are the "appliance kings" of East Los Angeles and have begun to think of expanding to a new market. Johnny Diego has just returned from Vietnam when the play begins, and he is ready to marry his childhood sweetheart, Bonita Zeveda, and secure the wealth and middle-class respectability that her family represents.

Johnny Diego is the all American (and Mexican) boy. The "When Johnny Comes Marching Home" song that accompanies his return is played initially in its traditional version but then moves quickly into a Mexican-flavored rendition with mariachi horns. The set, designed by Tia Torchia, is a kitchen that eventually transforms into what appears to be an altar where appliances on stairs on either side of the set lead up to the highest point at the center of the stage, where a small platform is topped with a television set, demonstrating the importance of consumerism in the life of the Zeveda family. This altar of appliances takes on even further religious overtones at the end of the play, when all lights go out and the final image is that of candles lit in each blender and coffee machine, rising up to the television. It is consumerism that has become the overriding religion for the Zevedas, although to maintain appearances of a decent Mexican American family (the father is, after all, running for public office), they make sure that traditional Mexican religious icons form part of their home. The Virgin of Guadalupe is next to the spice rack on the kitchen counter and a cross is hanging on the wall above the sink.

There is nothing particularly transgressive about the presentation of the erotic antics of the members of Johnny's family. No one is shocked by Johnny's sexual attraction to Mrs. Zeveda, to sisters Bonita and Teresa, and to brother Arnie. Reyes's lighthearted and witty approach to presenting gay and bisexual characters essentially robs them of their power to shock. The audience is not offended because no one is ever led to doubt the fundamental goodness of the characters themselves. The presentations are nonthreatening because they reinforce the dominant paradigm by demonstrating that hard work and basic decency will win out in the end. While the presentation of the message has been tweaked a bit, clothed differently, the message remains the same and it is one that

From the Arizona State University's 1998 production of *The Seductions of Johnny Diego*, written by Guillermo Reyes and directed by Joseph Megel. Photograph by Lyle Beitman.

is familiar to most Americans. This is a recurring theme in all the plays discussed here.

Johnny Diego becomes the successful businessman he aspired to be and yet doesn't sell out his heritage. Miguel/Michael of *Deporting the Divas* is able to pass his Spanish class and move up the rungs of the ladder to his own version of the American dream. The "Campus Borders"

From the Arizona State University's 1998 production of *The Seductions of Johnny Diego,* written by Guillermo Reyes and directed by Joseph Megel. Photograph by Lyle Beitman.

college student of *The His-panic Zone* is appointed the new chair of the Campus Committee to which he is recounting his story. All survive as winners in these classic American success stories, in which hard work and dedication to one's own principles triumph as long as Latino roots are not lost in the process. I will examine this in greater detail in the context of the staging of *Johnny Diego.*

In *Johnny Diego,* the comfort level is established with the public from the beginning and the audience is then receptive to the unfolding of the events. Reyes counts on this comfort level in order to introduce subsequently more absurd situations, ending in the final act with the introduction of Johnny's latest girlfriend, a blond puppet, *güera.* Clearly the objects Reyes elects to use throughout the play in an erotic fashion, such as the puppet or the vacuum cleaner with which Johnny dances (at one point unzipping the bag and sticking his hand inside with an expression of orgasmic fulfillment), lead themselves to any number of multiple sexual interpretations. And yet, while Johnny strains, or possibly even suspends the level of trust among some audience members, this is restored with his return to his wife by the end of the play. The performance begins and ends with these stock scenes, the first being the soldier returning from the war to his beloved, and the last being the man who reunites with his family with a renewed love and appreciation for his life, à la Frank Capra in *It's a Wonderful Life.* These sorts of scenes framing the play allow Reyes to slip in, I would argue, figures that might have been received less sympathetically in a different context.

In all three of the plays discussed here we have seen how Guillermo Reyes is able to write gay and bisexual characters who widen the spectrum of Latino representation in contemporary theater. He does so in a way that is not jarring for the public due to the multiple other points of reference that clearly place the audience members at ease. It is precisely because of this that his plays are ultimately so provocative. They showcase characters who are proud of their heritage while at the same time steadfast in their refusal to be defined merely on the basis of their sexuality or Latino blood. As Reyes himself has stated, "I'm uncomfortable with any form of proselytizing, anything that seeks to convert you" (Lockhart 1997, 118). The need to break free of limitations in order to negotiate one's way in life is a central tenet of Reyes's works, and he conveys this message in a manner that is both comical and thought-provoking.

NOTE

1. "Una representación teatral es pluridimensional. El espectador recibe simultáneamente palabras, espacio, color, movimiento, música, efectos de sonidos, en fin, todos los signos con que el director, técnicos y actores dan vida a un espectáculo. Este conjunto de signos require de una síntesis, interpretación y comprensión: en términos semióticos, una descodificación. Pero sabido es que los espectadores ven y oyen cosas diferentes y que su lectura del espectáculo depende de dónde fijan la mirada, de su capacidad de concentración, que varía a cada instante y de su competencia para descodificar los signos teatrales y culturales en juego, . . . el significado último del espectáculo depende exclusivamente del espectador" (A theatrical representation is pluridimensional. The spectator receives simultaneously words, space, color, movement, music, sound effects, all of the signs that the director, technicians, and actors use to make a performance come alive. This group of signs requires a synthesis, interpretation, and comprehension: in semiotic terms, a decodification. But it is known that spectators see and hear things differently and that their reading of a performance depends on where they are casting their gaze, their capacity for

concentration, which may change at every instant, and his/her competence in decoding the theatrical and cultural signifiers at work, . . . the final meaning of a performance depends exclusively on the spectator) (Rojas 1999, 187).

BIBLIOGRAPHY

Boney, Bradley. "The Lavender-Brick Road: Paul Bonin-Rodrigues and the Sissy Bo(d)y." *Theater Journal* 48, no. 1 (1996): 35–58.

Butler, Judith. "Imitation and Gender Insubordination." In *Inside/Out*, ed. Diana Fuss. London: Routledge, 1991.

Case, Sue-Ellen, ed. *Performing Feminisms: Feminist Critical Theory and Theater.* Baltimore: Johns Hopkins University Press, 1990.

Chávez-Silverman, Susana. "Tropicolada: Inside the U.S. Latino/a Gender B(l)ender." In Tropicalizations: Transcultural Representations of *Latinidad,* ed. Frances R. Aparicio and Susana Chávez-Silverman. Hanover, NH: University Press of New England, 1997.

Chávez-Silverman, Susana, and Frances R. Aparicio. Introduction to *Tropicalizations: Transcultural Representations of Latinidad,* ed. Frances R. Aparicio and Susana Chávez-Silverman, 1–17. Hanover, NH: University Press of New England, 1997.

Dolan, Jill. "Practicing Cultural Disruptions: Gay and Lesbian Representation and Sexuality." In *Critical Theory and Performance,* ed. Janelle G. Reinelt and Joseph R. Roach, 263–75. Ann Arbor: University of Michigan Press, 1992.

Foster, David William. "The Homoerotic Diaspora in Latin America." *Latin American Perspectives,* forthcoming.

Lockhart, Melissa Fitch. "Living between Worlds: An Interview with Guillermo Reyes." *Latin American Theater Review* 31, no. 1 (1997): 117–22.

———. "Queer Representations in Latino Theater." *Latin American Theater Review* 31, no. 2 (1998): 67–78.

McNulty, Charles. "The Queer as Drama Critic." *Theater* 2 (1993): 12–21.

Prieto Stambaugh, Antonio. "La actuación de la identidad a través del performance Chicano gay." *Debate Feminista* 7, no. 13 (1996): 285–315.

Ramírez, Elizabeth C. *Chicanas/Latinas in American Theater: A History of Performance.* Bloomington: Indiana University Press, 2000.

Reyes, Guillermo. *Deporting the Divas.* 1996. *Gestos* 23 (1999): 109–58.

———. *The His-panic Zone.* Unpublished manuscript, 1997.

———. *Men on the Verge of a His-Panic Breakdown.* In *Staging Gay Lives: An Anthology of Contemporary Gay Theater,* ed. John M. Clum, Boulder: Westview, 1996. 401–24.

———. *The Seductions of Johnny Diego.* Unpublished manuscript, 1997.

Rojas, Mario A. "La experiencia teatral como evento sociocultural: *El galpāo* y la búsqueda de una estética *sertaneja.*" In *Propuestas escénicas de fin de siglo: FIT 1998,* ed. Juan Villegas, 173–92. Irvine: Ediciones de Gestos, Colección Historia del Teatro 3, 1999.

Román, David, and Alberto Sandoval. "Caught in the Web: Latinidad, AIDS and Allegory in *Kiss of the Spider Woman, the Musical.*" In *Everynight Life: Culture and Dance in Latino/a America,* ed. Celeste Fraser Delgado and José Esteban Muñoz, 255-87. Durham: Duke University Press, 1997.

Sedgwick, Eve Kosofsky. *Epistemology of the Closet.* Los Angeles: University of California Press, 1990.

———. "Socratic Raptures, Socratic Ruptures: Notes on Queer Performativity." In *English Inside and Out: The Places of Literary Criticism,* ed. Susan Gubar and Jonathan Kamholtz, 122–36. New York: Routledge, 1993.

Svich, Caridad, and María Teresa Marrero, eds. *Out of the Fringe: Contemporary Latina/Latino Theater and Performance.* New York: Theater Communications Group, 2000.

I I

"Don't Call Us Hispanic"

Popular Latino Theater in Vancouver

Michelle Habell-Pallán

I'm twenty years old and I still look at myself in the mirror every morning wondering who the hell I am. Am I Mexican? Am I Canadian? Am I just plain Latino? Am I Mexican-Canadian? Am I Latin-Canadian?

　　　　　　　　　　　　　　　　　　—¿Que Pasa con la Raza, eh?

Well I've never been to Spain
so don't call me an Hispanic
. . . that name, refuse it
Never going to choose it
I just can't use it.

　　　　　　　　　　　　—El Vez and the Memphis Mariachis

LATINOS AT HOME IN CANADA

Chilean-born and Canadian-raised director Carmen Aguirre initiated Vancouver's Latino Theater Group (LTG) in 1995 after attending a conference in Brazil on Augusto Boal's Theater of the Oppressed.[1] Upon her return to Canada, she was inspired to establish a community theater workshop focused on Latino issues. The group first acted out improvisational street performances that called for audience participation to resolve enacted crisis situations. As LTG congealed, the collective playwriting process of *¿Que Pasa con la Raza, eh?* (What's up with the people?) emerged. Since each LTG member developed and performed a character based on their own experiences, the play's structure demanded innovation to register multiple Latino-Canadian experiences— specifically those of Guatemalan-, Chilean-, Salvadoran-, and Mexican-Canadian as well as ethnically mixed Latino-Canadians.

Analysis of ¿Que Pasa con la Raza, eh? serves as a launching point to examine the way the themes, iconography, and sounds of Chicano popular culture resonate in the northern reaches of the hemisphere within a framework of what scholar Angie Chabram-Dernersesian calls a critical transnationalism, one that considers "geopolitical and linguistic complexities" within "Las Américas," complexities "that arise from making strategic connections with other people of colour in the Americas."[2] This conceptual framework points to a nuanced understanding of the cultural effects of late-twentieth-century neoliberal economic restructuring on the continent of North America, and compels people of color in the Americas interested in issues of social justice to find the common ground for a transnational conversation. During the opening scene, the play immediately invites a transnational conversation with Chicanas and Chicanos by invoking the Chicana/o edict, "Don't call us Hispanic," and by reiterating El Vez's lyrics, "'cause we ain't never been to Spain." These gestures also urge Chicanos and other progressively minded U.S. Latinos to examine their relation to Latino diasporas and communities north of the border.[3]

In order to understand the significance of ¿Que Pasa con la Raza, eh? within its Canadian context, we need to note that the cultural production made by Latin Americans in Canada has been framed by the notion of exile.[4] The first major immigration of Latin Americans to Vancouver was composed of highly educated Chilean and Argentine leftists fleeing from persecution by the Pinochet dictatorship and the military juntas. During the 1970s and 1980s, Canada granted asylum to political refugees from all over Latin America.[5] The progressive nature of Latino/Latin American communities in Vancouver has been shaped by their progressive politics. Aguirre asserts, however, that the recent increase in undocumented immigration from Central America and the Caribbean has made the Latino/Latin American community more heterogeneous.[6]

Reflecting this change, the protagonist of ¿Que Pasa con la Raza, eh? has not been exiled from Guatemala for political beliefs, but instead is an economic immigrant.[7] In addition, each of the play's characters

From *¿Que Pasa con la Raza, eh?* Courtesy of Carmen
Aguirre. Reprinted by permission.

represents a different stage of the Latino/Latin American community's
integration into the greater Vancouver community. Some members of
LTG—whose ages run from sixteen to twenty-seven—are the children
of exiles. Their relation to Latin America and Canada and English (the
language of the play) differs significantly from that of their parents.
However, one LTG member explains, "The only way people see Latinos
is through the point-of-view of adults, and they have a totally different
view from youth."[8] Aguirre comments further, "Their parents describe

them as Canadian but they're not accepted by the mainstream, which sees them as Latino. So these kids are stuck in the middle, trying to find their own ground."[9] This play constructs a narrative that enables young Latinos to assert their rightful place in the local and national context (Vancouver, British Columbia, Canada) by making visible their connection to the larger geopolitical space and history of las Américas.

WELCOME TO THE AMÉRICAS

Six dancers, most under the age of twenty-five, jump on stage and begin to hip hop to "Mexican Power" by Chicano rappers Proper Dos as "Never Been to Spain" by El Vez (the innovative performance artist/musician from Los Angeles) fades out.[10] A series of slides of the internationally acclaimed Chicano comic novel series *Love and Rockets* by Los Brothers Hernandez flash behind them. The audience reads,

> The Latino theater group was created in 1994 to express our latino selves through theater. . . . We're a soulful bunch, full of Latino pride and lots of stories to share with you. . . . like, did you know that not all of us are actors! No, we're all like economists and cashiers and child care workers and high school students and college students and computer geeks and so on and so on. . . . In other words, we are the real thing from the real Vancouver Latino community here to tell you some real stories based on our real lives. . . . Welcome to the fire hall, in the downtown eastside of Vancouver, in the northwestern tip of the Americas, this continent that contains us all. . . . and remember, don't call us Hispanic, 'cause we ain't never been to Spain. . . . if anything, call us Americans, 'cause we are all from the Americas.

To emphasize the location of Vancouver, Canada, on both the cultural and geographical map of Nuestra América/Our America, an inverted, borderless map that locates Chile at the top and Canada at the bottom of the Américas remains center stage throughout the performance of the play. At its conclusion, text projected on the map states, "The borders have blurred, north is down and south is up: Welcome to the Americas."

¿Que Pasa con la Raza, eh? advances an alternative, counterhegemonic story concerning the culture of las Américas. The play also

employs commercialized forms of U.S. Latino and Chicano popular music to express grassroots narratives about the life stories of Latino-Canadian youth, narratives that are rarely given room for expression in the institutionalized form of media culture. Like the inverted map, the play seeks to disrupt outdated cultural conceptions about who constitutes Canada and to define a citizenship of the Américas. The reversed map also symbolically turns on its head the connection between Canada, the United States, and Mexico (and the rest of Latin America): it suggests that the audience will be given a glimpse of what economic restructuring, as exemplified by the North American Free Trade Agreement (NAFTA), looks like from the bottom up.[11]

¿Que Pasa con la Raza, eh? begins at the U.S.-Mexican border, where a coyote (border smuggler), ironically named Santo (Saint), guides a group of undocumented immigrants across the Río Grande to "el Norte." Only one immigrant, Guatemalan Rata, makes it through the doomed crossing. Once in Vancouver, the narrative is propelled by the impending deportation of Rata and attempts by his circle of friends to save him by organizing a marriage of convenience to ensure his Canadian citizenship. Characters enlisted in his aid include Sombra (Shadow), who left Guatemala after her parents were "disappeared"; Skin, a Canadian-born Chilean activist; Zap, a Mexican-Canadian bachelor; Dandelion, a Canadian-raised Jewish-Argentine environmentalist; and Julio, a recent political refugee from Guatemala. All the characters are in their early to mid-twenties, except for Julio, who is in his thirties, and almost all are in search of romance.

Using real-life *testimonios* (testimonies), the LTG distilled the experiences of forty members into *¿Que Pasa con la Raza, eh?* The two-act play mixes farce and performance art and each scene is punctuated by short dance breaks between acts. Because the play takes its cue from the Theater of the Oppressed, the combination of forms and content reflects the interests and experiences of the group. Theater of the Oppressed, a process rather than aesthetic or particular practice, assists disempowered communities in solving social crisis by providing a cultural space for dialogue and exchange of ideas.[12] By creating "a reflection on reality and a rehearsal for future politics," Theater of the Oppressed transforms everyday passive spectators into social actors.[13] It is popular, in the democratic sense of the word, in that it is a grassroots process. In *¿Que Pasa con la Raza, eh?* the group must collaborate to prevent Rata's deportation.

DON'T CALL US HISPANIC

To those familiar with the history of Chicanos in the United States, it comes as no surprise that memories that constitute *¿Que Pasa con la Raza, eh?* resonate with major themes addressed in Chicana and Chicano literature, *teatro*, music, and visual art; themes including border crossings, cultural identity crisis, critiques of transnational labor exploitation, and struggles for social justice. These themes remind us that it is impossible to take for granted the meanings of nation and citizenship. In fact, Chicana and Chicano cultural production emphasizes that the "concept of citizenship does not exist in a vacuum; rather, it is related to other aspects of a society, particularly where a society is marked and divided by racism and when race and national origin have determined who is awarded citizenship."[14]

¿Que Pasa con la Raza, eh? echoes these themes as it turns on a crisis of citizenship, albeit Canadian citizenship. The following excerpts demonstrate the way the play illuminates particular, yet familiar, conflicts and tensions that shape the lives of young Latinos north of the U.S. border in a historical moment when "accords like NAFTA have engendered profound disruptions that evoke the prospect of deepening social immiseration and marginalization on the one hand and the potential for cross-national popular organizing and resistance on the other."[15]

Mary Pat Brady argues that certain Chicana narratives provide "highly charged political critique of border mechanics," that is, of the U.S.-Mexico border's site-specific practices of terror and exclusion. *¿Que Pasa con la Raza, eh?* like the narratives Brady cites, takes the "U.S.-Mexico border seriously, seeing it as a process, not a static place" that impacts the lives of the characters.[16] The play begins in 1996 with a tragically familiar U.S.-Mexico border crossing. Here the coyote figure, Santo, is rendered as a greedy smuggler who extorts money and possessions from his five terrified clients, including Rata. Santo however, sees himself as "a guide, messenger, coyote, messiah." The role of the coyote (border smuggler), indispensable to border economies, has intensified during the latest phase of restructuring. In an attempt to rally customers, Santo evokes the utopic myth of "el Norte" that these economic immigrants desire:

Imagine a land where there are no twelve-hour lineups, where you pay a phone bill sitting at home, through the internet—I know you don't know what that means . . . everybody in the north has a computer. . . . Everyone in the north has or can find a job. Everyone is employed. They have positions for turkey watchers at the supermarkets during Christmas time. You can get a job waxing-apples.

To a certain extent, Santo tells the truth when he explains that beyond the Río Bravo lies "a land of great opportunity and wealth. Yes, riches beyond your wildest dreams." What he fails to mention is that those great opportunities and wealth are much easier to acquire if one holds the privilege of citizenship or legal residence, and do not necessarily trickle down to undocumented workers. He makes no mention of the massive inequalities that exist in the North or their constant vulnerability to deportation.

¿Que Pasa con la Raza, eh? constructs a border-crossing experience gone bad to portray the exclusionary mechanisms of "nation" at work and articulate the meaning of nation and citizenship from the perspective of the disempowered who are denied it. The crossing turns for the worse when Santo orders his five clients to strip and hand over their jewelry and wallets. The women reluctantly do so, but then panic when searchlights appear with sounds of helicopters and dogs. Chaos breaks out, Rata screams for them to "shut the fuck up! I want to get across." When the crossers emerge on the other side of the river, a daughter finds that her two parents have drowned. She begins to wail and another young crosser becomes hysterical and begins a laughing attack. Santo silences the laughing girl by punching her in the face and raping her, while Rata merely turns away. Her rape is interrupted by two U.S. Border Patrol agents, Rodrigo and Federico. They arrest all of them except for Rata, who slips away. Forced to their knees at gunpoint, the girls plead with them, "But you're one of us, both of you, are just like us. . . . you're not gringos, you're Latinos, aren't you ashamed? . . . We have done nothing wrong. . . . This land is ours and was taken from us." Insulted that the "lettuce-pickers" see a connection with them, they reply, "We are American citizens and proud of it. Born and raised. One more word out of any of you and we'll set you on fire. Let's go." This scene, not unlike the U.S. film *El Norte*, explores the very real tensions between the U.S.-born and the undocumented existing within Latino communities.[17]

While the immigrants understand their connection to the Mexican Americans in a much larger context—the history of colonization—the

Mexican American Border Patrol agents, in the height of anti-immigrant hysteria, cast up the privileges of citizenship and a nativist nationalism to override that possibility of solidarity. Rata eventually crosses over the "easy" border to Vancouver, but not before almost hitching a ride from a "friendly" Chicano trucker who picks up recently crossed immigrants. He finds Rata walking on the road and urges him to "get in my truck before you end up . . . back where you came from. . . . We all look out for each other out here." He advises him to "follow the coast, hitch rides, I hear you can pretty well walk right into Canada." However, he does not let Rata on until he pays him. As Rata hands over the money, the trucker thanks him with "We're all in this together, brother. Viva la raza!" Rata hops into a truck packed with other undocumented workers, but before it leaves, it is stopped by a highway patrol car. Rata jumps off and sneaks away as the others faint from the heat of the enclosed truck. By framing the experience of young Latino-Canadians in this way, ¿Que Pasa con la Raza, eh? parallels what Manuel Pastor, Jr., asserts is a recent trend in "Cultural production aimed at understanding the Chicano experience"; that is, it "is rooted increasingly in the notion of *frontera* (border)" and concerned with the "defense of the rights of undocumented immigrants, an agenda based implicitly on a notion of transnational (or noncitizen) human rights."[18]

Rata finally settles into Vancouver's Latino community in 1999. As an economic immigrant, Rata rejects his new friends' progressive politics. He describes himself as a free agent, "a man of the world" who passes over "L.A. and El Paso" because he "needed a new land." He fantasizes in front of his friends about buying a low-rider limousine complete with hydraulics, a pool in the back, and a boom system. He explains to them, "I want to drive it all the way to Chile so that I can have a limo business there." Rata has no desire to volunteer for community politics and fundraisers organized by his friends and cannot understand why they "don't want to keep any money for yourselves. . . . Volunteer? I didn't come all the way over here to give my money away." The irony is that as he espouses the virtues of American individualism, his fate depends on community help to acquire the documentation he needs.

Canadian-born Skin, the character most critical of Canadian nationalism and racism, pleads with their environmentalist friend Rocio Bernstein, nicknamed Dandelion, to marry Rata. Dandelion wants to know why Skin will not marry him herself, and Skin, exasperated, fumes, "Don't mock me. I renounced my Canadian citizenship, . . . I'm not going to be suckered in like you idiots to this imperialistic, capitalist, racist, white-wash, superiority-complex country." In a speech that gets her elected president of the college organization Shades of Revolution, formerly called Rainbow Nation (a name she rejects), Skin reveals the source of her anger:

> I don't feel like I'm part of the multicultural mosaic when I'm surrounded by bleeding hearts who suffer from amnesia about the history of their country. . . . We are living in Vancouver. A place where white supremacists beat an old Sikh brother to death, where they chase black brothers out of the Ivanhoe with baseball bats, where they beat the crap out of Filipino brothers in Squamish, where everywhere I look I'm portrayed as a fuckin' drug dealer 'cause I'm Latino. (12)

As Skin recounts these true incidents of racial hate crimes, she provides a relatively unknown counterhistory of life for people of color in Vancouver.[19] For Skin, the sole way of combating hate crimes against people of color in the Americas is through a coalition politics that recognizes Canada's role in the legacy of imperialism that has ravaged indigenous people throughout the Americas. In calling for solidarity across racial, ethnic, and national lines in antiracist struggles, Skin reiterates the desire of radical U.S. women of color for what Sonia Saldívar-Hull calls "border feminism."[20] Skin's activism in Canada on behalf of revolutionary struggles in Latin America parallels the transnational efforts of border feminists. Yet, despite her valiant efforts, Skin cannot immediately change the quandary Rata is caught in: without the privilege of the protection of citizenship she renounces, Rata will be deported.

The second act begins with an apparition of the Mexican Virgen of Guadalupe. Zap, short for "Zapatista, Emiliano Zapatista, Chiapas, Mexico, Resistencia," prays to the Virgen for help in solving "his cultural-identity crisis," even though Rata cannot understand why he has a problem, "You've got this land, this land's got you. Simple. You're Canadian." But Zap is caught in a situation explored by many Chicana narratives. Zap feels trapped "between two worlds." His national and cultural identities are at odds: "I'm twenty years old and I still look at myself in the mirror every morning wondering who the hell I am. Am I Mexican? Am I Canadian? Am I just plain Latino? Am I Mexican-Canadian? Am I Latin-Canadian?" As Zap considers the multiple identities he might embody, "Mexican, Canadian, Mexican-Canadian, etc.," he laments that he is so "mixed up." Though Zap is confused, he is on the verge of realizing that cultural identity is a process of becoming, that it is not a given.[21] He is what Guillermo Gómez-Peña calls "a child of crisis and cultural syncretism."[22] His presence engenders what Teresa McKenna calls a "new culture that repudiates both a monocultural and a binary existence."[23] Zap is in the initial stages of constructing a border identity, an identity that will allow him to negotiate life in Canada as a racialized other, where Latinos are categorized as a visible minority. After trying and failing, Zap realizes that he cannot resolve his identity through interracial dating. Although he likes the Canadian "suburban Brady bunch meets Melrose Place white girl" who wants him to "do his best Spanish accent in English," he realizes she demands a performance of a racist stereotype of Mexicanness—as do the customers in his aunt's Mexican restaurant for whom he is required to play the maracas while busing their tables.[24] He contemplates attending "a cross-cultural support group," but instead goes to Latin Lovers dating service, where he finally meets a Canadian mestiza like himself.

For all of ¿Que Pasa con la Raza, eh?'s open discussion of sexuality and safe sex, only passing references are to queer practices. When his friends kid Rata about marrying Zap to retain his citizenship, Rata responds, "I'm not even going to pretend I'm a fag." Skin tells Rata to "shut up" and Zap admonishes him "not to be such a homophobe." Rata is reassured by the fact that Canada prohibits same-sex marriages for its citizens: "It's 'illegal' for 'two Latin American males' to get married."

In act two of the play, Sombra confronts Rata's childhood friend Julio about her disappeared parents. Sombra and her friends question Julio at the sugar refinery where he works: she holds a picture to his face and demands, "Where are they?" Julio admits that "There were so many. They might be in a ditch, a river, or who knows where." As he leaves, Julio trashes the photo. But the group stops him and then beats him in slow motion to the rock en español song "Matador" (Killer) by the Argentine Los Fabuloso Cadillacs. Afterwards, Sombra rebukes Julio, "If you wanted to destroy . . . the desire for people to live better, you should have killed me . . . because I have my memory. I have my humanity." By publicly confronting this history, Sombra, with the support of her friends, walks out of the shadow of her past. Again, the incident the character describes is one that many Latino immigrants face. Yet, for

Sombra, asylum and the privilege of Canadian citizenship do not necessarily mean safety from the torturers she fled.[25]

THIS IS FOR LA RAZA

¿Que Pasa con la Raza, eh? articulates the heterogeneity of experiences
and values within Vancouver's Latino community in order to resist
stereotypical representations of Latinos, representations that originate
in the United States but spill into Canada and often influence the conceptual frame by which non-Latino Canadians see them. For instance, a
recent controversy involving stereotypical images of Chicanos and the
Toronto Police Association points to the ways images originating in the
United States inundate Latino-Canadian youth.[26] A provincial election
poster depicting "a gang from East L.A." urged voters to "help fight
crime by electing candidates who are prepared to take on the drug
pushers, the pimps, and rapists."[27] Members of the LTG affirm that the
circulation of images that equate Latinos with criminals affects their
everyday realities "Day after day, you see it in the media: Latinos, drug
dealers, Latinos, drug dealers. . . . I'll be walking around or standing on
a street corner, and I can feel that . . . not one day goes by without at
least one white person asking me to sell them drugs."[28] However, the
group finds anathema any suggestion that it is making victim art and
uses farcical humor as a strategy to avoid such representation. Aguirre
explains that by using farce "we are really highlighting the fact that
we're laughing at ourselves and our community . . . the show is all
about resilience."[29]

   ¿Que Pasa con la Raza, eh? also uses imported images to construct a
larger consciousness about North American Latinos living in las Américas. However, it is in alternative and oppositional Chicano and Latino
popular culture that the play finds the language to shape oppositional
representations of Latino-Canadian youth. U.S. Latino rap and hip hop
by Lighter Shade of Brown, Kid Frost, El Vez, Mellow Man Ace, and
Proper Dos reinforce the theme of each scene.[30] *¿Que Pasa con la Raza,
eh?*'s use of Chicano and U.S. Latino cultural production to underscore
their experiences speaks not only to the way that cultural production
travels and resonates across national borders, but also points to the innovative ways the Latino-Canadian youth culture interprets and cus-
tomizes forms of oppositional culture. *¿Que Pasa con la Raza, eh?* suc-

cessfully navigates what George Lipsitz calls "a dangerous crossroads, an intersection between the undeniable saturation of commercial culture in every area of human endeavor and the emergence of a new public sphere that uses the circuits of commodity production and circulation to envision and activate new social relations."[31] Why should the Latino-Canadian youth culture turn to the popular forms of Chicano youth culture? Perhaps, as María de los Angeles Torres reminds us, it is for the same reason Mexicans in Mexico find inspiration in it: "Mexicans in the United States have developed unique cultural and political skills as a result of the struggles they have had to wage against racism. . . . [H]ome countries can rely on these skills in developing cultural and political projects that offer an alternative to pervasive and often popular global market culture."[32]

The best of Chicano and Chicana cultural production responds compellingly to the historical moment from which it emerges. ¿Que Pasa con la Raza, eh? shares this quality in its desire to document a particular time, place, and sensibility around Latino youth culture. The play references themes found in the best of the third wave of Chicana and Chicano cultural production, a wave that finds no shame in expressing its love affair with the U.S. youth pop culture and that interprets it in unexpected ways.[33] ¿Que Pasa con la Raza, eh? attempts to activate new social relations between Latino youth in the United States and Canada by thinking beyond the nation and employing Chicano popular music and images, distributed through commercial circuits, to narrate the experiences of Latino youth in Canada. The ease with which Chicano themes speak to their situation demonstrates their experience as being part of a larger North American context. This is not to argue that young Latino-Canadians will, over time, become "Chicana" or "Chicano." We must remember that Chicano iconography emerges out of and responds to the specific historical and political context of the United States, specifically the annexation of most of the U.S. Southwest from Mexico.

In the end, Chicano cultural production acts as a partial mirror that helps the play express the experiences of Latino Canadians. For instance, the title, ¿Que pasa con la raza, eh? reads as an analogue for the way Chicano culture gets transculturated in Vancouver. The "eh?" in the title marks the inflection of Canadian English. Diane Taylor, elaborating on Cuban anthropologist Fernando Ortiz's definition of transculturation, explains that it "suggests a shifting or circulation pattern of cultural transference. . . . [I]t involves the shifting of sociopolitical, not just aesthetic borders; it modifies collective and individual identity; it changes discourse, both verbal and symbolic."³⁴ Recognizing the transculturation of Chicano cultural production outside the United States provides important feedback from Latinos in somewhat comparable social locations, thus compelling Chicano cultural studies to move beyond the U.S./Mexico framework into a hemispheric one. It also compels students of Chicano and Latino studies to see their concerns reflected in the world, the required initial step toward Chabram's "strategic connections with other people of colour in the Americas."

The play concludes at the Ukrainian Hall, where, historically, the Chilean exile community would hold its *peñas* (fundraising events) to support progressive struggles in Chile. Rata and Dandelion are wed at the hall a day before Rata is deported. As an allegory, the wedding suggests that the fate of the recent undocumented immigrants is linked to that of the Canadian-born Latinos and vice versa. As "La Raza" by Kid Frost plays, the newlyweds toast, "Que vivan los novios" shifts into "Que viva la Raza" (long live the people) and all the performers, echoing the opening scene, begin to dance—inventing new moves for the "land of a thousand dances" in our new América.

By invoking El Vez and locating the members of LTG as American, *¿Que Pasa con la Raza, eh?* employs Chicano popular culture to invent a critical transnational culture, one that reinforces a continental and, by extension, a hemispheric connection based on oppositional cultures of las Américas, instead of a connection based on nation. At the heart of the play is a critique of citizenship, and by extension, nation, nationalism, and transnational exploitation. The play articulates this critique by Latinos under the age of twenty-five living in Vancouver through modes of Chicano popular culture and by representing the trials and tribulations of their everyday lives. Ultimately, the play speaks the power of popular theater to articulate in everyday terms an oppositional narrative of Américan identity.³⁵

NOTES

1. Aguirre's solo performance *Chile con Carne* has toured Chile and Venezuela. Aguirre is featured in the film *Sabor a Mi/Savor Me* by Claudia Morgado Escanilla.

2. Angie Chabram-Dernersesian, "Introduction: Chicana/Latina Cultural

Studies: Transnational and Transdisciplinary Movements," *Cultural Studies* 13, no. 2 (1999): 183.

3. Carmen Aguirre, *¿Que Pasa con la Raza, eh*? In *Along Human Lines: Dramas from Refugee Lives* (Winnipeg: Blizzard, 2000). See also Néstor García Canclini, "Latins or Americans: Narratives of the Border," *Canadian Journal of Latin American and Caribbean Studies* 23, no. 46 (1998): 117–31.

4. For more on the theme of exile, see Alvina Ruprecht and Cecilia Taima, eds., *The Reordering of Culture: Latin America, the Caribbean, and Canada in the Hood* (Ottawa: Carleton University Press, 1995); and Lake Sagaris, "Countries Like Drawbridges: Chilean-Canadian Writing Today," *Canadian Literature* 142–43 (1994): 12–22.

5. See Thomas Wright and Rody Oñate, eds., *Flight from Chile: Voices of Exile*, trans. Irene Hodgson (Albuquerque: University of New Mexico Press, 1998). Also see Arch MacKenzie, "U.S. Crackdown Boosts Exodus to Canada," *Toronto Star,* 15 January 1987, A1, CP; "Central Americans Pour into Canada Seeking New Homes," *Toronto Star,* 15 January 1987, A1.

6. Carmen Aguirre asserts that Latinos are grossly undercounted and estimates that 40,000 people of Latin American descent live in greater Vancouver. The Canada Statistics 1996 Census counts 13,830 Latin Americans in the Visible Minority category. Canada Statistics: available www.statcan.ca/english/Pgdb/People/Population/demo40h.htm.

7. Latin Americans and South Asians are funneled into manual labor. See Karen Kelly, "Visible Minorities: A Diverse Group," *Canadian Social Science Trends* 37 (summer 1995): 2–8; and Tanya Basok, "Migration of Mexican Seasonal Farm Workers to Canada and Development: Obstacles to Productive Investment," *International Migration Review* 34, no. 1 (spring 2000): 79–97.

8. "The Latino Quarter: Carmen Aguirre's Theatre Troupe Subverts Stereotypes and Confronts Traumatic Pasts," *Georgia Straight,* 11–18 March 1999, 69.

9. Ibid.

10. Proper Dos, "Mexican Power," *Latin Lingo: Hip-Hop from La Raza* (WEA/Atlantic/Rhino Records, compact disc, 1995); El Vez, "Never Been to Spain," *How Great Thou Art* (Sympathy for the Record Industry, compact disc, n.d.). For more on the cultural significance of El Vez, see Michelle Habell-Pallán, "El Vez Is Taking Care of Business," *Cultural Studies* 13, no. 2 (1999): 195–210.

11. For an excellent collection that examines the effects of NAFTA, see Isabella Bakker, ed., *Rethinking Restructuring: Gender and Change in Canada* (Toronto: University of Toronto Press, 1996).

12. Augusto Boal developed Theater of the Oppressed in Brazil during the 1960s as a response to military repression against theater companies who did not support the dictatorship. It seeks to empower those whose point of view has been silenced. See Augusto Boal, "Theater of the Oppressed," *Unesco Courier* 50,

no. 1 (November 1997): 32–36; and Mady Schutzman and Jan Cohen-Cruz, eds., *Playing Boal: Theater, Therapy, and Activism* (New York: Routlege, 1994).

13. Augusto Boal, *Legislative Theater: Using Performance to Make Politics* (New York: Routledge, 1998), 9.

14. María de los Angeles Torres, "Transnational Political and Cultural Identities: Crossing Theoretical Borders," in *Borderless Borders: U.S. Latinos, Latin Americans, and the Paradox of Interdependence,* ed. Frank Bonilla et al. (Philadelphia: Temple University Press, 1998), 172.

15. Pedro Cabán, "The New Synthesis of Latin American and Latino Studies," in *Borderless Borders,* ed. Bonilla et al., 213.

16. See Mary Pat Brady, "The Fungibility of Borders," *Nepantla: Views from South* 1, no. 1 (2000): 181, 194.

17. Gregory Nava, prod., *El Norte/The North* (Farmington Hills: Independent Productions, 1984). For more on these tensions, see Lina Y. Newton, "Why Some Latinos Supported Proposition 187: Testing Economic Threat and Cultural Identity Hypothesis," *Social Science Quarterly* 81, no. 1 (March 2000): 180–93; and David G. Gutiérrez, *Walls and Mirrors: Mexican Americans, Mexican Immigrants, and the Politics of Ethnicity* (Berkeley: University of California Press, 1995).

18. Manuel Pastor, Jr., "Interdependence, Inequality, and Identity: Linking Latinos and Latin Americans," in *Borderless Borders,* ed. Bonilla et al., 18.

19. For details on the hate crimes Skin refers to, see Kim Bolan, "Phone Tip Led to Arrest of Racists in Temple Killing," *Vancouver Sun,* 3 October 1998, B5; and Kim Bolan, "Security Tight as Five Face Hearing in Temple Killing," *Vancouver Sun,* 6 October 1998, A5; Kim Bolan, "Racists Attack Three Blacks at Bar," *Vancouver Sun,* 6 June 1998, B1; and Lori Culbert, "Squamish Youths Say They're Not Thugs," *Vancouver Sun,* 6 June 1998, B1.

20. Border feminism recognizes the geopolitical interconnectedness of people of color in the Americas. See Sonia Saldívar-Hull, *Feminism on the Border: Chicana Gender Politics and Literature* (Berkeley: University of California Press, 2000).

21. See Rosa Linda Fregoso, *The Bronze Screen: Chicana and Chicano Film Culture* (Minneapolis: University of Minnesota Press, 1993), for cultural identity as process.

22. Guillermo Gómez-Peña, "Documented/Undocumented," in *The Graywolf Annual Five: Multicultural Literacy,* ed. Rick Simpson and Scott Walker (Saint Paul: Graywolf), 129.

23. Teresa McKenna, *Migrant Song: Politics and Process in Contemporary Chicano Literature* (Austin: University of Texas Press, 1997), 107.

24. See Michelle Habell-Pallán, "Family and Sexuality in Recent Chicano Performance: Luis Alfaro's Memory Plays," *Ollantáy Theater Journal* 4, no. 1

(1996): 33–42, for a discussion of Luis Alfaro's similar take on love and popular culture.

25. Ricke Ouston and Marina Jimenez, "Latinos Still Haunted by Ghosts of War," *Vancouver Sun*, 23 February 1998, A1.

26. Peter Small, "Police Union Ad May Break Rules," *Toronto Star*, 14 June 1999, edition 1, news sec.

27. Bruce DeMara, "Subway Poster Spurs Call for Hate Crimes Probe," *Toronto Star*, 16 June 1999, edition 1, news sec.

28. Jennifer Van Evra, "Young Actors Put Human Face on Political Strife," *Vancouver Courier*, 17 March 1999, 24.

29. "The Latino Quarter," 69.

30. Most of the tracks are on *Latin Lingo: Hip-Hop from La Raza*. Though the songs speak back to racist practices raged against U.S. Latinos, they remain unreflective about masculinity.

31. George Lipsitz, *Dangerous Crossroads: Popular Music, Postmodernism, and the Poetics of Place* (New York: Verso, 1994).

32. Torres, 178.

33. Examples of third-wave production include director Jim Mendiola's 1996 film *Pretty Vacant*, and the Marisela Norte, Alma Cervantes, Sandra D. Muñoz, and Luis Alfaro 2000 play script collaboration, *Black Butterfly, Jaguar Girl, Piñata Woman, and Other Superhero Girls Like Me*.

34. Diane Taylor, "Transculturing Transculturation," *Performing Arts Journal* 38 (1991): 90–104.

35. See David Román, "Latino Performance and Identity," *Aztlan* 22, no. 2 (fall 1997): 151–67; and Jose Muñoz, "No es Facil: Notes on the Negotiation of Cubanidad and Exilic Memory in Carmelita's Milk of Amnesia," *Drama Review* 39, no. 3 (1997): 77, for more on the relationship between identity, theater, and performance.

12

A Decidedly "Mexican" and "American" Semi[er]otic Transference

Frida Kahlo in the Eyes of Gilbert Hernandez

William A. Nericcio

Passing through ostentatiously . . .
Had I a curtain . . .
bound looseness . . .
the coarse cells of my heart . . .
subtle sting

—Frida Kahlo

CURIOUSLY ENOUGH, IT is *in* the artistic vision of Americans of Mexican descent, the spectacular semiotic hallucinations of Chicana and Chicano visual artists, that one witnesses the coming together of legacies and conventions of representation that all too often stay firmly anchored within their own isolated national, not to say nationalistic, estuaries. An examination of art, photography, and film by Americans of Mexican descent and by Chicanas/os (not always the same thing, as we know) reveals that those who wish to study arts created between and within Mexico and the United States need an eclectic and wide-ranging knowledge. For instance, in speaking to the rich graphic tendencies of late-twentieth-century Chicana/o art, one must be as sensitive of sixteenth-century Spanish altar design tendencies, and the adaptations these underwent in their introduction to the indigenous peoples of Meso-America via Cortés and Spanish Inquisition–era clerics as one must be of the impact Andy Warhol's Factory had on the First World art

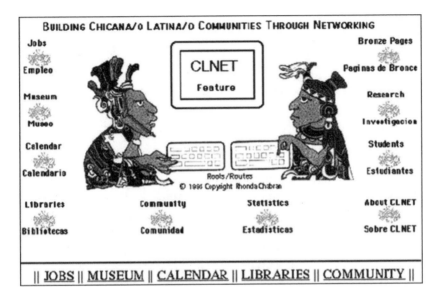

FIG. 12.1. Rhonda Chabran, "1999 Logo," CLNet: Building Chicana/o
Latina/o Communities through Networking. 14 December 2000, University
of California at Riverside. Downloaded 30 May 2001, http://clnet.ucr.edu.

market in the United States in the late sixties; as knowledgeable of the
role *retablos* and *lotería* play in northern Mexican cultural communities
as of the (some might say) similar role Elvis Presley played in the
atomic-era, Ike, and post-Ike suburban culture of the United States.
Consider, for instance, the semiotic etiology of the screenshot seized
from the Chicano/Latino World Wide Web site at the University of California, Los Angeles back in 1999 (figure 12.1).

The visual dynamics of this particular image are dense and diverse;
moreover, they span more than four centuries and at least two continents. A sophisticated marriage of pictograph and ideogram in its own
right, a Mexica graphic narrative couples with the graphic-user inter-
face of the World Wide Web: brought through the eye, pre-filtered
through an always already camera-inflected (or is it *infected*?) sense of
spectacle, yielding what is, in essence, a late-twentieth-century *mestizo*
Web page. With apologies to mathematicians everywhere, the semioti-
cally tinged version of this equation might look something like figure
12.2, where [glyph] + [a computer] + [the eye/I] + [camera] = World
Wide Web.

FIG. 12.2. Guillermo Nericcio Garcia, "Aztlán WebEquation." © 2001.

This awkward illustration does not appear here for merely melo-
dramatic purposes—though I am aware of the potential for that kind of
interpretation, and have, in the past, been guilty of such flourishes. The
maladroit logic of this fabricated equation or attractiveness gestures at
the kind of graphic fabrication that will be necessary on the part of the
critical community to document usefully just what happens when the
multivalent cultural legacies of the Americas are allied with an understanding of how advances in visuo-information technologies impact on
the arts, and on the artists producing these works.[1]

To be Chicana/o and, more important for the purposes of this essay,
to be a Chicana/o artist, is to live in the mix of more than two worlds, a
rich fractious legacy where the courts of Spain, the mute, dark cham-
bers of England, the dynamic cultural imperialism of the United States,
and the fractious, revolutionary history of Mexico merge. Said merger
is not without its profits.

Let us now quickly dash from the abstract to the specific and to the
work of Southern California native Gilbert Hernandez. We will narrow
our focus even further, electing to examine how the work of Mexican
arts diva/deity Frida Kahlo impacts on Hernandez's work. From the
start, we might note that Hernandez is somewhat at a disadvantage,
plying his trade in comic books, a genre most often associated with the
banal exploits of leotarded, steroidally enhanced musclemen (Superman, Spiderman, et al.), ditzy, hormonally gifted teenagers (Archie,
Betty, and Veronica), and outrageous dysfunctional animals (Uncle
Scrooge, Mickey Mouse). As such, he and his brother Jaime Hernandez's Dickens-like, fifteen-year serial graphic fiction project, *Love and
Rockets*, has only recently begun to receive the attention it deserves from
the community of literary critics and art historians in the United States
and abroad. Still, the Latino community as well as the Raza intelli-

gentsia has been a bit slow to note Los Bros Hernandez' literary output. Jaime Hernandez is candid about this Raza indifference in a 1993 interview: "Disappointedly, we've had little response from the [Chicana/o] community. The response we've had is that very few Hispanics read our comic books, that we know of. There's no backlash either, because our comic book isn't that important so they don't bother about it."[2] Frida Kahlo, of course, is another story. Few other artists of the late-twentieth-century have drawn the critical and popular acclaim this eccentric, gifted luminary of the Americas has received.

For an example of a flow of Mexican art onto and into the works of Mexican American artisans, there exists no better microcosm of the process of exchange than "Frida" (1988), the graphic biography of Kahlo authored and illustrated by Gilbert Hernandez: Kahlo, that most autobiographical of twentieth-century painters (only Van Gogh and Rembrandt come to mind as her competitors when it comes to the self-portrait), returns to us translated in a drawn biography by Hernandez, a Chicano born in Oxnard, California. "Frida" is Hernandez's homage to the dazzling Kahlo.[3] Using Hayden Herrera's Kahlo biography (1983) as a skeleton of sorts, Hernandez renders Frida in words and, more important, pictures.[4]

And this is where illustrator Hernandez and biographer Herrera part company, for it is the autobiographical insights gleaned from Kahlo's paintings that guide Hernandez's drawing hand as he writes the life of the late Mexican painter, more so than Herrera's prose. If this is a novelty (a visualized biography of one visual artist by another), one wonders why. How better to render the life of a painter than in pictures?

Hernandez's homage begins with a loaded frontispiece (figure 12.3)—the image is Buñuel-like in its subtlety, or better put, its lack thereof: Frida, in an adaptation of one of her many self-portraits, gazes out to us her spectators, surrounded by a constellation of symbolic keynotes (clockwise from top right): an allusion to Picasso's *Guernica*, which periodizes Kahlo in a world art context, a drawing of a bomb wrapped with a ribbon, a stylized ideogram of Andre Breton's now-famous quote about the Mexican painter (note also how drugs linger just to the left of the neatly wrapped bomb, signaling Kahlo's use/abuse of the same in the course of her many illnesses), a semi-erect devil with a pitchfork. Moving to the bottom left quadrant of the opening panel, Hernandez adds a bottle of booze, a rendition of Chester Gould's Dick Tracy nemesis, Flat Top (which, like the Picasso allusion, periodizes

FIG. 12.3. The first "splash" panel from Gilbert Hernandez's loving homage to the life and art of Frida Kahlo. Courtesy of Fantagraphics Books.

Kahlo, while also signaling Hernandez's autobiography, or, better put, auto-ergography, his own debt to a tradition of comic art in the United States). To close, the frontispiece also displays a chimera–Diego Rivera (frog and man), a Soviet hammer and sickle (glossing Kahlo's committed socialist politics), and last but not least, one of Mexican graphic artist José Guadalupe Posada's *calaveras*—Posada's works an inspiration for Kahlo and Hernandez alike.

Diligently working through the sources and inspiration for this portrait of Frida by Gilbert Hernandez, one sees at once the impact of Mexican, European, and American artists on the work of a Mexican American visual artist. Chester Gould, Andre Breton, Frida Kahlo: the rich, diverse tapestry fueling Hernandez, driving him to draw through the dizzying and myriad anxiety of influences, reminds art historians and cultural critics of how far we have to go in our efforts to interpret and, through our acts of curation, monumentalize the legacy of our Americas.

What I like about Hernandez's "Frida" is the way it problematizes the divide between the autobiographical and the biographical while also efficiently and succinctly retelling the life of a prominent twentieth-century artist. In painting, the self-portrait is the counterpart of autobiography in nonfiction prose—and certainly no little amount of ink has been spilled connecting the trajectory of Kahlo's development as a painter with the contours of her life history. But in painting Kahlo's story, Hernandez takes counsel as much from Frida's oeuvre as he does her published biographies, as much from his own experiences and development within the eclectic domain of comic book publishing as from Kahlo's self-portraits. Dick Tracy's "daddy," Chester Gould, has everything to do with Hernandez and almost nothing, save for chronology, to do with Kahlo: at once, biographical and autobiographical categories are fused as Hernandez retells the story of Kahlo's life even as he signals autobiographically his debt to Frida Kahlo.

Adapting here a smidgen, a semiotic tactic culled from the pages of bookmaking machine Jacques Derrida, we might venture that Gilbert Hernandez conjures the space of a collaborative semiotic *hallucination* wherein he and Frida reside and frolic simultaneously: "What we are talking about here is hallucination in painting. Does painting have to *let a discourse be applied to it that was elaborated elsewhere*, a discourse on hallucination. Or else must painting be the decisive test of that discourse, and its condition."[5] Displacing, however temporarily, the pages of Kahlo's various biographers, Hernandez creates a dizzying playground where *both* illustrators' lives *and* works *speak* or *show themselves* simultaneously.

FIG. 12.4. A detail from Hernandez's Kahlo biopic—here Chester Gould's Flat Top character appears armed, dangerous, and bracketed by a bottle of booze and a wine glass. Courtesy of Fantagraphics Books.

• • •

One of the most noted elements of Frida Kahlo's life is her contentious, erotic, and outrageous relationship with the inimitable Diego Rivera, who alternatively wore the hats of her mentor, lover, husband, friend, and nemesis through the years. In figure 12.5, Hernandez pictures the curious, bellicose, yet symbiotic links Kahlo shared with Rivera ("Frida," 36). Positioning both artists before unseen canvases—emphasizing momentarily their personal bonds as opposed to their aesthetic connections—here Hernandez literalizes the fusion of the two Mexican artists' twin destinies. In a way Hernandez's illustration can be seen to suggest something about Kahlo and Rivera's relationship that was already quite clear from Kahlo's oeuvre: that any permanent separation

FIG. 12.5. A devotee of expressionist and surrealist tactics, here Hernandez literalizes Diego and Frida's symbiotic ties that were both sexual and aesthetic. Courtesy of Fantagraphics Books.

FIG. 12.6. Kahlo often used blood in her paintings as a metaphorical symbol and literal organic object; enacting a semiotic transference with Kahlo, Hernandez here pictures Kahlo's communist allegiance with a bleeding hammer and sickle tatoo. Courtesy of Fantagraphics Books.

of the two could only come as the result of death. But, of course, there is even more going on in the panel: the various shapes Hernandez includes present also at once a *mise en scene* that evokes Kahlo and Rivera's symbolic universe (skulls, shadows, canvases, a discarded lover lurking in the background)—a uniquely Mexican aesthetic cosmos dominated by the artists themselves oddly frowning and smurking in the foreground.

Just as one would be at great pains to extract the affective coordinate of Kahlo's world from that of its aesthetic domain, one finds it equally difficult to tear the fabric of Kahlo's political intrigue from her aesthetic *and* libidinal drives. It is this fugue of politics, art, and desire that guides Hernandez's hand in our next panel where the Agoura, California–born seer renders that moment in Frida's life, August 22, 1940, when one Ramón Mercader viciously murdered the exiled Russian Communist Leon Trotsky—a man with whom Kahlo had shared time, ideas, dialogue, debate, and, not unimportantly, her body. Needless to say, Kahlo was shaken terribly by the dastardly act, the twelve hours of police questioning that followed doing nothing to sooth the mourning artist. Hernandez's version of the event (figure 12.6) tells us all this and more—communicating the violence of the assassination while simultaneously underscoring via the bleeding tattoo on her forehead Kahlo's links to Soviet Communism and Marx.

FIG. 12.7. Dada meets *The Brain That Wouldn't Die* meets Mexico. Worthy of Buñuel, his attested muse, Hernandez produces his most eloquent, moving, and disturbing portrait of Frida Kahlo: decapitated, intoxicated, wounded, and, most importantly, a spectacle! The stick figure peering through the window proxies our own witnessing subjectivities. Courtesy of Fantagraphics Books.

Hernandez's bleeding india inked shadows—clear political iconography sloppily dovetailing with a melodramatically rendered blood-stained hint of romance—provide a ready point of entry for a markedly important incident in Kahlo's life.

From politics, violence, and the libido, Hernandez's illustrated biography moves forward to consider the practice of autobiography in Kahlo's work. Our next sampled panel (figure 12.7) finds Frida Kahlo (circa 1946) during that late period of her life when her health was rapidly diminishing. Hernandez's rendition of this painful scene ("Frida," 37) artfully renders Kahlo's divided, decapitated body, simultaneously revealing the split self of an increasingly tortured artist. But even as he renders this scene, Hernandez belies his kitschy, Southern California, Hollywood sensibility as the template for this moving portrait of Frida comes from director Joseph Green's 1962 schlockfest/drive-in B-movie, *The Brain That Wouldn't Die*; a detail from the poster for this cold war classic reveals Hernandez's unlikely source (figure 12.8).

The most plaintive, pathetic figure in Hernandez's panel is the sketchy, confused protagonist, gawking at Frida through the window. This stickman (a proxy for you and me?), startled yet attentive, peers upon a fascinating, surreal scene. Note that the table on which Frida's head sits is a stylized altar of sorts—with Frida's head as chalice, flanked not by candles but by empty bottles of booze.

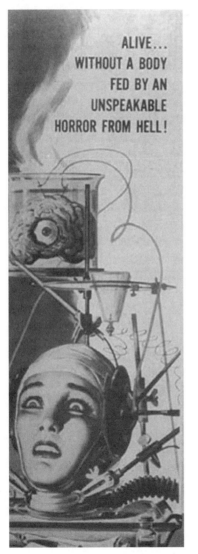

ALIVE...
WITHOUT A BODY
FED BY AN
UNSPEAKABLE
HORROR FROM HELL!

FIG. 12.8. Rex Carlton, *The Brain That Wouldn't Die* (sinage, detail), in *Daddy-O's Drive-In Dirt: The History Behind the Movies and Shorts on Mystery Science Theater 3000*. Downloaded 30 May 2001, http://www.mst3kinfo.com/daddyo/di_513.html. One of the original cinematic sources for Hernandez's mestizo imagination. We begin to understand how Hernandez's pen marries the visual archive of Hollywood black and white schlock films to the sensual contours of twentieth-century Mexican oil paintings.

FIG. 12.9. Frida Kahlo, detail from *The Little Deer* (1946), Museo Dolores Olmedo Patiño, Downloaded 23 October 2001, http://www.arts-history.mx/museos/mdo/okahloin2.html.

Moving briskly on this tour, with me your obedient prose docent, let us now jump between two illustrations, one a detail of a painting by Frida Kahlo, *The Little Deer* (1946); the other, an evocative riff played off the original, used by biographer Hernandez in "Frida" to bring off his narrative denouement (figures 12.9 and 12.10).

Note the movement from *autobiographical* self-portrait by Kahlo to the *biographical* portrait by Hernandez. A facial expression of angst in the first panel emerges remade as peaceful sleep in the second as Kahlo's documentation of an increasingly torturous life is recast by Hernandez as the no-less-violent yet somehow also hopeful scene of Frida's death. Note also how Hernandez has removed the deer's right leg to signal Kahlo's July 27, 1953, amputation, still on the horizon when *The Little Deer* was completed in 1946. Hernandez's comic book biography again tells the remarkable life of Frida Kahlo, but he also accomplishes much more. This consummate Chicano narrative wiz-

FIG. 12.10. Hernandez's transformation of Kahlo's *Little Deer*—note especially the amputated hind-leg which alters Kahlo's original painting but obeys the chronology of Kahlo's surgeries. Courtesy of Fantagraphics Books.

ard delivers what the French used to call a *haute nouveauté* (a superior, high novelty).

Of course it is not just Mexican artists who impact on Mexican American artistry. In Hernandez's *Blood of Palomar* (published in the United Kingdom as *Human Diastrophism*), Gilbert writes and draws the story of a serial killer run amok in Palomar, a fictional Central American community (imagine Faulkner's Yoknapatawpha south of the Rio Grande in García Márquez's Macondo).[6] But just as important in the novella (which appeared serially over a two-year period) is the coming-of-age story of Humberto, the literal portrait of an artist as a young man. Humberto's artistic talent is the featured sub-plot of this singular detective story/psychological novel, underscoring in an odd way the novella's concern with documenting the impact of murder on a small, insular (which is not to say provincial) community.

Figures 12.11 and 12.12 document the impact of Picasso, Grosz, Kandinsky, and modern primitivism on Gilbert Hernandez's India-inked lines. Picasso's hand in this stew is also quite interesting and noteworthy. Pablo Ruiz Picasso was born in 1881 in Málaga, Andalucía, Spain; his father was an art teacher and the precocious scribbler's first art instructor. In *Blood of Palomar* it is Heraclio, Humberto's friend, who plays master to the young talent, bringing him books by Mary Cassatt, Paul Klee, and Picasso to educate his young charge. Readers, screeners, seers all, we are confronted at once with a

FIG. 12.11. Hernandez's Picasso-influenced portrait of Luba, one of several key characters from his ongoing series of illustrated stories. This appears as the full-color, back cover of the novel-length tale *Blood of Palomar: Human Disastrophism*. Courtesy of Fantagraphics Books.

FIG. 12.12. Heraclio, a teacher, marvels at Humberto's artistic range in a key panel from *Blood of Palomar*. Courtesy of Fantagraphics Books.

decidedly delicious semio-/*geo-logicultural* ménage à trois: Oxnard, Califas (California, where Hernandez was born), Mexico (Kahlo's crib, though her father's German lineage ought to be thrown into the mix), and Spain, Mexico's motherland, Mexico's mother-tongue, that European behemoth responsible for remapping the globe in the fifteenth and sixteenth centuries. Look carefully at figures 12.13, 12.14, and 12.15.

I have sandwiched Gilbert Hernandez's drawing (in *Blood of Palomar*, it is an over-the-shoulder glance at a page from his budding artist/protagonist Humberto's sketchbook) between Kahlo's singular *Broken Column* and Picasso's ubiquitous *Don Quixote and Sancho Panza* so as to play up the intrigue amidst these three panels, one an oil painting, the second ink on paper, and the third a lithograph. This triptych evidences the depth of these circuitous allusions: the fractured, elided pudenda of a half-man, half-woman serial killer, Humberto's portrait of "Tomaso" in the center panel is informed by the syntax of fractured subjectivity Hernandez had learned from a careful perusal of Kahlo's oeuvre where Kahlo's broken, bifurcated nude form figures her torn psyche/matrix. Similarly, it was to Picasso's experimental pen strokes that Hernandez turned to represent the incipient talent of Humberto in his story. In Gilbert Hernandez's imagination and in the strokes of his pen, the lush sensual angst of Frida Kahlo is reimagined through the playful lens of Pablo Picasso's paintbrush—with the leering gaze of Miguel de Cervantes, an artist himself rather adept at wrestling with and manifesting the peculiarities intrinsic to the concept of representation, hovering just above this unlikely trio.

FIGS. 12.13, 12.14 & 12.15. *(left to right):* Frida Kahlo, *The Broken Column* (1944), Museo Dolores Olmedo Patiño. Downloaded 23 October 2001. http://www .arts-history.mx/museos/mdo/okahloin2.html. Gilbert Hernandez, two panels from *Blood of Palomar* (1987), india ink on paper. Courtesy of Fantagraphics Books; Pablo Ruiz Picasso, *Don Quixote and Sancho Panza* (1955), lithograph. © 2000 Estate of Pablo Picasso / Artists Rights Society (ARS), New York. Kahlo, Hernandez, and Picasso, a decidedly curious and utterly Chicano ménage à trois.

AFTERWORD

The borders dividing and defining Mexico and the United States as well as those no less real borders dividing high culture and popular culture cannot stop the surging of ink, the dance and coupling of photons as they bounce off canvases and comic book pages into the willing and willful eyes of their readers and viewers. *La migra's* starched green uniforms, those natty, nifty, and reactionary costumes, wardrobe progeny of the spume of Mussolini's fashion fascists, cannot bar the cacophony of the semiotic intercourse between Mexico and the United States.

EXERGUE

In an interview with Gary Groth and Robert Fiore, Gilbert Hernandez recalls the origins of his love of comics: "Our mom collected comics in the 1940s, and it's the old story, her mother—our grandmother—threw them out, so she didn't have any left and she'd always tell us about the old comics."[7]

A writer of a different age and the distinct cultural space of Texas, I walked a different path: It is the hot summer of 1966 in Laredo, Texas, and a four-year-old boy and his seven-year-old sister are playing on the bed of their father's mother. Our grandmother's name is Ana Juarez de Nericcio, and among the curious ceramic animals, old photographs, and dainty artifacts, we find a treasure chest of new and old comic books. Archie and Jughead, Betty and Veronica, Hot Stuff, Casper, Richie Rich—an odd Superman, Little Dot and Big Lotta; occasionally a Sad Sack falls our way. Here my sister Josie and I play and laugh and break things—Ana's precious little ceramic dog whose head I broke and Ana patiently repaired; I never remember her getting mad. Here I learn to read; here I learn to read another way—like José Arcadio Buendía with Melquíades, like Shelley's voyeur Wretch within his hidden cave. In the dark safe confines of my father's mother's house I am

FIG. 12.16. Ana Juarez de Nericcio, c. 1921. Photographer unknown. An I.D. photo, 1925 of my grandmother Ana Juarez de Nericcio, who introduced me to the world of comic books and forever infected me with curiosity for both the printed word and the printed image.

forever initiated into the sensual and colorful semiotic and semantic mishmash of word and image.

Gilbert Hernandez's evocative canvases send me back to this now lost Utopia of outrageous plots, garish colors, and yellowing cheap paper. It is a world as well of chocolate milk and hamburgers and the singularly selfless love of a beloved grandmother and my always special sister. The latter taught me to read and the former provided the fuel to consume that everlasting spark. The elegiac majesty of this reverie runs through my past and present, a pleasure- and pathos-filled borderzone of chaos.

NOTES

1. I address this more fully in William A. Nericcio, "Artif[r]acture: Virulent Pictures, Graphic Narrative and the Ideology of the Visual," *Mosaic: A Journal for the Interdisciplinary Study of Literature* 28, no. 4 (December 1996): 79–109.

2. Arthur Goldstuck, "The Brothers Speak," The Unlovely Love and Rockets Home Page, 1993, available http://www.web.co.za/arthur/losbros.htm (3 June 2000).

3. "Frida" is one of several experimental short stories by Gilbert Hernandez also collected in *Flies on the Ceiling: Volume Nine of the Complete Love and Rockets* (Seattle: Fantagraphic Books, 1991), 29–40. Page references in text will be to this edition.

4. Hayden Herrera, *Frida: A Biography of Frida Kahlo* (New York: Harper Perennial, 1991).

5. From "Restitutions," the last section of Derrida's *La vérité en peinture* (Paris: Flammarion, 1978), trans. Geoff Bennington and Ian McLeod as *The Truth in Painting* (Chicago: University of Chicago Press, 1987), 366.

6. Journalistic accounts of Gilbert Hernandez's literary roots repeat time and again the connection between the magic streets of his Palomar and those of a now legendary Macondo invented by García Márquez. Jaime Hernandez, Gilbert's artist-brother, bursts our osmotic-sensitive sensors: "[he] read [García Márquez], but he didn't know about him till someone told him that they wrote similarly. It was really ironic: Gilbert had never read him but people were telling him this. I think it was more being raised on the same wavelength" (Goldstuck 2000). What García Márquez and Gilbert Hernandez do share is a fascination with the Latin American motherlands, the Latino mother tongue. In Gilbert Hernandez's own words, "The interest was always there. But I . . . refined it doing stories about the old country, doing stories about the old people, and the stories of Hispanic culture, particularly Mexican, I think it has me thinking about it every time I draw." On another note, for a first-rate recent critical con-

sideration of Hernandez's Palomar series, see Charles Hatfield, "Heartbreak Soup: The Interdependency of Theme and Form," *Inks: Cartoon and Comic Art Studies* 4, no. 2 (1997): 2–17.

7. Gary Groth and Robert Fiore, eds., *The New Comics: Interviews from the Pages of "The Comics Journal"* (New York: Berkley Books, 1988), 302.

13

Performing Multiple Identities

Guillermo Gómez-Peña and His "Dangerous Border Crossings"

Juan Velasco

GUILLERMO GÓMEZ-PEÑA is one of the few Mexican performance artists who, since he came to the United States in 1978, has been able to create and explore the merging of visual language and text in the complexities of cross-cultural identities through controversial issues. Labeled by some as one of the most significant performance artists of the late twentieth century, he uses multiple media: video, performance, installation art, and bilingual poetry. In his "Performance Diaries" he explains the process of performance in his work as "a vast conceptual territory where my eclectic and ever-changing ideas and the ideas of my collaborators can be integrated into a coherent system and be put into practice. It's radical theory turned into praxis through movement, ritual, gesture, sound, light and spoken text" (Gómez-Peña 2000, 7).

His writings, like his performance work, point toward the dangers of commodification of indigenous and Latina/o identities into easily consumed pop culture products, and interrogate the redeeming potential of the poetics of hybridization in a world increasingly dominated by globalization. His best-known books include *Warrior for Gringostroika* (1993a), *The New World Border* (1996b), *Friendly Cannibals* (1996a), *Temple of Confessions* (Gómez-Peña and Sifuentes, 1997), and *Dangerous Border Crossers* (2000). Gomez-Peña's performance work has moved the term "border art" to the center, simultaneously exploring the complexities of the rich cultural and ethnic past of Latinas/os in the United States.

I will give special attention to the 1992 performance piece *Two Undiscovered Amerindians Visit . . .*, which became the video documentary (directed by Coco Fusco and Paula Heredia) *The Couple in the Cage* (1993), the performance and video documentary *Border Brujo* (1988, 1990), and his last book, *Dangerous Border Crossers* (2000). It is in these works that Gómez-Peña is able to link the very complex issues that make him controversial, going as far back as the colonial past when the notion of "Indian" was created as an empty signifier, a symbol of Otherness ready to be used for the Europeans' colonial ambitions, and fueled by the early development of capitalism. But the particularities of the performance work shape also the reenactments of the "modern" Other: "the dangerous border crossers." I will address Gómez-Peña's acts of interrogating the *mestizo's* otherness, the challenge to reflect on its multiple conditions, and its relationship with the indigenous past, especially through the more modern theoretical discourse of Xicanisma.

The Couple in the Cage, created in collaboration with Cuban American performance artist Coco Fusco, goes beyond criticism of the Quincentennial celebration of Columbus's voyage. Their successful tour through Europe and the United States translates the performance piece into "a critical intervention into the repertoire of displays and representations of 'the authentic Other'" (Kelly 1999, 125). Furthermore, Gómez-Peña and Fusco use the "Indian" as a beginning notion, a term that since the mid-sixteenth century is created as part of the discourse on the Other and the subsequent legitimization of its exploitation. More specifically, the performance piece is exposing the notion of "Indian" as linked to a "new world order."[1]

As part of these critical interventions of the past, *Border Brujo* addresses the new Other of the modern world: the border crossers, the presence of Latina/o culture and its physical bodies as perceived by the imperialist gaze of the United States. If the film *The Couple in the Cage* interrogates indigenous identities today, *Border Brujo* addresses some of the complexities of the term "Latina/o," its multiplicity, and the possibilities of further creation of identities surrounding the term "Indian."

Two main issues arise in the discussion of the performance works as they relate to the narrative strategies employed by Gómez-Peña and Fusco: Gómez-Peña and Fusco's impulse to interrogate how identity is constructed, performed, and commodified in visual and written culture; and their examination of the indigenous and the Latina/o subjects today as well as the dangers of erasure and recolonization implicit in some of its most recent projects of cultural representation.

THE INDIAN IN THE CAGE

Two Amerindians reminds us of the apocalyptic nightmare envisioned by Adorno when confronted with the prevalent rise of popular culture and the end of the modernist utopia. Guillermo Gómez-Peña and Coco Fusco take us to a world where the audiences' isolated consumerism of images and products cannot distinguish between artificial and real images of modern "Indians," especially when they are being transformed into spectacle and reduced to a cage. This move is a devastating critique of imperialism as the initial performance takes place in 1992, in Columbus Plaza, downtown Madrid. This is at its best a very significant year and area of Madrid, since it has been invested in the colonial imagination with a meaning assigned to its unique use of space. Looking from the Biblioteca Nacional (the National Library), the plaza is strategically situated. It is at the crossroads of two of the main arteries of downtown Madrid: Calle Serrano and Calle Colón. On the left side, walking from the library, you can see a statue of Columbus suspended in the air, so high you will almost miss it. On the right side of the plaza, gigantic monoliths of reddish stone with inscribed pre-Columbian symbols appear as América. Their presence is overpowering, but also alien to the European architecture that surrounds the plaza: Europe and pre-Columbian America, air and earth. If there was ever an intention of balance, their dialogue seems too strenuous, artificial, and difficult to situate. The meaning of the plaza escapes most walkers.

In 1992 Guillermo Gómez-Peña and his collaborator, Coco Fusco, crafted a performance, *Two Amerindians*, which was looking to bring new attention and meaning to this plaza in Spain. *The Couple in the Cage* constructs the "Indio" as a hybrid being; the elements of the performance emphasize and resemble the format of a turn-of-the-century freak show.

Presenting themselves as caged natives, as aboriginal inhabitants of an imaginary island in the Gulf of México, the performance artists reverse "traditional" tasks assigned to an "Indian" identity. In fact, the performance shows how Indian identity has been exploited, commodified, and exhibited over the last five hundred years throughout Europe and the United States. As explained in *Warrior for Gringostroika,*

> Coco Fusco and Gómez-Peña lived for three days in a golden cage at Columbus Plaza in Madrid as "Amerindians from the (fictional) island of Guatinaui." They were taken to the bathroom on leashes and hand-fed through the bars. Audience members could ask for "an authentic dance," a "story in Guatinaui," or a Polaroid. This piece was also performed at Covent Gardens, London; the Walker Art Center, Minneapolis; the Smithsonian Institution, Washington, D.C.; the Museum of Natural History, Sydney, Australia; the Field Museum, Chicago; the Whitney Museum of American Art, New York; and at other locations. (Gómez-Peña 1993a, 137)

Audiences all over the world contemplate the performers watching television, using the computer, or dancing, and "this performance piece staged the two in an ironic, reflexive gesture to the still widespread allure of native authenticity" (Kelly 1999, 114). The role of the audience becomes especially revealing since the "drama" of colonization is restaged in this encounter. The audience of modern times becomes part of the performance as they reproduce the role of the spectators in museums, circuses, world's fairs, and freak shows in Europe and the United States during the colonial and postcolonial periods: "The drama of discovery and display of native bodies—then and now—serves various functions. The indigenous bodies perform as a 'truth' factor; they 'prove' the material facticity of an 'other'" (Taylor 1998, 163).

As Indian identity becomes the physical embodiment of the Other, the scenarios envisioned by the colonizers become also part of a theatrical narrative that reveals how social, political, and racial hierarchies are justified. Moreover, both Fusco and Gómez-Peña disclose in this work the performative nature of identity, the "theatricality" of the encounters with different colonial powers, and "the aesthetic, political, and perspectival structures within which the characters are positioned and perform their prescribed roles" (Taylor 1998, 165).

To the film audience (to us), *The Couple in the Cage* is a metaphor to describe the Europeans' and Americans' inability to deal with the Indian's "difference." To the audience of the performance the Indians in the cage resemble the puzzling encounter with the Other because they do not know they are the audience, and they are unaware it is a performance. The voice of the narrator in the film speculates about the Western attempts to categorize and define the "differences" observed by Europeans and Americans as they analyze the native bodies, and how these attempts are conceptually mapping modern discourses on race.

Colonial discourse, created as an undeniable binary of "fixed" oppositional cultural identities, justifies the exploitation of the colonized, but it also reassures the cultural apparatus ultimately destined to maintain the superiority of the colonizers. As this radical separation is established, at least at the beginning, in the colonizers' mind the "Indio" is the savage, the inhabitant of a myth, and becomes a part of the discourse of the invention of America. And as such it develops as an empty signifier, a conceptual space ready to be employed as discourse on the legitimization of exploitation.

The Couple in the Cage then interrogates further the notion of "Native" as defined by colonial narratives, its moral integrity, and the modern responses of the audience to the contemporary dimensions of its definition. In doing this, Fusco and Gómez-Peña's theatrical "discovery" of the native bodies is also addressing the realm of cultural identity, and especially its performative nature. Showing caged natives as a legitimate spectacle in the twentieth century, and in the most "civilized" cities around the world, takes us also into the realm of the present-day notion of the "Indio." As I see it, Fusco and Gómez-Peña show us that in 1992, as in 1492, the Subject is still unable to understand indigenous nations as separate (from the Subject) cultural and social entities. In fact, this performance turns the ironic gaze inward, as we understand in this context that the notion of the "Indio," as the product of a colonial intervention (it takes the form of a nightmare or a dream), is still the result of a drastic separation between colonizers and colonized.

For Fusco and Gómez-Peña, the politics of identity should be translated and understood within the colonial context in which they were created. Thus, for the colonizers, law and order depend on the practices that reinforce this difference. For the colonized, survival depends on not recognizing this discourse, and the formation and continuation of their identity need to be understood in the context of an increasing fluidity and diversification that allow multiple forms of resistance. In physically reenacting this, Gómez-Peña and Fusco's notion of "performance of identity" very closely resembles the practices of agency and social identity exercised by indigenous groups. I see an identification between their work's continuous reenactments, its fluidity and positionality, and the practical reality of the creation of an "indigenous" consciousness since the colonial period.

THE PUEBLO'S MANY PRACTICES OF IDENTITY

What seemed from the point of view of imperial discourse a binary opposition becomes in the reality of the colonized a negotiated and interdependent practice, as illustrated by the formation of Pueblan identity after the Pueblo Revolt of 1680. This historical moment is crucial for the creation of an "indigenous" consciousness because it validates the indigenous claims to resist the invaders and the ability to redefine the patterns of construction of the Indians' multiple identities (Jemez, Hopi, Taos, and so on).

The 1680 revolt, then, is significant for two reasons: mainly because it is the first triumphant indigenous sedition within the modern territory of the United States, but also because it created a precedent for "indigenous" practices of resistance. Though Popé was considered by many the leader of the revolt, the actions were carefully planned between decentralized communities.

Cooperation and defiance resulted in the first Indian war of independence. For twelve years, Pueblans' freedom and autonomy also reinforced linguistic and cultural differences between nations. Yet the period was critical for the survival of their unified identity since it created the boundaries between "Hispanic" and "Pueblan" consciousness, between accommodation and resistance.

As the new situation developed, the multiple choices made by the different nations indicated that the boundaries were also flexible within the Pueblan community. In 1691 some representatives were petitioning for a Spanish return; others embraced a more syncretic Kiva religious practice (Sando 1991, 69). The "negotiated" Pueblan identity allowed them to re-create an energetic but flexible response to European aggression.

Identity became then a blueprint that was testing the limits of the impossible, given the new colonial situation, and the available forms of resistance. As such, the response to the new situation is always in transition and refuses to be defined within the boundaries of the colonial binary structure of identity. The performative nature of the process of deterritorialization of identity is understood and assigned different meanings depending on the historical actors (Gutiérrez 1991, 69). Looking at the agreements of 1706, Joe Sando reports that to what colonial forces considered a pact, some of the indigenous nations responded with the celebration of victory dances (1991, 80).

As the Pueblans were in the process of resisting the invasion, they also entered the process of reinventing and modeling multiple forms of identity that changed according to the different needs of the communities. Pueblan events of 1680 show the resistance to the invasion but also the flexibility and mobility by which the different nations viewed themselves. What is certain is that they never allied themselves with the dichotomy posited by the colonial's discourse of the Other, and Pueblan identity sought to challenge the advance of Western colonial ambitions with the display of its fixed binary notion of identity.

Fusco and Gómez-Peña's engagement in a counterhegemonic redeployment of norms in clearly significative ways shows us the changing notions of cultural identity and "the popular," and the strategies by which contemporary colonized groups can subvert the binary established by colonial powers. In this context I see Fusco and Gómez-Peña's notion of "performance of identity" as a crucial one. The notion of performance of identities in their work exposes the many layers by which we produce "the 'savage' body, and it historicized the practice by highlighting its citational character" (Taylor 1998, 5). Gómez-Peña's work is increasingly ambitious as his process of destabilizing meanings addresses also the *mestizo* experience, especially through *Border Brujo* and *Dangerous Border Crossers.*

BORDER BRUJO: INTERROGATING MESTIZO'S OTHERNESS

The same way *The Couple* exposes the discourse of exploitation and simultaneously interrogates indigenous identities, *Border Brujo* also interrogates and exposes the prejudice exercised on the "modern" Other:

> the so called "Border Crossers." *Border Brujo* is a performance piece
> that shows the multiple experiences and forms of Latina/o identity. As
> expressed in *Warrior for Gringostroika, Border Brujo* is a ritual, linguis-

tic, and performative journey across the United States/México border.
. . . *Border Brujo* puts a mirror between the two countries and then
breaks it in front of the audience. (Gómez-Peña 1993a, 75)

We should see these works as complementary since they interrogate two of the most significant cultural signs in terms of the representation of the Latina/o experience: the "Indian" and the "border." The
redeployment and simultaneous disruption of their liberatory potential
beyond the binary "cage" make these pieces (both performances and
textual narratives) some of the most relevant artistic contributions to
discussions on representation and identity.

Simultaneously, the development of the notion of "borderlands"
not only displaces notions of "border" connected to fixed constructions
of sexuality and race, but also brings into the center of the American unconscious the cultural and biological hybrid. As stated by Claire F. Fox,
"Gómez-Peña transforms himself into fifteen different personas to ex-
orcize the demons of dominant cultures. In English, Spanish, Spanglish,
Ingleñol and Náhuatl-bicameral" (1996, 232).

The metaphorical power of the crossing of geographical, spiritual,
cultural, and sexual borders is clearly demonstrated by Gloria Anzaldúa's autobiography, *Borderlands/La Frontera* (1987). For Anzaldúa's
narrative, the border is the central element in the process of self-con-
figuration of her identity. In fact, Anzaldúa rewrites the territory of
the border as multidimensional and uses the different levels of her experience to reflect and explore its ideological layers. Anzaldúa's *Bor-
derlands/La Frontera* not only redefines the space of the Borderland as
a more inclusive utopia, but also reinvents a different hero, the new
mestiza:

> That focal point or fulcrum, that juncture where the mestiza stands, is
> where phenomena tend to collide. It is where the possibility of uniting
> all that is separate occurs. . . . In attempting to work out a synthesis,
> the self has added a third element which is greater than the sum of its
> severed parts. That third element is a new consciousness—a mestiza
> consciousness. (79)

In comparing both works and their reconstruction of the border
trope, we see that what is truly remarkable is their unwillingness to

sustain the notion of "place" as the embodiment of cohesive and unified experiences of culture. Anzaldúa recuperates the border trope as a space in which experience (as opposed to the "frontier," the site of separation) can transcend individual "difference" to be reconstructed as a site of collective practice. The performance *Border Brujo* embodies and complements Anzaldúa's articulation of a new notion of "border" based on theories of syncretism and *mestizaje*. In both works, the artist assumes whiteness as a basis for "American" identity, and includes their cultural production within the Latin American tradition of *mestizaje* for empowerment and resistance.

The difference between both projects, though, should be attributed to the nature of the "heroes" who inhabit these borderlands. Following the Latin American tradition established by José Vasconcelos (in his analysis of America's heterogeneous cultural roots as essential characteristics of Latin American culture), Anzaldúa (1987) argues in "Towards a New Consciousness" that "From this racial, ideological, cultural and biological cross-pollinization, an 'alien' consciousness is presently in the making—a new 'mestiza' consciousness" (77). The *brujo* created in *Border Brujo*, on the other hand, seems uneasy about taking a role once it has taken over the space of the border. According to Claire F. Fox,

> The Brujo incarnates a mosaic of parodic characters including a *mojado*, a *cholo*, a Texas redneck, and a transvestite, who are differentiated from one another by variations in costume, body movement, and speech. The idea of alternation among personae, spaces, and languages is in fact so integral to the performance that it raises the issue whether Gómez-Peña would really like to see borders eliminated, or whether his work is indeed dependent upon borders to uphold the oppositions that he critiques. (1996, 233)

I would argue that the performative value of both his sole-authored and collaborative work is to destabilize the very specific idea of creating a new identity. In the light of *The Couple*, the performance becomes a rewritten space that underlines identity as a continual interrogation, rejecting all types of monolithic or fixed thought by dissolving its multiple meanings. Borrowing Garcia Canclini's 1995 critique of a depoliticized notion of hybrid cultures, Gómez-Peña seems skeptical of *Border Brujo* as a positive model of cultural hybridity, especially in the context of American culture and politics, "precisely because its elasticity and open nature . . . can be appropriated by anyone to mean practically anything" (Gómez-Peña 1993b, 62).

It is his positionality as a "dangerous border crosser" that characterizes the *brujo's* multiple Latina/o identities. The performance emphasizes the need constantly to reterritorialize the space, and calls for a constant interrogation of the conventional disguises of identity.

The performative value of these projects and the project's experimentation with new notions of identity should also be framed as the avant-garde of new works that examine *mestizo*-indigenous relationships. Among others, cultural critics had worried that the discourse of multiculturalism, as a progressive reappropriation of *mestizaje* by official discourse (under the new "multiracial" category), displaces the fluidity of Latina/o identities, eliminating the racial difference on which social justice is based.

Gómez-Peña's reconstruction of the border and its consecutive emphasis of Amerindian culture carries forward not only the importance of decentering privileged Eurocentric assumptions about nation and identity, but also the need to initiate the conditions for a critical form of Latina/o performativity that alternates between sincerity and subversion, irony and compliance. Gómez-Peña is not alone in this project, as other Latina/o cultural critics in the last few years have responded to the progressive reappropriation of the discourse of hybridity by the state with the notion of Xicanisma: a call for a return to the Amerindian roots of most Latinos as well as a call for a strategic alliance to give agency to Native American groups.

Roberto Rodríguez's *X in La Raza* (1996) includes three chapters: "Who Declared War on the Word 'Chicano'?" "The Missing X in the Treaty of Guadalupe," and "The X in Xicano." In "A Continuation of Indian Removal," Rodríguez states that "Mexicanos—independent of the statistical and ideological manipulations of burrocrats—are Indians" (40). Implicit in the "X" of more recent configurations of "Xicano" and "Xicanisma" is a criticism not only of the term "Hispanic" but of the racial poetics of the "multiracial" within Mexican and American culture.

As the United States progressively reappropriates the multiracial (or *mestizo*) identity as part of the "popular," the multiracial-multicultural discourse is no longer Eurocentric. In many ways, *The Couple* and *Border Brujo* ally themselves with the new Xicanistas.

In "The 'X' in Race and Gender," I argued that if we compare racial theories of "Mexicanness" from classics such as José Vasconcelos and Alfonso Reyes to the recast of the ethnic self produced by contemporary Xicano texts in the United States, we find a new emphasis on the "X" as signifier of race (1996, 221). While for Reyes and Vasconcelos the project for racial and cultural *mestizaje* would fully develop the construction of a homogeneous, *mestizo* national identity, for the Xicanistas, Reyes and Vasconcelos's project becomes a theoretical and integrationist mechanism formulated to negate the "Indian" through conformity and nationalism.[2] For these new Xicanistas, the "X" is associated not with the politics of *mestizaje* but with the recuperation of the racial and cultural Indian self: "'X' could have the same value to Raza as it does to African Americans—representing the indigenous names, the language and our history that was taken from us" (Rodríguez 1996, 86).

Likewise I would like to emphasize the role of the indigenous figure in Ana Castillo's *Massacre of the Dreamers: Essays on Xicanisma* (1994). While avoiding the elitist theories of Me(x)icanness developed by Vasconcelos, this literature redefines the "X" as the signifier of race in a significative way. In *Massacre of the Dreamers* Castillo states that the core of her Latina identity is found when "I stand firm that I am that Mexic Amerindian woman's consciousness" (17). Furthermore, Castillo uses the metaphor of the *tapiz* to further develop her concept of "Mexic Amerindian woman" and Xicanisma. The "X" of what Castillo calls the "conscienticized poetics" of the Xicanista corresponds with a new notion of color and identity that involves a revision of theories of *mestizaje* to reevaluate the Indian woman as the very core of the racial identity. In the same line, the work of Gómez-Peña calls for a more complex and situational *mestizo* subject.

Returning to the performance *The Couple in the Cage*, I would argue that the title more accurately refers to the dichotomy that the two symbols of the Columbus Plaza in Madrid are trying to encapsulate. The small statue of Columbus suspended in the air as symbol of the Subject and the heavier, gigantic, pre-Columbian rocks on the plaza as a symbol of the Other have become the couple that have been condemned to constantly redefine each other since 1492, trapped in the cage set up by colonial ambitions. Fusco and Gómez-Peña's performance piece also aims at escaping the binary structure provided by colonial discourse in recasting cultural and racial differences of *mestizo* people in terms of positionality. The redefinition allows the audience to dismantle the notion of the Other, to open a new space from which to claim the historicized experience of Latinas/os from a position of "border crossing," and to act accordingly.

This rhetorical operation as applied to culture constitutes itself as a new subject within the paradigm of a dynamic and fluid identity in constant motion. The *brujo* (ultimately Gómez-Peña) becomes the representation of the "dangerous border crosser." Continued analysis of these performances together with the many books produced by Gómez-Peña offers multiple layers of complexity. The diverse meanings behind the notion of the Other in his work also seem to change as the context of the political circumstances changes. As his work becomes an invitation to keep questioning in the final and dangerous act of border crossing, I would ask if Fusco and Gómez-Peña are manipulating the image of the *Indio* in *The Couple in the Cage* in order to help them reconcile their own particular raw feelings of the *mestizo*'s Otherness in Europe and the United States. Or perhaps they are looking at the "Indianness" of the performance in *indigenista* terms, using the signifier of colonial times to shock the audience, creating a chronicle of our collective responsibility for the erasure of the Indian in the present?

NOTES

1. Coco Fusco further explores this link in her performance collaboration with Nao Bustamante called "Stuff" (1997).

2. For some references to a critique of Chicanos' use of Indigenous images, see "An Open letter to Chicanas: On Power and Politics of Origin," by Hernández-Ávila (1992).

BIBLIOGRAPHY

Aldama, Frederick Luis. "The New Millennial Xicano: An Interview with Guillermo Gómez-Peña." *Xcp: Cross-Cultural Poetics* 5 (1999): 7–11.

Anzaldúa, Gloria. *Borderlands/La Frontera*. San Francisco: Aunt Lute Books, 1987.

Castillo, Ana. *Massacre of the Dreamers: Essays on Xicanisma*. New York: Plume/Penguin, 1994.

Cohen, Sarah R. "Performing Identity in the Hard Nut: Stereotype, Modeling, and the Inventive Body." *Yale Journal of Criticism: Interpretation in the Humanities* 11, no. 2 (1998): 485–505.

Fishman, Jenn. "Performing Identities: Female Cross-Dressing in She Ventures and He Wins." *Restoration: Studies in English Literary Culture, 1600–1700* 20, no. 1 (1996): 36–51.

Fox, Claire F. "Mass Media, Site Specificity, and the U.S.-México Border: Guillermo Gómez-Peña's *Border Brujo* (1988, 1990)." In *The Ethnic Eye: Latino Media Arts,* ed. Chon Noriega. Minneapolis: University of Minnesota Press, 1996.

Fusco, Coco, and Nao Bustamante. "Stuff." *Drama Review* 41, no. 4 (winter 1997): 63–82.

García Canclini, Néstor. *Hybrid Cultures: Strategies for Entering and Leaving Modernity.* Trans. Christopher L. Chiappari and Silvia L. López. Minneapolis: University of Minnesota Press, 1995.

Gil-Gómez, Ellen M. *Performing La Mestiza: Textual Representations of Lesbians of Color and the Negotiation of Identities.* New York: Garland, 2000.

Gómez-Peña, Guillermo. *Warrior for Gringostroika: Essays, Performance Texts, and Poetry.* St. Paul, MN: Graywolf, 1993a.

———. "The Free Art Agreement/El Tratado de Libre Cultura." *High Performance* 63 (fall 1993b): 58–63.

———. *Friendly Cannibals.* San Francisco: Artspace, 1996a.

———. *The New World Border: Prophecies, Poems, and Loqueras for the End of the Century.* San Francisco: City Lights, 1996b.

———. *Dangerous Border Crossers: The Artist Talks Back.* New York: Routledge, 2000.

Gómez-Peña, Guillermo, and Roberto Sifuentes, eds. *Temple of Confessions: Mexican Beasts and Living Santos.* New York: powerHouse Cultural Entertainment, 1997.

Gutiérrez, Ramón. *When Jesus Came, the Corn Mothers Went Away: Marriage, Sexuality, and Power in New Mexico, 1500–1846.* Stanford: Stanford University Press, 1991.

Hernández-Ávila, Inés. "An Open Letter to Chicanas: On Power and Politics of Origin." In *With-out Discovery: A Native Response to Columbus,* ed. Ray González. Seattle: Broken Moon Press, 1992.

Johnson, Anna. "Guillermo Gómez-Peña and Coco Fusco." *Bomb* 42 (1993): 36–39.

Joseph, May. "New Hybrid Identities: Performing Race Gender Nation Sexuality." *Women and Performance: A Journal of Feminist Theory* 7–8, no. 2 (1995): 14–15.

Kelly, Mary Kate. "Performing the Other: A Consideration of Two Cages." *College Literature* 26, no. 1 (1999): 113–36.

Limón, José. "Selena: Sexuality, Performance, and the Problematic of Hegemony." In *Reflexiones 1997: New Directions in Mexican American Studies,* ed. Neil Foley. Austin: University of Texas Press, 1997.

Neustadt, Robert. "(Con)fusing Cultures: Guillermo Gómez-Peña and the Transgression of Borders." *Mattoid* 3217 (1998): 65–79.

Rodríguez, Roberto. *X in La Raza*. Albuquerque: Roberto Rodríguez, 1996.

Sando, Joe S. *Pueblo Nations: Eight Centuries of Pueblo Indian History*. Santa Fe: Clear Light, 1991.

Taylor, Diana. "A Savage Performance: Guillermo Gómez-Peña and Coco Fusco's 'Couple in the Cage.'" *Drama Review: A Journal of Performance Studies* 42, no. 2 (1998): 5, 160–75.

Vasconcelos, José. *La Raza Cosmica/The Cosmic Race*. Los Angeles: Centro de Publicaciones, Department of Chicano Studies, Los Angeles, California State University, 1979.

Velasco, Juan. "The 'X' in Race and Gender: Rethinking Chicano/a Cultural Production through the Paradigms of Xicanisma and Me(x)icanness." *Americas Review* 24, nos. 3–4 (1996): 218-30.

Vercoe, Caroline. "Agency and Ambivalence: A Reading of Works by Coco Fusco." In *Body Politics and the Fictional Double*, ed. Debra Walker King. Bloomington: Indiana University Press, 2000.

Wolford, Lisa. "Guillermo Gómez-Peña: An Introduction." *Theatre Topics* 9, no. 1 (1999): 89–91.

SPORTS

14

Learning America's Other Game

Baseball, Race, and the Study of Latinos

Adrian Burgos, Jr.

BECOMING PART OF THE GAME

Baseball has been hailed as the U.S. national pastime since the late nineteenth century. Many Americans have invested it with symbolic meaning, making the game representative of larger ideals, values, and beliefs. Americans have imagined baseball as a sport that literally separated the men from the boys. They have also idealized the game as a melting pot that forged Americans out of a nation of immigrants. Seizing on these beliefs, social commentators have proclaimed the sport "America's game." As a popular cultural institution, professional baseball has thus served as a principal site where ideas of national identity, masculinity, and race were performed on green playing fields before a national audience.

At the end of the nineteenth century, sporting goods entrepreneurs such as A. G. Spalding joined a chorus of "progressive" reformers who believed baseball should "follow the flag" as the United States expanded overseas in search of new markets. These advocates for America's game believed the sport would teach new subject peoples in Puerto Rico, Cuba, and the Philippines about American (U.S.) culture and values. Their belief reveals that baseball was always more than just a game.

Anyone watching coverage on professional baseball provided by the nation's premier sports networks (e.g., ESPN or FOXSports) is left with an indelible impression: baseball surely followed the flag. The globalization of America's game is evident in the presence of players from the Spanish-speaking Americas, Asia, and Australia in Major League uniforms. Latino players have been particularly noticeable among these "foreigners." The sport's All-Star Games seemed a virtual showcase for Latino players such as Pedro Martínez, Alex Rodríguez, Nomar Garciaparra, Bernie Williams, and Sammy Sosa, to name a few. For some observers, the Latino presence is a reflection of baseball's continued place as America's game. Others frame it in terms of another recent phenomenon—the "Latin boom," the "discovery" by the mainstream culture. For many North Americans, Sosa, Garciaparra, and Orlando "El Duque" Hernandez in baseball are as hot as Ricky Martin, Marc Anthony, and Jennifer Lopez in music.

Hosted by salsa singer Marc Anthony, the July 15 telecast of Fox's All-Star Game edition of *This Week in Baseball* demonstrated the linking of baseball with the "Latin boom." His songs interwoven throughout the telecast, Anthony interviewed Sosa and Garciaparra among other Latino all-stars who spoke with pride about representing Latinos and their respective homelands, be it Puerto Rico, the Dominican Republic, or the United States. This show illuminated the way these men self-identified in transnational ways; Anthony himself discussed the meaning of the Puerto Rican anthem "Preciosa," a song he described as capturing his pride as an American and a Puerto Rican. Baseball and salsa became further intertwined at a concert where Bernie Williams, a classical guitar player, joined Marc Anthony onstage. The show captured a current theme in U.S. popular culture: "Latinos are in."[1]

Taking into consideration the dominant narrative about baseball as a popular cultural institution, we can understand professional baseball as a playing field where different ethnic groups sought to gain acceptance as fellow Americans. The current popularity of players like Sosa and others belies the fact that the path to the "big leagues" has also meant facing a peculiar set of issues regarding their racial and national identity. This chapter links the contemporary issues Latinos face with the experience of the first U.S.-born player from the Spanish-speaking Americas to play in the Major Leagues, Vincent Nava. In particular, I discuss how Nava's racial and ethnic identity was viewed by his contemporaries and how twentieth-century baseball historians have often placed him within the black and white binary, thereby explaining away the "brownness" that his contemporaries acknowledged. In so doing, we gain an appreciation for the similarities between the treatment of Nava and the way contemporary Latino players are confronted with a conundrum when they enter the U.S. playing field: I am black or white. How they deal with this question and still maintain their appeal to North American fans, the media, and advertisers to reap (financial) rewards reveals how they too learn how to play "America's game."

WHO WAS "SANDY" NAVA?

I first came across Nava several years ago while perusing a special pictorial dedicated to nineteenth-century baseball. The periodical contained a photograph of the 1884 Providence Grays baseball team.[2] Included in the photo was a "Cuban" player, Sandy Nava, the team's reserve catcher. Nava was a relative unknown in the annals of baseball. I had not previously come across him in my initial years of dissertation research on Latinos in North American professional baseball. His name did not appear in published lists of Latin American or Latino Major Leaguers who played prior to Jackie Robinson and the breaking of baseball's color line in 1947, a short list in either case. Thus, his place in Latino baseball history intrigued me, prompting follow-up research on the mysterious mustachioed player in the photograph.[3]

Nava's nationality and identity represent a mystery whose solution could significantly alter our historical knowledge about the participation of Latinos in the U.S. national pastime. Born in San Francisco on April 12, 1850, he was no more than a modest talent who was never a full-time starter in the Major Leagues; he was among the early contingent of West Coast players to appear in the National League—the highest-ranking professional league in the United States.[4] Adding to the mystery surrounding his identity, somewhere along his travels Nava acquired the nickname Sandy—a name that would be a source of confusion for historians.[5] This confusion was manifested in Nava's entries in the standard baseball encyclopedias that listed his name as Vincent Nava, Sandy Irwin, and even Irwin Sandy.[6] Clearly not of "Spanish" origins, the name "Irwin Sandy" alluded to the possibility that this player was not even Latino.

Our understanding of the construction of Latino identity not only strongly affects Nava's place in baseball history, it also gives us cause to reconsider the spread of America's game. At one level, if Nava was indeed a U.S.-born Latino, his participation in the Major Leagues signified the game's spread westward to California and into its Latino population. This expansion westward in the 1860s and 1870s paralleled baseball's transport south to Cuba.[7] Thus, the history of the game's spread initiated a process whereby in the twentieth century many Latinos on either side of the U.S. territorial borders would share baseball as a common cultural practice—a distinction separating them from most European immigrants, who came from non–baseball-playing cultures. This distinction, moreover, facilitated the articulation of a Latino identity as a pan-ethnic identity in North American professional baseball during the twentieth century.

The question whether he could be labeled a Latino and/or the first Mexican American Major Leaguer raises several methodological concerns about the ethnic identity of players from the Spanish-speaking Americas. First, the issue of his identity speaks to the issue of how Latino identity is articulated in the United States at the individual level. Second, it raises the issue about theorizing a foundational base upon which Latino identity is shared by these players from throughout the Spanish-speaking Americas. These concerns beckon examination of the reception of these players in North American professional baseball circles, specifically, whether fellow Major Leaguers, league management, baseball fans, or the print media viewed the Latino players who performed in the segregated Major Leagues as different from themselves in terms of national or racial identity.

In the hope of locating additional documents that would help decipher the mystery, I scoured through Nava's biographical player file at the National Baseball Library. Holding few documents, it did contain important clues as to his ethnic identity, a copy of his 1906 death certificate. The certificate stated that his mother was born in Mexico and his father in "America." Since Nava died unmarried, his housemate of over a decade, Thomas Healy, acted as the informant who shared the deceased's family history.[8] The death certificate thus provides hearsay evidence, since Healy could only share what he had learned from Nava. Considering the ballplayer's 1850 birth date, one can estimate that his father was probably born between the late 1810s and early 1830s. Given this time frame, the elder Nava's birthplace, "America," in all likelihood referred to the geographical region then known as the "American frontier"—territories not yet officially incorporated as part of the United States. Thus, the death certificate clarified part of the confusion concerning his identity. Born to a Mexican mother and an "American" father, Nava could lay claim as the first Mexican American in the Major

Leagues. This claim requires further validation, especially if his contemporaries did not consider him different in terms of their identity as white Americans.

Nava traveled a long way to make his initial appearance with Providence's National League squad in 1882—the league had no team west of Chicago. When he arrived in the National League circuit, the ballplayer's physical appearance, noticeable "foreignness," and possible racial difference prompted intrigue among the league's following. The racial and ethnic cues they read from the catcher's physical appearance and personal background led aficionados, newspaper scribes, and fellow players to consistently refer to Nava as "the Spaniard."[9]

Journalists from throughout the country emphasized several aspects of the catcher's difference from the white mainstream. At various points in its coverage the *New York Clipper* referred to him as *Don* Irwin, the little Spaniard, and *Señor* Irwin. Writers from the *Chicago Tribune* echoed this description of Nava, calling him "the little Spaniard," while the baseball columnist from the *National Police Gazette* chimed in by identifying him as "Nara [*sic*] the plucky little Spanish catcher."[10] In addition to phenotypical features, sportswriters alluded to language practices in constructing the California native's difference. One *National Police Gazette* column mocked an attempt by John Montgomery Ward to coach Nava, his "Spanish protégée": "Hi, Senor! quito offi il firsto basilo et makadagio towardso secundo basilo liki hellio!"[11] This portrayal is curious considering Nava's birth in San Francisco, his fluency in English according to census records, and the fact that the ballplayer lived his entire life in the United States. Another cogent example of the construction of Nava's difference came in the form of a lyrical parody entitled "Nava Pinafored," originally published in the *Detroit Free Press* and later reproduced in other contemporary periodicals such as the *Chicago Tribune*:

NAVA PINAFORED

I am the catcher of the Providence club.

Chorus—
And a very good catcher, too.

Solo—
You're very very good,

And be it understood,
    There's one thing he don't do.

Chorus—
He's very very good,
And be it understood,
    There's one thing he don't do.

Solo—
Tho' at wielding the ash
I seldom make a dash,
    And sometimes pop an easy fly,
When I don my little mask
I'm all you can ask,
For I Nava let a ball go by.

Chorus—
What, Nav

Solo—
No, Nava

Chorus—
What, Nav

Solo—
Well, hardly Ava.

Chorus—
Hardly Ava lets a ball go by;
Then give three cheers, and a rub, dub, dub,
For the Spanish catcher on the Providence club.[12]

Publication of these lyrics in newspapers throughout the National League circuit confirmed several ideas about the cultural response of North Americans to the entry of Spanish-speaking Americans. First, the published lyrics illustrated how the sporting press actively participated in marking Nava as different, and how the print media circulated ideas of racial and/or ethnic difference. Second, these lyrics offer a vivid example of how baseball fans, the sporting press, professional players, and league management were made aware of the "Spanish" presence in the Major Leagues. This practice of marking individuals from the Spanish-speaking Americas continued into the twentieth century, as seen in the reception of the more than fifty Cuban, Puerto Rican, Mexican, and Venezuelan players who entered the segregated Major Leagues prior to 1947.

BECOMING "LATINO" IN THE MAJOR LEAGUES

The nineteenth-century racialization of Vincent Nava—the construction of his foreignness—set a precedent for the racialization of Latinos in the twentieth century. The approach required to establish the cultural significance of Latino players in baseball history illuminates the need for an interdisciplinary methodology. Long neglected within studies of American popular culture, evidence of Latino participation must be culled from a variety of sources that were produced in the U.S. mainstream and Latino communities as well as throughout the Spanish-speaking Americas. These sources move us closer to the world Latino players inhabited, including their interactions at different points along their travels and others' reactions to their presence.

The U.S. English-language sporting press encountered some difficulty covering a cohort of "foreign" players whose primary language was not necessarily English. The result of their coverage has greatly affected the scholars who followed. Although the U.S. sporting press attempted to present objective coverage of Latino Major Leaguers, language difference presented a barrier that often prevented clear communication between reporters and players. Yet the problem was not just language difference. Many North American reporters perceived and wrote about these players through the perspective of the period's popular racial ideology. A mixture in reporting resulted. Some reporters employed ideas of cultural supremacy and notions of racial hierarchy in describing the play and personality of players from the Spanish-speaking Americas. Such writing often exoticized these players, portraying them in their "native," uncivilized settings and on numerous occasions as inarticulate, indolent "hotheads"—a label most Latino players, even Sammy Sosa, have had attached to them during their careers. Often relying on ethnocentric notions of race, civilization, and Americanness, these portrayals present an image shaped more by cultural notions of where these players were from (Spanish-speaking countries) than the players' abilities.

The images of Latino players produced by the U.S. sporting press have a particularly wide historical range. Scholars who examine baseball's twentieth-century history are left with primary documents (newspapers and magazines) incapable of fully capturing the experience of Latinos, particularly the Spanish-dominant player's perspective. Subsequently, written histories based on primary documents from the U.S. English-language media have tended to marginalize Latinos. For example, in their discussions of race relations in professional baseball, historians have particularly focused on Jackie Robinson and the project of baseball's integration.[13] In becoming the twentieth century's first black Major Leaguer, Robinson faced the brunt of white player hostility and institutionalized racist practices. Initiating the radical transformation of professional baseball's workplace, Robinson's successful entry was heralded in numerous corners as a significant change in social practice and an important advance in racial tolerance in the United States. Contrary to popular perception, however, Robinson was not the century's first player "of color" in the majors.[14] Over fifty players from the Spanish-speaking Americas appeared in the majors before Robinson in the segregated Major Leagues. Yet an in-depth analysis of their impact on professional baseball's racial system has remained beyond the scope of most discussion of the integration of America's game. Stating that the "Latin" players who entered were white, most historians mute the conflicts that often arose with the entry of these different players.

The tendency to pigeonhole Latinos into categories of black or white reflects the dominance of the black-and-white paradigm among U.S. baseball historians.[15] At the surface, the racial binary enables the explanation of racial prejudice and the persistence of Jim Crow segregation in professional baseball. However, as the lived experience of Latino and Native American players bore witness, there also existed "brown" and "red" racial categories during Jim Crow baseball. The existence of these two categories presented room for negotiation around the color line such that the league's rank and file was not exclusively white. In the case of individuals from the Spanish-speaking Americas, most of whom were seen as racially ambiguous, this meant an opportunity to enter the Major League playing field by strategically emphasizing their foreignness, thereby placing themselves outside the dominant binary. The result for more than fifty players was access, although not quite acceptance as fellow whites. Indeed, their positioning outside the binary also meant that they would never quite be either fully white or black in the U.S. sense. Just as significant, the manner in which these players gained entry illuminated the complicity of Major League organizations, particularly the Cincinnati Reds and the Washington Senators, who had approximately half of the Latino players debut in their uniforms during Jim Crow. These organizations and the players did encounter resistance at the Major League and minor league levels, as the cases of Rafael Almeida and Armando Marsans with Cincinnati and Luis Padron with New Britain (Connecticut League) illustrate.

ENTERING THE U.S. PLAYING FIELDS: LESSONS LEARNED

Newspaper coverage of the Cincinnati Reds' 1911 signing of two Cuban players, Rafael Almeida and Armando Marsans, illuminates resistance to their incorporation into Major League baseball. The arrival of the Cuban duo in towns throughout the National League circuit pricked the consciousness of fans, players, management, and the sporting press. A number of them were uneasy about Almeida and Marsans, expressing suspicions about the Cuban players' racial ancestry. Such reaction was typical within professional baseball. As early as 1908, when they played as part of a Cuban quartet for the Connecticut League's New Britain club, U.S. fans vocalized suspicions.[16] The clamor reached such a level that after the league's 1908 season, the team owners reinstituted a color line. Concerned with the league's edict, New Britain's owner traveled to Cuba during the 1908–1909 winter to verify his players' racial status, conducting family interviews and checking players' birth certificates. Only one of the four Cubans, Luis Padron, failed the test, prompting the exclusion of the lone "Negro" from the league. Padron resurfaced the following season (1909) in the Negro Leagues, where he played over the next three decades.

A further indication of the limitations of the U.S. black and white binary, is the fact that concerns about the race of Cuban players did not subside. When the Cincinnati Reds became interested in signing Almeida, the process of verifying his race began anew. The organization's interest in the Cuban infielder began in Cuba, where a barnstorming team composed of Reds players led by Frank Bancroft was competing against Cuban professional teams. Impressed by Almeida, Bancroft wrote a letter to Cincinnati's team president, Garry Herrman, that included a scouting report that concluded, "Wish we had him. He is not colored."[17] Intrigued by the prospect, Herrman sent inquiries to sportswriters who covered the Connecticut circuit. Among those who replied, the terse letter written by J. F. Sullivan typified the ambivalence toward the incorporation of Cuban players into the white professional leagues. Offering some basic information on Almeida, Sullivan observed, "Were he a white man, he might be good for the big show. He is a Cuban, all right, not a nigger. But I find the presence of these Cubans breeds discontent here and I think it would do so even more on a major league club."[18]

Sullivan's letter raised several red flags that would have deterred most Major League officials from pursuing Almeida any further. First, it warned about the divisiveness the Cuban presence would cause among Major Leaguers, a principal warning that segregationists offered in seeking to maintain the status quo. Second, his letter reiterated the racial difference between whites, African Americans, and Cubans. Sullivan's and Bancroft's, descriptions of Almeida captured the cognitive dissonance in U.S. racial perception toward the Cuban infielder specifically and Latinos in general. Despite the varied opinions about Almeida's talent and the concerns about his racial stock, Cincinnati pressed forward. Concerned about public perception, local supporters of the Reds' signing felt compelled to demonstrate their support. In defense of the signing, one *Cincinnati Enquirer* reporter wrote,

> Ladies and Gentlemen, we have in our midst two descendants of a noble Spanish race, *with no ignoble African blood* to place a blot or spot on their escutcheons. Permit me to introduce two of the *purest bars of Castilian soap* that ever floated to these shores, Senors Alameda [*sic*] and Marsans.[19]

The article lauding the racial stock of Almeida and Marsans proved necessary. A full-page story published in several large urban newspapers, including the *Detroit Free Press* and the *Philadelphia Inquirer*, carried a photograph of the two Cubans in full Reds uniform. Evidently, their appearance in print unsettled some observers, for the photo rendered their "race" visible. At the very least, it reiterated that Almeida and Marsans, his countryman, were not white in the U.S. sense.

Examination of contemporary press coverage as well as the coverage of Nava and Almeida unveils the racialization of Latino players and disputes the claim that Latino players who have participated in America's game fit within the black-white binary. Simply declaring those who played during Jim Crow white contradicts their placement into ethnoracial categories and their experience of being the target of racialized ethnic slurs while African Americans remained excluded.[20] The black-white paradigm thus fails to capture how race has operated as a "metalanguage" in the United States.[21] The press and fan treatment of individuals from the Spanish-speaking Americas gave further evidence of the flexibility of the U.S. racial system beyond black and white. In the context of the Major Leagues, the presence of Latinos forced baseball's racial system to expand by forming new racial/ethnic categories such as "Castilian" that conferred a circumscribed whiteness or revising older categories such as a notion of "Spanish" identity that emphasized that certain "Latin" players came from Spanish descent of pure blood with no intermixture with Africans (blacks).

The way Latinos demonstrated the lessons they learned from playing America's game—baseball—and performing racial identities—has been lost on most baseball historians due to the lack of an integrated approach that incorporated transnational identity and cultural practices. What has often occurred in studies of "Latins" in professional baseball is that those born in U.S. Latino communities are treated as a distinct group; that is, historians have tended to separate them from their compatriots born outside the United States. This occurs despite the history of racialization where individuals from the Spanish-speaking Americas have tended to homogenize the group within U.S. professional baseball. This typically affects Puerto Ricans born stateside as they are often excluded from the category of "Latin" while those born on the island are included, although Puerto Rico has been a U.S. territorial possession since 1898. Consequently, current Major Leaguers like Bobby Bonilla and Jose Rosado—born in New York and New Jersey, respectively—are not identified as "Latins" in some historical treatments, even though in the case of Rosado his family moved to Puerto Rico while he was still a toddler.[22] This geographically determined notion of identity fails to take into account the role of migration as a critical aspect of Latino experience and identity in the twentieth century, especially as U.S. economic activity took on a more pan-American operational character. Similarly, such a notion does not capture the ways Latinos, regardless of country of birth, identified themselves in transnational ways. Wherever they moved, Latinos formed new bonds of affinity by creating social, political, and cultural institutions such as Spanish-language newspapers, mutual aid societies, bilingual church congregations, and baseball teams that bore the names of their native towns. These institutions reflect how Latinos maintained their ethnic ties and identity connected to their land of origins while living in the United States; however, it has not meant that they saw themselves as any less American.

The popular representation of Latinos in baseball today and its presentation as a recent phenomenon tend to overlook the history of Latino participation that dates back to the 1870s. Surface-level discussion of their presence today as an indication of baseball's continued role as a melting pot misses a much longer history of participation by individuals from the Spanish-speaking Americas. Their entry onto the game's greatest stage has not necessarily translated into acceptance of Latinos in everyday life. The Pedro Martinezes and Sammy Sosas of the baseball world are somewhat easier to accept than those bearing the same names but who work in the fields or factories or are on the poverty rolls. Latinos in U.S. society continue to face questions posed in a manner that forces them to decide between black and white (and that excludes their self-identification as something more akin to being brown). It is a choice that has taken on new significance as we enter the twenty-first century, when Latinos are poised to become the largest minority group in the United States and the 2000 census still imposed a dichotomy that falls beyond the pale of the racial experience of Latinos. In the world of professional baseball, closer examination of the careers of Latino ballplayers unveils a history of countless slights, misunderstandings, and recriminations for being different from both white and black Americans. As such, it is not a recent phenomenon; individuals from the Spanish-speaking Americas involved in America's game have long struggled to gain equal footing as fellow Americans and also to gain recognition for being "brown" in a black and white "field of dreams."

NOTES

A number of individuals and institutions contributed to this chapter. The University of Michigan's Rackham Graduate School provided a discretionary grant to fund a research trip to Cooperstown, New York. Thanks to the National Baseball Library and Archive's research staff, in particular Tim Wiles and Scot Mondore. Jerry Malloy, Joel Franks, and Bob Timmerman shared important documents and insights about Vincent Nava and nineteenth-century baseball. Thanks to the editors of this volume for their insightful reading and comments. Finally, thanks to Dolly Túa-Burgos, who always challenges me with insightful questions and pushes my writing in important ways.

1. The issue of applying contemporary labels such as "Latino" versus "Spanish" hints at some of the difficulties historians encounter when dealing with people from the Spanish-speaking Americas in a U.S. context. "Latino" captures more adequately the intermixture of cultures and race(s) that "Spanish" fails to connote. As labels of identity, "Spanish" and "hispano" tend to privilege Hispanic culture or were used to imply direct lineage from Spain.

2. John Thorn and Mark Rucker, eds., "Special Pictorial Issue: The Nineteenth Century," *National Pastime* 3, no. 1 (1984): 54.

3. Nava was not the first player from the Spanish-speaking Americas to appear in the U.S. "Major Leagues." That distinction belongs to Cuban-born Esteban Bellán, who picked up the game while receiving his secondary-level and collegiate education at New York City's St. John's College, present-day Fordham University.

4. Nava played with Providence until 1884 before briefly appearing with Baltimore (American Association) in 1885 and 1886. Nineteenth-century baseball clubs typically had fourteen-player rosters. Roster size along with the rudimentary protective equipment made the position of catcher physically demanding, and doubly important for a team to have an able reserve catcher. Thus, Nava represented a valuable member of the Providence team.

5. Joel Franks, a researcher of professional baseball's history in California, suggests that Nava's nickname, Sandy, could have been an Anglicization of Vincent. Personal communication with Franks, August 1998.

6. Some of this confusion may have been exacerbated by the fact that Nava occasionally played infield positions in nonleague games and that one of his Providence teammates was Arthur "Sandy" Irwin, the team's regular shortstop. The two played together during the 1883 and 1884 seasons and are clearly identified in the 1884 team photograph.

7. Baseball arrived in Cuba in the mid-1860s, transported primarily by students returning from their studies in the United States. Tensions surrounding issues of national independence, slavery, and economics fueled external immigration during the 1860s and 1870s as the Ten Years War (1868–1878) was fought between Spanish and Cuban insurgent forces. During these two decades, Cuban émigrés in the United States gained their first extensive exposure to baseball. In 1879 a professional league was established. During the thirty years of insurgent activity for independence (1868–1898), Cuban migrants transported the game throughout the Spanish-speaking Caribbean Basin. On baseball in nineteenth-

century Cuba, see Louis A. Pérez, "Between Baseball and Bullfighting: The Quest for Nationality in Cuba, 1868–1898," *Journal of American History* 81, no. 2 (September 1994): 493–517; and Roberto González Echevarría, "The Game in Matanzas: On the Origins of Cuban Baseball," *Yale Review* 83 (July 1995): 62–94. On the Dominican Republic, see Rob Ruck, *The Tropic of Baseball* (Westport, CT: Meckler, 1991); and Alan M. Klein, *Sugarball: The American Game, the Dominican Dream* (New Haven: Yale University Press, 1991).

8. Nava player file, National Baseball Library and Archive (hereafter NBLA), Cooperstown, NY. Evidently, Nava and Healy were friends for a number of years. They are listed as sharing a residence in the 1900 U.S. census at 363 Davis, and according to the Baltimore City directory they shared another residence at 219 Bathe in 1906. Thanks to Bob Timmerman for sharing these important documents.

9. "Eighteen-Inning Game and Only One Run Made," August 1882; and "The Opening Game of the Base Ball Season in Providence," 8 April 1883; Nava player file, NBLA.

10. *New York Clipper*, 25 March 1882, 5; 22 April 1882, 74; *Chicago Tribune*, 21 May 1883, 10; 31 May 1883, 7; 10 June 1883, 16; and 22 June 1883, 8; and *National Police Gazette*, 4 October 1884, 11.

11. *New York Clipper*, 27 March 1883.

12. This version of the Nava song appeared in *Chicago Tribune*, 25 June 1882, 9. Thanks to Jerry Malloy, who shared this version; a slightly different version appears in Lee Allen, *The Cincinnati Reds* (New York: Putnam, 1948), 96–97.

13. The seminal work on baseball's integration continues to be Jules Tygiel, *Baseball's Great Experiment: Jackie Robinson and His Legacy* (New York: Oxford University Press, 1993). For other scholarly studies of Robinson, see Arnold Rampersad, *Jackie Robinson: A Biography* (New York: Knopf, 1997); Jules Tygiel, ed., *The Jackie Robinson Reader: Perspectives of an American Hero* (New York: Plume Books, 1997); and Joe Dorinson and Joram Warmund, eds., *Jackie Robinson: Race, Sports, and the American Dream* (New York: M. E. Sharpe, 1998).

14. Thanks to the work of Negro League historians, most baseball enthusiasts know about nineteenth-century African American players, such as Moses Fleetwood Walker, who appeared in the Major Leagues. Their effort historicized a once neglected area, the experience of African American players who fell victim to the color line in the nineteenth century. On black baseball, see Sol White, *Sol White's History of Colored Baseball, with Other Documents on the Early Black Game, 1886–1936* (reprint, Lincoln: University of Nebraska Press, 1995); and David W. Zang, *Fleet Walker's Divided Heart: The Life of Baseball's First Black Major Leaguer* (Lincoln: University of Nebraska Press, 1995). Pioneering works on the Negro Leagues are Robert Peterson, *Only the Ball Was White: A History of Legendary Black Players and All-Black Professional Teams* (reprint, New York: Oxford University Press, 1992); John Holway, *Blackball Stars: Negro League Pioneers*

(reprint, New York: Carroll and Graf, 1992); and Donn Rogosin, *Invisible Men: Life in Baseball's Negro Leagues* (reprint, New York: Kodansha, 1995).

15. Works that have begun to address the void by focusing on the impact that Latino players have had on the Major Leagues are Peter Bjarkman, *Baseball with a Latin Beat: A History of the Latin American Game* (Jefferson, NC: McFarland, 1996); Samuel O. Regalado, *Viva Baseball: Latin Major Leaguers and Their Special Hunger* (Urbana: University of Illinois Press, 1998); and Marcos Bretón, *Away Games: The Life and Times of a Latin Ball Player* (New York: Simon and Schuster, 1999).

16. Newspaper clipping, "Some Inside Facts in Cuban Players in America," Marsans biographical player file, NBLA. (Since it refers to Marsans possibly playing the following season with the New York Giants, the article was most likely written in early 1915).

17. Bancroft letter, 14 December 1910, "1080 1914" file, Garry Herrman Papers, NBLA.

18. J. F. Sullivan letter, 2 January 1911, "Unmarked Letters" file, Garry Herrman Papers, NBLA.

19. *Cincinnati Inquirer* passage quoted in Lisa Brock and Bijan Bayne, "Not Just Black," in *Between Race and Empire: African-Americans and Cubans before the Cuban Revolution,* ed. Lisa Brock and Digna Castañeda Fuertes, 185 (Philadelphia: Temple University Press, 1998). Player photo found in Almeida player file, NBLA.

20. See Daniel C. Frio and Marc Onigman, "'Good Field, No Hit': The Image of Latin American Baseball Players in the American Press, 1876–1946," *Revista/Review Interamericana* 9, no. 2 (September 1979): 199–208, and "Baseball Triumphs of Latin Players Obscured by Ethnic Slurs, Jokes," *Washington Post,* 5 March 1978. Also see Regalado, "Béisbol en el Norte," chap. 3 in *Viva Baseball,* 19–38.

21. Evelyn Brooks Higginbotham, "African American Women's History and the Metalanguage of Race," *Signs* 17 (1992): 251–74.

22. Interview with José Rosado, June 1996, Bronx, New York. The growth of the Dominican population in the United States along with the circular migration over the last twenty years has had a similar effect, where historians employing a territorially-defined version of Latin and/or Latino could group family members into different categories.

15

Fútbol Nation

U.S. Latinos and the Goal of a Homeland

Christopher A. Shinn

U.S. LATINOS COMING from diverse homelands throughout the Americas nonetheless speak a distinct and widely popular Latin idiom: "fútbol."[1] As the world's most popular sport, the game of fútbol enables Latinos to maintain strong social and cultural ties to Latin America, building upon a long-standing sports history that recalls the beginnings of the World Cup in Uruguay in 1930 and counts a remarkable half of the World Cup titles won by South American countries (Brazil, Uruguay, Argentina).[2] The sport itself necessitates a paradigm shift because, historically speaking, the United States never became a fútbol nation as did many of its neighbors in the South. Indeed, the game has often instilled particularly fierce loyalties and deep divisions throughout Latin America in its celebrated and checkered sports past. Close to four thousand casualties resulted in the summer of 1969, for example, when El Salvador mobilized armed forces and invaded Honduras in the so-called Central American Soccer War following the outcome of a qualifying round of the World Cup championship, a clear indication of just how serious this type of play can be.[3]

The wide popularity of fútbol among Latinos, then, might be best understood within the larger cultural and historical framework of the game's privileged position among the various and dispersed peoples of Latin America. For Latino communities, given the history of fútbol in Latin America and their ties to this history, the game clearly constitutes a source of Latino/a pride, cultural tradition, popular folklore, and psychic and social connection to distant homelands. Thanks to media and closed-circuit television, Guatemalans in the United States can continue to follow the Central American games (CONCACAF), while Mexican Americans can watch Mexican fútbol matches on Univisión, Fox Sports, World Español, or Galavisión.[4] At the same time, as a spectator sport, the game provides intimate occasions for Latino/a fans to congregate in clearly defined *U.S.* Latino/a social spaces such as the home, the taqueria, the cantina, or the local community center in order to follow their favorite national teams and players in Latin America. The sport thus actively engages what is culturally specific among Latinos and leads us to ask how fútbol contributes to the shared and discrepant meanings of the terms "Latinoamericano" and "U.S. Latino." Their entanglement becomes a matter of deep play, for the game captures the sense of movement and flow appropriate to the dynamic exchange of diverse Latin American and U.S. Latino/a identities.[5] The prominence of fútbol among a growing immigrant and native Latino/a population, I will argue, coincides with a deep and abiding transnational connection with Latin America and symbolizes the cultural future for Latinos, forging new gendered, pan-ethnic, and corporate structures that seek to create and capitalize on an emerging sense of homeland in the United States. I will pay special attention to the establishment of Major League Soccer and the growth of Latino fútbol leagues in Washington state in order to indicate how Latinos themselves participate in a complex process of intercultural and transnational exchange with multiple homelands.

PRELIMINARY CONSIDERATIONS: FÚTBOL AND LATINO/A POPULAR CULTURE

Rather than debate the degree of actual connectedness to distant homelands that the game may or may not allow, one might note simply how, by definition, the game creates a space of exaggerated meanings through the element of play and always exceeds the boundaries of what it is. The game thus imagines popular Latino/a alliances that reflect the experiences of migrating peoples and the cultural traditions that come to define them. The sense of pan-Latino-ness, Latin male sentimentality, and the comradery of aficionados globally, for instance, are based in part on the game's romance as it comes to represent the "passion of the people," the "beautiful game," or, in the Uruguayan Eduardo Galeano's poetic words, "soccer in sun and shadow."[6] Within this romance, fútbol

allows for an imaginary sense of peoplehood among Latinos that frequently becomes a lasting expression of the sport's popular nostalgia.

To love fútbol, then, is essentially to take part in what it means to
be, or not be, culturally "Latino" in the Americas and ask how U.S.
Latino communities define or reinvent themselves in relation to the
game. The issue of gender clearly remains a critical factor in this equation. The love of the game coincides with the practice of established
male rituals that are part of Latino socialization. Traditionally, the game
follows conventional male codes of homosocial bonding and behavior,
including such popular subcultural trends as wearing solid colored jerseys and shiny shorts along with black hip hop styles. U.S. Latinas and
women in Latin America in turn participate in the sport primarily as
fans and supporters, spectators and on-site vendors, and occasionally
as referees.[7] Latin American women are largely discouraged from playing fútbol (except in locations such as Brazil, where the women's national team has achieved some prominence internationally), while soccer in the United States has become the leading sport among women.
Latina contributions to the game demonstrate how women can
uniquely participate in and observe the game, testing the boundaries of
place and purpose against a traditional Latin male sports world. This
participation usually means, however, that Latinas must challenge conventional norms of femininity and sexuality in order to revise what Barbara Cox and Shona Thompson have referred to as the standard male
"soccer body."[8]

While soccer is the largest growing sport among women in the
world, the World Cup champion U.S. women's soccer team did not include a single Latina player.[9] Ironically, Mexico, by contrast, chose to recruit ten Mexican American women, that is, U.S. citizens of Mexican
descent, to play fútbol for the national team under the direction of former California State Los Angeles coach Leonardo Cuellar, filling a vacuum created by the absence of women players in their own country.[10]
Although local fútbol leagues in U.S. Latino communities include a
very small percentage of women (less than 10 percent in the Los Angeles area, for example, compared to Latino soccer programs among
men), recent trends suggest that the presence of U.S. Latinas in the
sport is increasing—in part as a result of the visibility of women's
World Cup soccer.[11] The same slow but incremental gains for women
can also be seen in Latin America as national pride becomes a factor in
reclaiming territory associated with the game as it is played among

Latin American men. As Patrick Escobar, vice president of the Amateur Athletic Foundation in the United States, predicts, "You're going to see national pride take over [in women's World Cup soccer]. Mexico and Brazil are not going to want to be relegated to fifth or sixth place."[12] The game of fútbol is indeed a major battleground for international competition in the form of women's and men's amateur and professional sports. Such international appeal, as we shall see, represents the guiding force behind the development of Major League Soccer (the official governing body of professional soccer in the United States) as well as the growth of local fútbol leagues among U.S. Latinos. While these organizations retain their local character, they promote and market national and transnational networks and alliances, part of the way that Latinos create and contest the imaginary spaces of homeland both on and off the field.

MAJOR LEAGUE SOCCER AND U.S. LATINO/A FANS

As the official soccer league of the United States, Major League Soccer (MLS) welcomes a fan base of an estimated 40 percent Latinos, imprinting a unique Latino presence on the game.[13] MLS openly courts Latino/a populations in the United States as fans and players according to their multiple national allegiances, capitalizing on the game's popularity among diverse Latino communities across the Americas and promoting the growth of soccer in the United States. Indeed, the MLS organization strategically markets the game according to the national backgrounds of U.S. Latino/a fans. As former MLS commissioner Doug Logan explained in 1997 to *Hispanic* magazine,

> Mexican goalkeeper Jorge Campos and Salvadoran Muricio Cienfuegos [play] for the Los Angeles Galaxy (since the metropolis has huge Mexican and Salvadoran communities), while Bolivian midfield star Marco Etcheverry is with the D.C. United (since Washington, D.C. is a city with a vibrant Bolivian community), and Colombian player Antony de Avila is with the MetroStars in New York (since there's a sizeable Colombian and South American community in Queens).[14]

Hence, MLS seeks to build upon the popularity of fútbol among U.S. Latinos in a larger effort toward making the magical crossover into the

American mainstream, transforming the United States into a competitive fútbol nation.

Most U.S. soccer clubs notably reside in metropolitan areas in which Latinos constitute a significant proportion of the population: the Los Angeles Galaxy, the New York/New Jersey MetroStars, the Miami Fusion, the San Jose Clash, the Chicago Fire, the Dallas Burn, and the D.C. United, among others. This fact has been a logical part of the marketing of MLS from the beginning in hopes that the popularity of the sport itself, building upon its traditional Latino/a fan base, would expand and become self-generating in the United States as a whole.[15] The fact that the United States hosted the World Cup in 1994 has bolstered MLS's vision and has helped gain a small but increasing level of interest among Anglo audiences. Among Latino/a fans, the presence of Latino players on the United States national team gave further reason to follow the United States' performance in the 1994 and 1998 World Cup. Latino players such as Marcelo Balboa, Fernando Clavijo, Hugo Perez, Tab Ramos, and Claudio Reyna were celebrated members of the 1994 United States soccer team, while Mexican-born Martin Vasquez, a former player on the Tampa Bay Mutiny, became a midfielder on the 1998 United States team.[16]

As the marketing strategy of MLS indicates, the construction of a fútbol nation depends on an imaginary projection of a nation itself—otherwise known as the "national league." Ironically, because of the ownership of players and the benefits of free agency, the players are not necessarily from the countries they come to represent. MLS has lost its better young players to European clubs (a condition quite familiar to Argentina and Brazil), while European players—such as Lothar Matthaus and Hristo Stoichkov, for instance—have been courted to play for the United States teams.[17] Martin Vasquez, noted above, once played for the Mexican national team in the World Cup until he was granted citizenship in the United States to play for the Tampa Bay Mutiny, then later became part of the U.S. national team, while defender Diego Sonora left the D.C. United to play for a Latin American team.[18] In short, the game retains its sense of peoplehood according to a nationally defined, though internally differentiated, sports organization where the players do not always hold to the nationality they come to defend. This condition reflects the wider multinational corporate structure of the game, in which the level playing field is broadly organized by the free market. While the United States might not be victorious on the field, it can nonetheless market the Latino athlete's iconic status and control the game according to the $135 million it contributes to MLS.[19] At the World Cup level the Nike Corporation, for instance, can use its considerable leverage, as it did to force the famed Brazilian player Ronaldo Luis Názario de Lima from his hospital bed during the 1998 World Cup finals so that he could showcase Nike's new line of shoe, the R-9, in front of an estimated two billion fans.[20]

Despite the corporate influences and controlling mechanisms surrounding the sport, fútbol alliances bring together nations and peoples that also cut across more restrictive definitions of "Latin Americans" and "Latinos." Who can forget the 1970 World Cup finals in Mexico City, for instance, in which the Brazilian player Pelé was hoisted on the shoulders of Mexicans who carried him off the field wearing a Mexican sombrero? Pelé was essentially deemed an honorary Mexican citizen, participating in a larger Latin American collectivity. While the term "Latin America" normally excludes Portuguese-speaking Brazil, the term "Latin" generally refers to the Romance languages, which include, among others, Spanish- and Portuguese-speaking peoples.[21] Brazil remains the largest country in South America—a país-continente—and so the question remains: why would Brazil not be included among the countries of Latin America?[22] In a general sense the game of fútbol has already created popular alliances under a larger *regional* configuration that speaks to other possible transnational and cross-cultural linkages.

Along these lines, we might ask why "U.S. Latino" excludes U.S. Brazilians and whether this distinction is in fact necessary. To address this question, we might examine a second related example: when Mexico lost to Germany in the sixteenth round of the 1998 World Cup, U.S. Latino communities, which had been supporting the Mexican national team, subsequently realigned their popular allegiance to Brazil in the finals against France. Why did Latino/a fans overwhelmingly root for Brazil and why not France? The nationalist rivalries among countries in the Americas yield to a larger regional imaginary within a global context as the circle of play expands to include countries from around the world. The game reinforces alliances in the Americas created by hemispheric models of play and brings together various American countries according to the long-standing cultural affinities shared among diverse Latino/a peoples. By contrast, the Old World comes to represent the *other* continent, if not more pointedly, the empire of the colonial past. As C. L. R. James reminds us, the playing field enacts social and political dramas in which present and former colonized countries often take re-venge on their historic oppressors.[23] Indeed, Iran's defeat of the United States in the 1998 World Cup symbolized a conquest of the "Great Satan" himself.[24]

LATINO FÚTBOL LEAGUES IN WASHINGTON STATE: IS THE PLAYING FIELD LOCAL, NATIONAL, OR TRANSNATIONAL?

In spite of soccer's indelible association to professional players and or-ganizations in the United States and Latin America, the game has also cut across the Americas and the globe and has made its way into one's very own home and neighborhood, public parks and fields, schools and locally sponsored soccer leagues. Here the people represent not the all-star players who remain larger than life, but the game's romance for everyday folks who constitute members of the local community. In a more localized world, Latinos participate in spontaneous "pick-up" games known as *cascaritas*, though much focus tends to be placed on the emergence of soccer leagues throughout the country. La Liga Hispana, based in Seattle, Washington, for instance, has expanded into thirty-six teams and over six hundred members as part of a larger statewide Latino membership that includes close to two hundred teams and more than three thousand players.[25] Latino communities, hence, create sub-cultures and enlarge other sporting alliances to engage diverse Latino/a populations into a new—or renewed—sense of homeland.

The growth of soccer leagues in the state of Washington attests to the arrival and settlement of diverse native and immigrant Latino/a populations that increasingly need and value leisure in the form of Latino/a communal life. Mexican service workers—approximately 125,000—travel the migrant circuit to Washington each year in order to labor for long hours in the fields, supporting the state's $5.23 billion agricultural economy. Undocumented Mexican workers constitute 70 percent of all seasonal pickers, arriving in eastern Washington (i.e., Yakima Valley) from such rural villages as Pajacuarán, in the state of Michoacán, which sends a third of its residents to work in the United States.[26] These workers often spend Sundays, their only day of rest, on the fútbol field, participating, for example, in Yakima's Liga Mexicana

and Sunnyside's League of the Lower Valley.[27] Many foreign- and native-born Latinos have also moved to western Washington—to places
like King County and Seattle and its suburbs. Washington's overall
Latino population has experienced an unprecedented boom as a result
of two key historical events. In 1986 Congress made legal residents out
of about 2.3 million Mexican migrant workers nationwide, allowing for
Mexican immigrants to bring their families to the United States. Then,
in an immigration backlash in the early 1990s, California passed Proposition 187 in the wake of economic recession, prompting Latino immigrants to move north to Washington.[28] According to Marc Ramirez, staff
writer for the *Seattle Times*, "From 1990 to 1997, Washington's Latino
population grew by nearly 50 people a day, almost four times the rate
of the overall population. In that seven-year period, the number of Latinos statewide rose 58 percent, from 214,568 to 339,618."[29]

The growth of fútbol leagues has come to represent the cultural future for many Latino immigrants as the game fosters gradual but steady
movement toward local, community-based activity, leading to national
affiliation and the establishment of homes in the United States. In a featured *Seattle Times* article, "Viva la Liga! Viva la Liga!—Local Soccer
League Mirrors Latinos' Growing Prominence around the Country,"
the *Times* notes,

> As the population takes root, so do the community staples that echo
> home for new arrivals and give others cultural anchors: Spanish-lan-
> guage video stores and church services, Latin markets and radio sta-
> tions. With more Latinos carving out lives in Seattle and its suburbs,
> what you see on playing fields from Kent to Mountlake Terrace is a
> snapshot of the future—a population with increasing moments of
> leisure, a community coming of age.[30]

Local sponsors, who are themselves part of the Latino community, promote an already traditional sport among Latino/a fans. Members of
the Hispanic Business Chamber and restaurant owners support La
Liga Hispana and participate in developing Latino/a communities
and their independently owned businesses.[31] Team jerseys advertise
Latino nightclubs, car dealers, La Española market, or the Azteca and
Jalisco restaurants.[32] On the other hand, as the popularity of fútbol
continues, the leagues increasingly demand larger corporate sponsors

in order to survive. The Liga de Fútbol de Pasco in Washington state, for example, consists of teams whose names are called "Albertsons," "Budweiser," or "Best Foods" instead of "Morelos," "El Aguila," and "Hidalgo."[33]

Despite the U.S.-based corporate sponsorship of these teams, the relationship between the local community and the wider affiliations of homeland created by fútbol indeed remains integral to the game. Local teams in the United States often take the name of fútbol clubs in distant homelands: teams in the Liga de Fútbol de Pasco, for example, assume names such as "San José," "Guadalajara," and "Mexico," to reinforce important symbolic equivalences.[34] The Guadalajara Chivas are so named after the Mexican First Division team, and the Pasco jerseys bear the likeness of the Mexican team.[35] This close association is not simply an expression of popular nationalist nostalgia, but is a further attempt to re-create Mexico in the United States. Indeed, many local players emigrated from the cities of Guadalajara and San José and have subsequently made Pasco, Washington, their home. The Mexican government itself frequently sponsors fútbol tournaments through the Programa para las Communidades Mexicanas en el Extranjero and the Mexican consulate.[36] The annual tournament "Copa México," held in Washington and throughout the United States, for instance, brings together local teams under a wide array of jurisdictions, corporate and national sponsorships, and mass media. The players and audiences generally belong to local communities throughout the Washington area but have migrated from multiple homelands. The radio station La Deportiva (KXPA—1540 AM) provides Raúl Sandoval's distinct play-by-play commentary, while local vendors sell products and programs to U.S. Latino/a fans. The fútbol leagues are supported by businesses such as Rosella's Produce and *La Voz* or *Siete Días*, popular Latino newspapers in the Pacific Northwest. At the same time, the games are sponsored by larger multinational corporations such as BuenaVista Travel and TELMEX, among others.[37] The regional winner of "Copa México" eventually moves on to compete on a national stage, bringing together Mexican American communities throughout the United States.

As with other forms of Latino/a cultural life from food to popular folklore, athletic competition reflects deep nationalist feelings even at this local level. In La Liga Hispana, national and ethnic pride often turns violent when teams collide on the field over loyalties to homeland. As the *Seattle Times*, for instance, notes, "La Española's players [of

La Liga Hispana] have seen civil wars erupt on opposing squads between teammates claiming superiority for the mother countries. Some say La Española itself is targeted for having so many non-Latinos on its roster."[38] Among these "non-Latinos" are often second-generation Mexican Americans, whose Latino ties to the homeland are challenged by recent Mexican immigrants.[39]

The weekend soccer league, moreover, can facilitate a process of Latino/a cross-cultural fertilization. Just as the consumer can purchase his or her mole, plantains, and guaraná all in the same ethnic grocery store, the game can also form multiethnic and transnational communities that emerge among those living in the same neighborhoods and playing the same game. La Liga Hispana includes players with roots in Mexico, Brazil, Chile, Nicaragua, and Ecuador as well as foreign and native-born Latinos and non-Latino players.[40] Though predominantly Mexican American, La Liga Hispana nonetheless includes a range of Latinos from Latin America and a few Anglos from the United States. This cross-section of Latinos not only reveals a shared history of migration and settlement in the United States but also creates local leagues with a distinct international flavor united by a common love of the game. In this instance, the game of fútbol serves as a popular site of U.S. and Latin American transcultural formation that links the United States and Mexico, parts of the Caribbean, and Central and South America.

The game of fútbol thus remains entangled in the popular projections of multiple Latino/a identities, national affiliations, and sporting alliances. The interrelatedness of the controversial terms "Latino/a," "American," and "Latin American," among others, applies to the game and its players in relation to the popularity of the sport throughout the United States and Latin America. This wider context of the Americas informs the introduction of Latino stars in MLS and explains the strong interest and consumptive patterns of U.S. Latino/a fans and players. The growth of Latino soccer leagues attests to the continuation and alteration of long-standing cultural traditions in Latin America and contributes to the formation of distinct U.S. Latino/a identities. Fútbol promotes as well as undermines the popular construction of nationality as U.S. Latino/a fans' allegiances are subsequently redrawn according to a wider, regionally based Latino/a configuration. Throughout the United States, the growth of fútbol coincides with an evolving sense of Latino/a identity that has indeed traveled down field as it continues to pursue the far-reaching goal of a homeland.

NOTES

I would like to thank Paul Cerda, Michelle Habell-Pallán, Ana Patricia Rodríguez, and Mary Romero for their helpful comments and suggestions in writing this piece.

1. I use the term "U.S. Latinos" to distinguish between Latinos in the United States and Latinos throughout Latin America. When the term "Latinos" or "Latinas" is not specified, it will refer generally to "U.S. Latinos" or "U.S. Latinas" unless otherwise indicated.

2. Michael Morrison et al., eds., *ESPN Information Please Sports Almanac* (New York: Hyperion ESPN Books, 1998), 751.

3. Mary Jeane Reid Martz, *The Central American Soccer War: Historical Patterns and Internal Dynamics of OAS Settlement Procedures* (Athens, OH: Center for International Studies, 1978).

4. CONCACAF stands for the Confederation of North, Central American and Caribbean Association Football.

5. Clifford Geertz, *Interpretation of Cultures* (New York: Basic Books, 1973), 432.

6. Tony Mason, *Passion of the People? Football in South America* (New York: Verso, 1995); Eduardo Galeano, *Soccer in Sun and Shadow,* trans. Mark Fried (New York: Verso, 1999). Brazilians popularly refer to fútbol as *jogo bonito,* meaning "the beautiful game."

7. See, for example, "Referee Endures Rough Start—Latin American Woman Thrives as Professional Soccer Official," *Seattle Times,* 5 December 1999, weekend edition, Sports sec., p. C2; Martha Liliana Toro of Colombia became the first professional female referee in Latin America.

8. Barbara Cox and Shona Thompson, "Multiple Bodies: Sportswomen, Soccer and Sexuality," *International Review for the Sociology of Sport* 35, no. 1 (2000): 10–12.

9. Anne-Marie O'Connor, "A Cultural Snub for Women's World Cup; Latinos: Reaction Reflects Traditional View outside U.S. That Soccer Is a Men's Sport," *Los Angeles Times,* 16 July 1999, home edition, p. 1.

10. Ibid.

11. Ibid.

12. Ibid.

13. "Logan's Run," *Hispanic,* October 1997, 19.

14. Ibid., 20.

15. Ibid.

16. Morrison et al., 739–40.

17. "More Like the Real Thing," *World Soccer* 40, no. 8: (2000): 71.

18. Morrison et al., 739–40. See also Steve Goff, "Sonora Probably Will

Leave United after 1st Round of Playoffs," *Washington Post*, 21 October 1999, final edition, Sports sec., p. D-8.

19. This amount will be allotted to Major League Soccer over a five-year period. "More Like the Real Thing," *World Soccer* 40, no. 81 (2001): 71.

20. Galeano, 214.

21. For a brief discussion of the term "Latino," see Geoffrey Fox, *Hispanic Nation: Culture, Politics and the Construction of Identity* (Secaucus, NJ: Birch Lane Press, 1996), 12–15.

22. The phrase *país-continente* is used by Lourdes Martínez-Echazábal to refer to the immense size of Brazil in relation to other Latin American countries.

23. Cyril L. R. James, *Beyond a Boundary* (London: Stanley Paul, 1963; Durham: Duke University Press, 1993).

24. Morrison et al., 734.

25. Marc Ramirez, "Viva La Liga! Viva La Liga! Local Soccer League Mirrors Latinos' Growing Prominence around the Country," *Seattle Times*, 29 August 1999, final edition, Scene sec., p. L1.

26. Lynda V. Mapes, "Under Two Flags: Mexican Workers in Washington Fields," *Seattle Times*, 18 June 2000, final edition, News sec., p. A1.

27. Ramirez.

28. Ibid.

29. Ibid.

30. Ibid.

31. Ibid.

32. Ibid.

33. Liga de Fútbol de Pasco divisions, available from http://www.3-cities.com/~rbocan/pascosch.htm (updated 1 August 1998; cited 25 April 2001).

34. Ibid.

35. Ross Courtney, "Chivas Hold Off Mexico in the Finals 4-2," *Tri-City Herald*, 12 October 1998.

36. "El Fútbol: Torneo de Fútbol 'Copa México 2000' se Realizará el 17 y 18 de Junio en Redmond," *Deportes*, 8 Junio 2000.

37. See "Copa Mexico 2000," *La Voz*, 15 Junio 2000.

38. Ramirez, L1.

39. Ibid.

40. Ibid.

16

Boxing and Masculinity

The History and (Her)story of Oscar de la Hoya

Gregory Rodriguez

AT THE DAWN of the new millennium as Chicanas/os consider the possibilities and paradoxes of their place in an evolving global culture, some Chicana/o scholars are delineating the contours of what they claim is nothing less than a Chicano cultural "renaissance."[1] The renaissance is not a renaissance at all, to the extent that it marks a "rebirth." Chicanas/os have been a cultural force in the West since the seventeenth century. The renaissance instead reveals in large part generations of ethnic Mexicans branching out together in forms of intercultural communication such as popular music, theater, sport, art, poetry, dance, and literature, to name but a few. This flourishing of popular cultural forms serves to reconnect individuals to their communities and helps them construct forms of identification that are often political and capable of bridging generational, national, and class divides. In other words, the swell of popular cultural activity is not just about entertainment. While it might be "fun," it tends to be a form of "serious fun." Latina/o popular cultural icons have based lucrative careers not just on their abilities as actors, musicians, performance artists, and athletes, but also on their ability to identify with fans as proud members of Latino communities in often hostile United States cultural settings.

Yet popular culture not only offers a domain for the affirmation of ethnic identity, it also offers a means to affirm, shape, and contest gender identity. It provides us with chances to express ourselves and intervene in cultural processes that shape what it means to be male or female, masculine or feminine. These relationships of gender often revolve around issues of ethnicity, which often revolve around issues of gender and sexuality, making identity something difficult to understand unless we consider a wide range of specific historical circumstances.

Chicana/o boxing offers one form of serious fun where we see people at work constructing or deconstructing ways of being this or that kind of "man," or this or that kind of "American," or this or that kind of "Latino." The career of Los Angeles boxing champion Oscar de la Hoya is a perfect example of a popular cultural process in which fans have been imagining new ways of being Latina/o in the United States.

In the first half of the twentieth century, Los Angeles boxing contributed to a sense of ethnic belonging among Mexican-descent people much the way flags, anthems, religious icons, geographical boundaries, commonality of language, political structures, and the ideas of a shared culture did. In the second half of the century, movements for Mexican American self-determination in the United States heightened awareness of group differences; nationalistic and ethnic expressions in boxing permitted the blurring of differences and helped to unite a multiethnic people behind a single sporting ideal. By the 1970s the great unifying quality emerging in boxing was that it offered a community of involvement that provided a place for everyone, whatever her age or station, whether fan or player. The sport came to represent the dreams of ethnic Mexicans who were White or Black, middle-class or working-class, older or younger, "right-wing" or "left-wing," male or female, "gay" or "straight." By the 1980s new ethnic Mexican boxing idols emerged within a postindustrial era where a corporate order manufactured their celebrity within an ever-expanding media network. The career of Oscar de la Hoya emerged from this rich boxing history of Mexican Los Angeles.

Oscar de la Hoya was a second-generation Mexican American born in Los Angeles in 1971. Vicente de la Hoya, Oscar's *abuelito* (grandfather), came to Los Angeles in 1956 and, among other jobs, worked as an auto mechanic in a garage at Seventh Street and Central Avenue. In 1957 he had saved enough to open a small Mexican restaurant half a block away that he named Virginia's Place. Shortly thereafter he entered the demolition business. He would bid on home demolition jobs, knock the houses down, haul the scrap lumber to Mexicali, and sell it. According to one of Oscar's cousins, lots of families live in Mexicali homes that were built of lumber hauled there by Oscar de la Hoya's grandfather. Vicente de la Hoya, who boxed as an amateur in Durango, Mexico, following World War II, ultimately returned to Mexico, retiring in Mexicali. Oscar's father, Joel de la Hoya, was sixteen when he arrived in Los Angeles in 1956. He went to Roosevelt High School, learned to box in East L.A. gyms, turned pro, and fashioned a 9-3-1 record. Like so many ethnic Mexican fighters before him, he too boxed several times at L.A.'s world famous Olympic Auditorium. In 1975 he became a dispatcher for an Azusa firm that made industrial heating and air-conditioning systems and would remain in that job until his son made sure that he would never have to work again.[2] Oscar de la Hoya first competed in boxing in 1979, at the age of eight, in tournaments at the Pico Rivera Boys Club. In his amateur career he won 223 bouts and lost only five. In 1992 he won Olympic gold at Barcelona and in less than nine years has earned four world titles and established a record of thirty-three wins and two losses.[3] In 1992 he was estimated to be worth close to $100 million.[4] Today in 2001 he is worth at least twice that amount. Even after two recent losses to Felix Trinidad and Sugar Shane Mosely he remains the number one draw in the boxing world today and ranks second only to the recently retired Michael Jordan and golf star Tiger Woods in endorsement earnings by sports figures.

De la Hoya appealed to many corporate sponsors because he was telegenic, family-oriented, and wholesome. His promoters portrayed him as "all-American," the antithesis of the stereotypical, threatening Mexican masculinity so often represented by the media. Part of de la Hoya's fanfare involved repetitive references to de la Hoya as a "good Mexican," and this must be understood in part as a reference to his ethnicity and gender. Reports repeatedly recorded the quote from de la Hoya's father that "Oscar's a very good boy, he doesn't smoke, drink, fool around—he's very dedicated to boxing and his schoolwork."[5] Much was made of de la Hoya's dedication of his Olympian quest to his "best friend," his mother, who died a year before he became a professional champion. He was encouraged to speak publicly to "inner-city kids" about the importance of family, as well as education, in instilling values necessary for success in life. "The most important thing in life," he once told an elementary school gathering, "is to love and listen to your parents. When you go home, give your mom a big hug and tell her that you love her and tell your parents, 'Thanks for taking care of me.' They'll love you even more."[6] Carol Koshi, de la Hoya's elementary school teacher at Ford Boulevard Elementary School, gave a glowing report of de la Hoya's own school behavior. "He was so nice," she said. "He did everything I asked of him. And he didn't get into fights."[7] The story of Maria Elena Tostado, a former nun who was de la Hoya's principal at Garfield High School, circulated in numerous accounts. "He knew what he wanted from Day 1," she was quoted as saying. "He always had a goal and worked toward it. I mean, nonstop. His mother . . . must have seen he had special qualities. He really is a single-minded young man. . . . He's never, ever once complained about what he was doing or how much it was taking of his life."[8] De la Hoya's "golden boy" image was so attractive that he was made into a parody of the quintessential "American." "He doesn't look right," an astonished Jim Murray observed:

> Look at him! You ever see a prizefighter like him? Even Dempsey bragged a little. Joe Louis too. Not our Oscar. . . . I mean, who does he think he is, mother Teresa? So far as anyone knows, Oscar never even stole a Hershey bar. What kind of record is that for a champion? It's un-American. . . . He should learn to scowl a lot. Travel around with an entourage. Trash his opponent. Talking trash has become an American hallmark. . . . It's part and parcel of the way we compete. . . . Oscar doesn't have to work on his jab, his uppercut, but he has to work on his vocabulary. He has to learn his opponent is a bum, the referee a crook, and that bad manners sell tickets. I don't say he has to go to prison, but maybe a 2 a.m. difference of opinion with a bartender is indicated.[9]

Although de la Hoya's image spoke to idealized forms and styles of masculinity that varied according to the cultures in which they were framed and performed, his public conflicts with ethnic Mexican fans over the meaning of manhood in boxing provide good examples of these debates in everyday life. Some fans expected de la Hoya to reproduce the warrior image they had cultivated in Los Angeles boxing for over eighty years, a distinctive East L.A., working-class form of masculinity that resonated with the lives of ethnic Mexican males beyond the ring. As comedian Paul Rodríguez put it, "A lot of my Chicano friends misunderstand being shy for arrogance. Oscar is not a very talkative guy. Oscar is reserved and shy, and he's not the kind of guy to go out to Lincoln Park and have Budweiser with the boys. That's what they want. But he can't do that, it's not in his system."[10] World champion and Mexican national Julio Cesar Chávez, on the other hand, was thought of as being "down with the boys," because he knew when "to hit the *cerveza* instead of the heavy bag."[11]

According to Paul Rodríguez, when in 1996 de la Hoya was billed to meet Chávez in the ring, the split in fan allegiances reflected roughly the split between Mexican nationals and Chicanos in East L.A. But when a reporter for the *Los Angeles Times* tested this theory among a sample of Mexicans, Chicanos, and one Nicaraguan, none "specifically mentioned de la Hoya's country of birth as an issue. Instead, the main theme was that Chávez [had] stayed true to the Latino ideal—and that de la Hoya [was] aiming for success as measured by Anglo-America."[12] One way to think about debates over the "Latino ideal," especially in boxing, is as a struggle over the meaning of manhood.

When de la Hoya became rich and moved from the barrio of "East Los" (as it was known among Chicanas/os) to a suburban home to the south in Montebello, a number of East L.A. fans felt snubbed, interpreting his actions as unmanly. Consequently, the moment it was announced that de la Hoya would face the legendary Mexican champion Julio Cesar Chávez, Chávez was instantly embraced as the hero of *barrios* everywhere. "What was the first thing [Oscar] did after he came back from the Olympics?" asked Gladys Martínez, who attended neighboring Roosevelt High at the same time that de la Hoya attended Garfield. "He moved out of here and went to the Montebello Hills. He couldn't drive that Corvette or whatever fast enough out of here. All the people that I know, they want Julio to beat his butt."[13] Sugar Ray Leonard, who experienced some of the same coldness in his neighborhood in Maryland until late in his career, believed that most of the strong feelings emanated from East L.A.'s deep affection for the "workmanlike" boxing style of Chávez, who never moved from his impoverished hometown of Culiacan, Sinaloa. "I think it's all about the perception here that Chávez, his background and his culture, really is blue-collar." Leonard suggested. "And Oscar is a white-collar fighter. I kind of went through a little bit of that with Tommy Hearns. The way it was with me wasn't on this grand of a scale. . . . But, tell you what depending who wins this fight and how impressive it is, there's room to change."[14] Deemed "Kid Barrio" by an adoring public, Chávez enjoyed a popularity that transcended national identities, at least within the ethnic Mexican community. As one Mexican American high school student argued, "I don't like de la Hoya at all. He's too much of a showoff. I used to like him when he won the gold medal. You look at Chavez, and see he hasn't changed. De la Hoya? He left East L.A., didn't he?"[15] According to Tim Kawakami,

Chavez embraced the barrios—and the people embraced him right back, fervently. On a walk with Chavez down Olvera Street in downtown Los Angeles one afternoon, through a narrow corridor lined with outdoor booths, it seemed like arms and hands were everywhere, reaching out to him and touching him and chasing him. Chavez soaked it all up, jubilantly yelling to the crowd, and the crowd rapturously chanted back to him.[16]

De la Hoya, on the other hand, had a much different experience walking the streets of his hometown. "You go down to the neighborhood and you shake people's hands," he said.

> And they say good luck and this and that—kick his butt, beat him for us. And you turn around and they're saying, "Oh, he's going to lose." You sense it right away. I mean they're just after you for your autograph, let's take a picture. But, when you're not looking, "Oh, he's going to get his butt kicked."[17]

Ethnic Mexican fans and fighters also read boxing style as another distinguishing feature of a prizefighter's masculinity. De la Hoya disrupted the hopes of some ethnic Mexican fans by varying widely from the traditional "slug-it-out" style (or, as Sugar Ray Leonard called it, "workmanlike" style) that had been popularized in local arenas. His approach to boxing reflected middle-class values whereby the body is seen less as a means to an end–as in the working body–than as an end in itself; that is, de la Hoya endorsed an approach to boxing as a means to a fit, healthy, and beautiful body. The stereotypical boxing style of ethnic Mexicans, on the other hand, sacrificed the body in order to "work inside," attacking the body and allowing oneself to be attacked. "Chavez was exactly what Mexicans loved in a fighter," noted Tim Kawakami:

> To hit you, he would allow you to hit him with everything you had. Then he would batter you, body part by body part, until, at the very end, you were swallowing your own blood and dizzy from the experience. To the people of those [Los Angeles] streets, to the immigrant Mexicans and the fight fans of the Latino populace, Chavez stood for Mexican pride. When Chavez bled, they believed, he bled for them. . . . De la Hoya, meanwhile, had just commissioned the design of his

own private bus, painted with his face. And he wouldn't even comment on the hot-button issue of the day–the California proposition [187] that . . . was widely viewed as part of a slightly veiled anti-Latino movement. De la Hoya didn't think about such things, and he surely never talked about them. If de la Hoya ever bled, the people of the barrio never saw it, and they knew it wasn't for them, anyway.[18]

In a *Playboy* interview, de la Hoya explains that

the tradition is that you're going to see a brutal fight and you have to go in there and bleed. I'm not going to give them that. I'm going to go out there, be careful and not get hit. I'll get it over with and that's it. If fans don't like that, I'm sorry. I'm not just any fighter. I want to make my money and I want to live well, but I'm not going out there to put on a brutal show. If I looked like a fighter, if I had scars," he continues, East Los Angeles "would accept me more."[19]

In defying the stereotypical image of the "Mexican boxer who fights with his face," de la Hoya challenged commonly held assumptions about masculine pride and raised the profile of the "pretty boy." De la Hoya—with his millions of dollars, movie-star looks, love of golf, and seeming devotion to women and children—cultivated what he believed to be the best "heroic ideal" to fit his time and place. Consequently, in constructing his own sense of masculine difference de la Hoya chose to emulate the career of an African American, not a Mexican American. "As a champion, in and out of the ring," he announced, "I want to be like Sugar Ray Leonard. I would like to be the way he made his money and was very smart–exactly like that. Stay clean. I think he got cut one time, that's it. . . . I want to have as few fights as possible and make the most money. My image is like a star image."[20]

Nonetheless, de la Hoya continually thought of himself as both "Mexican" and "American" and clearly had set his mind on trying to be "both." This meant possibly being both a "macho Mexican" *and* a "pretty boy American," or a "pretty boy Mexican" *and* a "macho American." As Gloria Anzaldúa has argued about life in the borderlands, the desire to be free to express a complex identity grows strong in a world that makes such hybrid expressions possible. To Anzaldúa, history and culture in the ethnic Mexican experience involves processes of *mestizaje*, or cultural syncretism, in which survival has meant negotiating identities in the borderlands of racial, sexual, and national power. The result has been an ethnic Mexican community with rich cultural resources and an increasingly panoramic vision of social change.

De la Hoya's "difference" mattered because in defining and challenging dominant representations of boxing masculinity he, along with his fans and detractors, raised awareness of new conditions and possibilities for gender identification. No other boxing champion has had his masculinity called into question like de la Hoya. He, according to Jim Murray for the *Los Angeles Times,* was "more priest than pug, more altar boy than home boy," leading "some [to] question whether Oscar loves [boxing] that much. He talks vaguely of becoming an architect. Or maybe archbishop."[21] To Vic Ziegel writing for *Playboy,* de la Hoya was "the thinking man's fighter."[22] Some men openly embraced de la Hoya's more genteel approach to masculinity inside and outside the ring. They took pleasure in de la Hoya as a "cerebral" boxer. For example, one fan, José Angel, expressed his confusion over the reaction of East Los Angeles boxing fans to de la Hoya. "Why do so many from Oscar's hometown claim they want to see him take punches? Is that manly?" he asked. "Well, we in Houston think he's too smart for that. All staying clean means is that he knows how to kick ass with his brain. Keep outsmarting 'em Oscar!"[23] Thus, some ethnic Mexican men found in de la Hoya a fitting example of a redefinition of their own sensibilities as ethnic men. De la Hoya's projection of the "damn near perfect man," as comedian Paul Rodríguez once described him, opened up space for ethnic Mexicans to imagine and celebrate the more sensitive and intelligent aspects of the violent masculinities of the ring. Males and females found in de la Hoya a masculinity constructed in prizefighting that could be upheld beyond the ring.

While it is difficult to ascertain to what extent women challenged social conventions in their roles as boxing fans, we can be sure that their enthusiasm for Oscar de la Hoya was unprecedented.[24] His apparent openness to the influence of women in shaping the production and consumption of his career generated a widespread female following. Females especially appreciated stories about de la Hoya's ostensibly progressive relationships with the women in his life. A founding story of his fandom centered on his mother. Almost immediately following his professional debut, de la Hoya drew criticism from males and praise from females for being a "momma's boy." He always claimed that the focal point of his inspiration was his mother, Cecilia, who died of breast cancer in 1990. "She was more than my mother," he claimed with conviction, "she was my best friend."[25] During the Olympic Games, after each of his victories de la Hoya fell to his knees and blew a kiss toward the sky to let his mother know he was working on keeping his promise to her of winning the gold medal. In his professional career, at the start of his fights de la Hoya stared into the skies, where he believed his mother watched over him. Stories about the ways de la Hoya kept the memory of his mother alive were elaborated in the media by a girlfriend, Veronica Peralta. "In some ways, I think he will always be lonely," she noted.

> Nobody will ever be able to replace the loss of his mother. He says sometimes that he has so much now that he wishes his mom had just a tiny part of it. If his mom was around, she would be his counselor, helper, friend. Sometimes when we go to the cemetery, he'll just sit there. I wonder, "God, what is he thinking? Is he talking to her?"[26]

Portrayals of de la Hoya as a rich, lonely boy in need of mothering that infuriated so many male boxing fans made him an attractive commodity to females.

As the media hyped the issue of de la Hoya's relationship to his deceased mother, female fans began lavishing praise on de la Hoya as a model of manliness and filial pride. Early in his career de la Hoya held special workouts for female audiences. A reporter described one such workout:

> His sisters, cousins and aunts seemed startled at the pistol shot-like noise de la Hoya's gloved fists made in the closed gym when he hit trainer Robert Alcazar's sparring mitts. They responded with polite applause. Then he made the speed bag sound like a machine gun for about 10 minutes. Polite applause. Next was a demonstration of high speed rope-jumping. More polite applause. Then he lay on his back, on a towel, while Alcazar hammered his stomach with judo chops. More polite applause. Finally, de la Hoya stood on his head in the corner. Good for the circulation, he says. More polite applause.[27]

Again and again, females demonstrated their devotion to de la Hoya because of his sex appeal and his boxing skills. In 1995, when he made his way into the ring to fight Genaro Hernández, he met "shrieks of joy from the girls, boos from some of their boyfriends."[28] In 1998, when he fought Patrick Charpentier, "His every move [was] closely monitored . . . especially by the female population."[29] According to Fred Albers, of the local television station KTSM, de la Hoya's effect on El Paso, especially on the females of the city, was without precedent. "I've never seen anything like this. This is beyond boxing. This is like lust," said Albers, as he pointed to the female fans who were yelling and screaming and waving as de la Hoya sparred a few rounds in the ring.[30] Sports journalist Tim Kawakami offered "one huge, demographically obvious reason why de la Hoya was scoring the monster box-office numbers. Women. Thousands of them who had never even thought of watching boxing were sure they watched de la Hoya."[31]

The public recognition of female participation in de la Hoya's career opened space for female fans to be key articulators of the masculine hierarchies taking shape in boxing. They were now playing fundamental roles shaping masculinities in boxing as they had always done in their ethnic Mexican families and communities. For example, female fans made it known to de la Hoya that they shared his desire that he box *and* stay "pretty."[32] One fan, Lorraine, praised de la Hoya, exclaiming, "You make boxing worth watching. Stay safe, cover that face!!!!!!!"[33] Amber wrote, "From all of the sexy fans in west Texas, the big city of Odessa. We are like a little El Paso. We will pay top dollar to see you prance around in white boxers. We love you!!!!!! And we will keep you in our prayers always!!"[34] Another fan, Sue, proudly announced, "we love him in our household. He has a great left hook and he's gorgeous."[35] Even de la Hoya's opponents began to fear the impact of de la Hoya's unique cast of female supporters. For example, Pernell Whitaker, after losing a decision to de la Hoya, blamed the undue influence of women in attendance for his demise. "Tell you what," Whitaker said at the postfight press conference that was broadcast on the public address system to the thousand or so fans still in the arena, "Oscar ought to thank every one of those girls who were screaming for him the whole fight. He missed, they screamed. And those judges reacted. '*Oooooh*, Oscar!' And he never hit me."[36]

At times, however, female fans were more critical and ambivalent in their assessments of de la Hoya's chosen profession. For example, the somewhat faulty logic of becoming a boxer with the hope of preserving one's face was not lost on female fans. "I am truly proud of your success. I admire you, you are a great role model," wrote Stephanie. "I hope to attend one of your fights someday. . . . I'm Mexican too. I relate to you in so many ways though. . . . Can I ask you a personal question? Do you ever worry that in the long run boxing will do damage to your physical health? Anyway, good luck in the future. I love you!"[37]

We cannot be sure de la Hoya's popularity among females is unprecedented in Mexican American boxing history. We do know, however, that females have used de la Hoya's career to challenge and debate the meaning of ideal masculinities. Evidence of this abounds in boxing Web site chat rooms. In 1998, for example, Loretta Barela, a fan of de la Hoya, argued that "it is probably true that the only reason you [men] hate him is because every female including myself thinks that he is fine. I think the critics should look at him and see what a real man looks and acts like."[38] We get a real sense from de la Hoya's female fanfare of the important role women play in the reproduction and instantiation of dominant forms of manhood as they engage them in their everyday lives. De la Hoya attracted females precisely because he seemed willing to join them in denaturalizing the links between sport, men's power over women, and the social distribution of violence. One way de la Hoya attempted to prove this was to encourage his onetime girlfriend, Veronica Peralta, a former Miss Mexico–Los Angeles, to elaborate on her critical insights into Oscar and their private lives together. Her interviews made public a particular ethnic Mexican female's prescription of what an ethnic Mexican man ought to be as much as what de la Hoya actually was. "I remember when I first met him," she reminisced:

> [H]e was only 19 and he was a wild one because he used to love to go out, hit the party scene and meet the girls. I think since he got famous quick and he got rich quick, it was something he wasn't exposed to before. He had to learn how to deal with it. Those girls who go after him . . . don't realize what he really is, don't know him when he's lonely, when he's sad, when he's depressed. [Another thing] I hate that Lamborghini [of his] so bad. I fear for him when you have so much power . . . I tell him "You know what? I don't need you to be king of the ring so you can die on the road."[39]

The influence of his mother, his girlfriend, his female fans, and his understanding male friends, combined with his instant wealth and popularity, produced a moment in de la Hoya's life when he could have challenged systems of gender domination that he confronted in his everyday life. But de la Hoya would capitulate to the wishes of his father, brother, and close advisers, who pressured him to avoid a long-term relationship at any cost. Only Jesus Rivero, the legendary Mexican trainer and mentor to de la Hoya, tried to keep the young man aware of life's options by pointing out that "changing women was not like changing clothes."[40] In time, however, de la Hoya capitulated to the wishes of his father—who never hid his antipathy for Peralta—by breaking off his long-standing relationship with her. According to Tim Kawakami, de la Hoya's biographer, the champion's male entourage

> didn't want Oscar to connect with anything that could lead him away from his father, his trainer, and [automobile dealer and close adviser] Mike Hernandez. They wanted him up in the mountains and tethered to no one and nothing but themselves. They wanted him alone, and making money. They didn't care so much about boxing history, but about making money for themselves and protecting their precious treasure.[41]

"I thought Veronica was magnificent and independent and exactly right for Oscar," recalled Jesus Rivero, "but they pushed her away to keep exploiting him. I call them *sanganos*, like the bees who don't do anything but eat. They are a bunch of leeches, parasites that surround him. His dad is a parasite. He gets 9 percent for every fight. Yes, they're all a bunch of snakes. They're thieves. And I would always tell Oscar that."[42]

In the fall of 1997 de la Hoya became engaged to an eighteen-year-old "virgin" who was willing to stay in the background during his high-profile endeavors. He and his father and brother were happy that his new fiancée was not like his old girlfriend. Peralta, he explained, "loved attention. I could see that right away. I'm aware of it. I'm very careful about that. My father hated her. My brother hated her guts. They would always see what she was trying to do to me, and I didn't want to believe it."[43] Swayed by the men in his family, de la Hoya now sought out a different kind of partner. "I want her very low profile," he said about his fiancée, "and she told me too. 'I don't want to be a picture in the news. I don't want anybody to know me.'"[44] When asked how he picked his bride-to-be, de la Hoya responded, "Man, it almost has to be like a hunch. Sometimes, I kind of test them, you know, to see if they're interested in money . . . she passed the test."[45]

In the end de la Hoya would not marry his virgin bride, breaking off his relationship as he joined the ranks of the other troubled men in his family. "My brother was blind—he finally broke up with his girl-friend," he claimed. "I was blind. So I hope my father realizes he's blind, and breaks up with [his wife]. We're the de la Hoya boys . . . the breakup boys, eh?"[46] But de la Hoya's father and brother would even-tually reconcile with their partners while de la Hoya would not.

In spite of his intense female following, de la Hoya has not yet openly embraced a feminist cause for gender equity. His critique of eth-nic Mexican boxing masculinity did not make him a true champion of women, but only a sexually attractive commodity. He was not con-sciously the champion of women and of working-class men, but in-creasingly seen as an icon of middle-class, Mexican American mas-culinity. Some working-class men, however, praised de la Hoya for his assimilation, revealing their own desires for and imagination of mid-dle-class life. Boxing fan Ray Rivera of Monterrey Park explained why he admired de la Hoya: "I'm glad he's doing commercials. I don't see too many Mexican Americans doing commercials. I'm not jealous of him, I'm happy for him. He's living everybody's dream. . . . He's living *my* dream."[47] Another fan on the Home Box Office Web site claimed,

> It's so obvious to any self-respecting East LA Mexican that the only reason so many despise de la Hoya is because he has made it. How many can truly say they'd rather be down with raza doing nothing than enjoying fast cars and fine clothes or playing golf in Cabo? Let's face it, Oscar can never be a rich white pretty boy in this country be-cause he's Mexican. He can only be a bad ass Mexican American. YOU GO OSCAR!!![48]

If for some de la Hoya's masculinity eschewed the signs of the life of struggle by appearing as a conscious removal of the signs of the barrio streets, such as composure, banter, and gait, for others this represented a positive, uncompromising refusal to conform to the will of others. In this way, de la Hoya resonated with the tastes of middle-class ethnic Mexican males and females, or males and females who simply aspired to be middle-class. Nevertheless, de la Hoya's signification of the pre-tensions of middle-class life intensified the tension in his relationship with working-class ethnic Mexicans on the streets of East Los Angeles. On one level de la Hoya's wealth and good looks threatened the working-class masculinities of the streets. On another level, de la Hoya was threatened. "I'm scared to go back to East L.A. because of that group," he claimed.

> Because I don't feel welcomed. I don't. I just don't feel welcomed. If I want to go back to my favorite place to eat tacos, King Taco, I always hide. I'm always hiding. If I'm in a car with a bunch of friends, I'll stay in the car. I don't feel welcomed. It's an ugly feeling. I just don't feel welcomed. They're driving me away. It's their fault, not mine. They're driving me away. I'll go anywhere around the world and I'll guarantee you they love me. Anywhere except East L.A., and it'll never change. Never, never. I know it won't. There's always going to be that jealousy, always. And it's that younger crowd, that crowd that has the pretty girlfriend and, "Oh, we're afraid that Oscar's going to take her away." Maybe it'll change when I get married. Maybe they'll respect me then.[49]

Unfortunately for de la Hoya, even among his most adoring fans his golden boy image would tarnish in a short period of time. A number of de la Hoya's actions did not bode well for him in the eyes of fans. His refusal to fight rematches did not win him the favor of fans. His moves to Montebello, then to Newport Beach, then Pasadena, and finally to Bel Air, where he currently occupies a mansion in Los Angeles's most expensive neighborhood, were always sure to draw criticism. Though he dreamed of becoming an actor, he decided to pursue a bilingual singing career that has yet to materialize into anything other than his self-eroticization and his repeated disparagement in the media and among fans. Although it may seem ridiculous to think that de la Hoya's best legacy was the attraction and elevation of female boxing fans to the level of expert authorities, on issues ranging from boxing technique to the business of boxing, we know that he was the subject of (her)story.

Yet it was precisely these female boxing aficionados who would begin launching criticism at de la Hoya that would permanently discredit him, at least in the present moment. Much of this criticism focused on his treatment of women. He drew the ire of loud female fans when he admitted that he fathered a daughter, whom he intended to raise from a distance, and whose mother he had no intention of marrying. During his frequent trips to Cabo San Lucas, Mexico, he developed a reputation for carousing and lascivious behavior. On one of these trips he allegedly raped a fifteen-year-old female, who is currently pursuing charges against him in court. As one fan, "boxinglady," put it, "He is, quite clearly, precisely the type of person he said he would never be."[50] Another fan responding to boxinglady noted that de la Hoya's "smile [and] charm cannot cover the deficits he always had. . . . Oscar tried to establish himself as the perfect citizen, fighter and person. . . . I consider Oscar a 'Corporate Fighter.'"[51] Another fan, "riveraa," responding to boxinglady: "The Spanish radio stations are driving me crazy with Oscar's CD," riveraa noted.

> Oscar played it wrong, cuz he kicked out his living [*sic*] girlfriend and son [*sic*] out of his house. But he did not speak to her, he sent one of his workers to do the job for him. What a man??? . . . He is self-centered and does not care about anybody, but himself. Wake up Americans and Mexicans, Oscar is not worth a penny, do not waste your time buying a CD from the "fraud master."[52]

"Ditto, riveraa!!" responded boxinglady. "I heard the single, 'Ven a Mi,' too! That album has more filter than a pack of cigarettes!! Dang, he threw out his OWN DAUGHTER? Well, what goes around comes around. Karma is like an angry divorced woman looking for alimony, Oscar better watch out!"[53]

The play of stereotypes such as those above and throughout this chapter should not be understood as merely falsehoods to be corrected. The voices we have heard can teach us to think about how stereotypes function to unite and divide communities. Oscar de la Hoya's major achievement involved the opening of space for females to disrupt or re-inforce stereotypical thinking and to intervene in a realm of masculin-ity once thought sacrosanct. Although it remains unclear whether or not females have won widespread approval as legitimate boxing experts, one thing is certain: for women a prizefighter's career signifies a great deal more than just boxing.

NOTES

1. David R. Maciel, Isidro D. Ortiz, and María Herrera-Sobek, eds., *Chicano Renaissance: Contemporary Cultural Trends* (Tucson: University of Arizona Press, 2000).

2. Earl Gutskey, "Relative Humility," *Los Angeles Times*, 1 July 1992, sec. C, 1.

3. Ibid., 10.

4. Tim Kawakami, *Golden Boy: The Fame, Money, and Mystery of Oscar de la Hoya* (Kansas City: Andrews McMeel, 1999), 253.

5. Earl Gutskey, "Thoughts of Gold in East L.A.," *Los Angeles Times*, 31 October 1990, sec. C, 1.

6. "De la Hoya Doesn't Pull Punches on Education during Visit to School," *Los Angeles Times*, 24 June 1997, sec. B, 4.

7. Ibid.

8. Tim Kawakami, "Boxing's Twister: De la Hoya Has Stormed the Sport, but He Plans to Cut a Wider Swath," *Los Angeles Times*, 2 June 1996, sec. C, 1.

9. Jim Murray, "He Doesn't Look Right—Until He Gets in the Ring," *Los Angeles Times*, 6 June 1996, sec. C, 1.

10. Ibid.

11. Jim Murray, "Have No Fear, Julio Cesar Is Here," *Los Angeles Times*, 7 June 1996, sec. C, 1.

12. Tim Kawakami, "Scorn in East L.A.? Not Much de la Hoya Can Do about It," *Los Angeles Times*, 6 June 1996, sec. C, 5.

13. Ibid.

14. Murray, "Have No Fear, Julio Cesar Is Here."

15. Kawakami, "Scorn in East L.A.?" 5.

16. Kawakami, *Golden Boy*, 220.

17. Kawakami, "Scorn in East L.A.?" 5.

18. Kawakami, *Golden Boy*, 220–21.

19. Vic Ziegal, "Golden Boy," *Playboy*, July 1996, 159.

20. Tim Kawakami, "$8 Million Later, Oscar de la Hoya Says He's Still Hungry," *Los Angeles Times*, 30 April, 1995, sec. C, 8.

21. Murray, "He Doesn't Look Right," 1, 5.

22. Ziegal, "Golden Boy," 116.

23. José Angel, Home Box Office World Championship Boxing Website, Boxing Fan Forum, 13 June 1998. Hereafter HBOWCBW.

24. This is attested to in numerous accounts, many of which are neatly summarized in Kawakami, *Golden Boy*.

25. Gutskey, "Relative Humility," 10.

26. Kawakami, "Boxing's Twister," 10.

27. Gutskey, "Relative Humility," 10.

28. Kawakami, *Golden Boy*, 191.

29. Steve Springer, "No Cutting de la Hoya Off at El Paso," *Los Angeles Times*, 12 June 1998, sec. C, 16.

30. Ibid.

31. Kawakami, *Golden Boy*, 278.

32. The responses of females at any of de la Hoya's Web sites, or in the discussion forums and billboards dedicated to him at the leading sports Web sites, prove this point.

33. Lorraine, HBOWCBW, Boxing Fan Forum, 13 June 1998.

34. Amber, HBOWCBW, Boxing Fan Forum, 13 June 1998.

35. Sue, HBOWCBW, Boxing Fan Forum, 13 June 1998.

36. Kawakami, *Golden Boy*, 275.

37. Stephanie, HBOWCBW, Boxing Fan Forum, 10 June 1998.

38. Loretta, HBOWCBW, Boxing Fan Forum, 13 June 1998.

39. Kawakami, "Boxing's Twister," 10.

40. Kawakami, *Golden Boy*, 196.

41. Ibid., 280–81.

42. Ibid., 281.

43. Ibid., 250.

44. Tim Kawakami, "After a Near Tragedy, a Recent Engagement and the Prospect of Fatherhood, de la Hoya Gets a Reality Check," *Los Angeles Times*, 12 September 1997, sec. C, 11.

45. Ibid.

46. Kawakami, *Golden Boy*, 250.

47. Kawakami, "Scorn in East L.A.?" 5.

48. Javier, HBOWCBW, Boxing Fan Forum, 13 June 1998.

49. Kawakami, *Golden Boy*, 231.

50. Boxinglady, HBOWCBW, 28 September 2000.

51. Kevnight, HBOWCBW, 28 September 2000.

52. Riveraa, HBOWCBW, 1 October 2000.

53. Boxinglady, HBOWCBW, 2 October 2000.

Contributors

ADRIAN BURGOS, JR. is an assistant professor of U.S. Latino history at the University of Illinois, Urbana-Champaign. He earned his Ph.D. in history from the University of Michigan and is currently at work on a book entitled *Playing America's Game: Latinos, Baseball, and the Performance and Policing of Race.* His work examines the intersection of race, culture, and diaspora in the Americas since the mid-nineteenth century.

LUZ CALVO is an assistant professor of comparative studies at Ohio State University. She teaches courses on Latino/a studies.

ARLENE DÁVILA is an assistant professor of anthropology and American studies at New York University. She is the author of *Sponsored Identities: Cultural Politics in Puerto Rico* and *Of Latinos, Inc.: The Marketing and Making of a People,* among other works looking at the commodification of culture and the cultural politics of U.S. Latinidad.

MELISSA A. FITCH holds a Ph.D. in Spanish and Latin American literature from Arizona State University. Her secondary specialization is in Portuguese language and contemporary Brazilian literature. Her research interests lie in the representation of gender and sexuality in contemporary Latin American theater, narrative, and film. She has published critical essays on these topics in *Latin American Theater Review; Gestos: Teoría y práctica del teatro hispánico; Chasqui: Revista de literatura latinoamericana; Ollantay;* and *Romance Languages Annual* and in the book *Interventions: Feminist Dialogues on Third World Women's Literature and Film* as well as in numerous reference texts. She is coauthor of the book *Culture and Customs of Argentina.*

MICHELLE HABELL-PALLÁN, currently a WWNF/Mellon Foundation Fellow, is an assistant professor of American ethnic studies and an affiliated faculty in Latin American studies at the University of Washington. Her forthcoming book examines contemporary transnational social dynamics through the lens of Chicana/o and Latina/o performance culture. She has published several articles on Chicana/o and Latina/o performance art, theater, and popular music.

TANYA KATERÍ HERNÁNDEZ, a professor of law at Rutgers University School of Law–Newark, received her J.D. from Yale University and her A.B. from Brown University. She is the author of "An Exploration of the Efficacy of Class-Based Approaches to Racial Justice: The Cuban Context," in *U.C. Davis Law Review*.

JOSH KUN is a writer and cultural critic whose work has appeared in *SPIN, Rolling Stone,* the *Village Voice, LA Weekly, CMJ New Music Monthly,* and *Color Lines*. His weekly arts column, "Frequencies," appears in the *San Francisco Bay Guardian* and the *Boston Phoenix*. He is an assistant professor of English at University of California–Riverside and is currently completing a book entitled *Strangers among Sounds: Music, Race, and American Culture*.

FRANCES NEGRÓN-MUNTANER is an award-winning filmmaker, writer, journalist, and cultural critic. She holds master's degrees in visual anthropology and fine arts from Temple University, and a Ph.D. in comparative literature from Rutgers University–New Brunswick. Negrón-Muntaner is a recipient of Rockefeller, Pew, Ford, and Truman fellowships. Among her films are *AIDS in the Barrio* and *Brincando el charco: Portrait of a Puerto Rican*. She has edited several books, including *Puerto Rican Jam: Essays on Culture and Politics*. Her new book, *Passing Memories*, is forthcoming from NYU Press in 2002.

WILLIAM A. NERICCIO is an associate professor of English and comparative literature at San Diego State University, where he also serves on the faculty of the Department of Chicana and Chicano Studies and the Center for Latin American Studies. His most recent published work was "Autopsy of a Rat: Odd, Sundry Parables of Freddy Lopez, Speedy Gonzales, and Other Chicano/Latino Marionettes Prancing about Our First World Visual Emporium," in *Camera Obscura: A Journal of Feminism, Culture, and Media Studies*.

RAQUEL RIVERA is a print and radio journalist. She received a Ph.D. in sociology from the City University of New York Graduate Center and is completing a book entitled *New York Ricans from the Hip Hop Zone* based on her dissertation. Her articles on hip hop culture have been published in *Stress* magazine, *El Diario/La Prensa*, *Hoy*, the *San Juan Star* and *El Nuevo Día*.

ANA PATRICIA RODRÍGUEZ is an assistant professor in the Department of Spanish and Portuguese at the University of Maryland, College Park, where she teaches classes in Latin American, Central American, and U.S. Latino literatures. She received a Ph.D. in literature from the University of California–Santa Cruz. She has received a postdoctoral fellowship in Latino studies from the Smithsonian Institution and a grant-in-aid from the University of Houston's "Recovering the U.S. Hispanic Literary Heritage" project. Her comparative work focuses on the cultural expressions of Central Americans in the isthmus and in the United States. She has presented her work at conferences in the United States and Latin America. A forthcoming article entitled, "Refugees of the South: Central Americans in the U.S. Latino Imaginary," will appear in *American Literature* and other works are in preparation for various anthologies and journals.

GREGORY RODRIGUEZ is an assistant professor of Mexican American studies at the University of Arizona. He holds a Ph.D. in history from the University of California–San Diego and is revising his dissertation, "'Palaces of Pain': Arenas of Mexican-American Dreams: Boxing and the Formation of Ethnic Mexican Identities in Twentieth-Century Los Angeles," for book publication.

MARY ROMERO is a professor of justice studies at Arizona State University and a Carnegie Scholar with the Carnegie Academy for the Scholarship of Teaching and Learning. Her research and teaching interests are feminist and racial justice, law and narrative, and Latina/o studies. She is the author of *Maid in the U.S.A.* and coeditor of *Women's Untold Stories: Breaking Silence, Talking Back, Voicing Complexity; Challenging Fronteras: Structuring Latina and Latino Lives in the U.S.;* and *Women and Work: Exploring Race, Ethnicity and Class.* Several articles have recently been published in *Journal of Gender, Social Policy and the Law,*

University of Miami Law Review, Chicago-Kent Law Review, Denver University Law Review, Signs, NWSA Journal, and *Harvard Educational Review.*

ALBERTO SANDOVAL-SÁNCHEZ is a professor of Spanish and U.S.-Latino literature at Mount Holyoke College. He received his Ph.D. in 1983 at the University of Minnesota. His bilingual book of poetry, *New York Backstage/Nueva York Tras Bastidores,* was published in Chile and in 1993 Mount Holyoke College produced his theatrical piece *Side Effects,* based on his personal experiences with AIDS. He has also edited a special issue of *Ollantay Theater Magazine* on U.S. Latino theater and AIDS. He has published numerous articles on U.S. Latino theater, Latin American colonial theater and colonial identity formation, Spanish baroque theater, Puerto Rican migration, Latino theater on AIDS, Latina theater, and images of Latinos in film and on Broadway. He is the author of *José Can You See? Latinos On and Off Broadway* and coeditor with Nancy S. Sternbach of *Puro Teatro: A Latina Anthology.* His latest book is *Stages of Life: Transcultural Performance and Identity in Latina Theatre,* also in collaboration with Sternbach.

CHRISTOPHER A. SHINN is an assistant professor of American literature at Florida State University. His research focuses primarily on comparative ethnicities and the study of popular culture. He is currently working on a book project entitled, *Black Dragon: Towards an Afro-Asiatic Imagination,* which traces the cross-cultural routes of the African and Asian diasporas in the context of colonial and postcolonial history.

DEBORAH R. VARGAS, a Ph.D. candidate in the Department of Sociology at the University of California–Santa Cruz, is a Dissertation Fellow in Chicana/Latina studies at the University of California–Davis and a recipient of the Smithsonian Institution's Pre-Doctoral Fellowship in Latino Studies, National Museum of American History. Her dissertation, "Las Tracaleras: Tejanas and Tex-Mex Music in the Making of Tejas," is a feminist exploration of Texas-Mexican music throughout the twentieth century. She will serve as a guest curator for *Tejanos Hoy,* the inaugural exhibition of the Alameda National Museum of Latino Art and Culture in San Antonio, Texas.

JUAN VELASCO is an assistant professor at Santa Clara University. He teaches courses in contemporary Latin American and Chicano/a literature, composition, and film, and has published articles on issues of ethnicity, race, and nationalism in Mexican-American texts. He received his Ph.D. from University of California–Los Angeles where he specialized in contemporary Chicano/a literature. The title of his dissertation was "Labyrinth of Mexicanness: The Construction of Ethnicity in Contemporary Chicano/a Autobiography."

Index